PROFESSIONAL

Data Privacy Law in Hong Kong

GUIDE

Mark Berthold

&

Raymond Wacks

FT

LAW & TAX

Asia Pacific

Published by **FT Law & Tax Asia Pacific**
An imprint of **Pearson Professional Asia Pacific**

Suite 1808 Asian House
1 Hennessy Road
Wan Chai
Hong Kong
Tel: (852) 2863 2600
Fax: (852) 2520 6646
Internet: pphkg@hk.super.net
Web: www.pearson-pro.com.hk

First edition 1997

Printed in China

ISBN 962 661 040 9

To Aida and Penelope

About the Authors

MARK BERTHOLD was educated at the University of Wellington and Monash, and practised in the fields of criminal and civil law in New Zealand and Australia. He joined the Hong Kong Attorney General's Chambers in 1985 and was appointed full-time secretary to the Law Reform Commission of Hong Kong's newly established privacy sub-committee in 1990. He conducted the extensive comparative research which facilitated many of the committee's proposals, and drafted its report on data privacy which formed the basis of the Ordinance.

In 1994 Mr Berthold acted as legal adviser to the Secretary for Home Affairs to assist the Legislative Council Bills Committee in the process that culminated in the enactment of the Ordinance in 1995. The following year he was appointed legal adviser to the Office of the Privacy Commission for Personal Data, the body charged with implementing the new law. He is a member of the editorial panel of *Privacy Law and Policy Reporter*, and now advises on compliance with the Ordinance and other privacy-related issues.

RAYMOND WACKS is Professor of Law and Legal Theory at the University of Hong Kong where he was Head of the Department of Law from 1986 to 1993. Educated at the University of the Witwatersrand, the London School of Economics, and University College, Oxford, his major interests are legal theory, and human rights, in particular the protection of privacy on which he is a leading international authority. In March 1997 he was awarded a Higher Doctorate in Law (LLD) by the University of London for his publications in law and legal theory.

Professor Wacks' major works in the field of privacy are *The Protection of Privacy, Personal Information: Privacy and the Law, Privacy* (an edited two-volume collection of essays) and *Privacy and Press Freedom*. He is a member of the committee of the Law Reform Commission of Hong Kong currently examining this subject, and of the Personal Data (Privacy) Advisory Committee. Professor Wacks is Editor of the *Hong Kong Law Journal*. He is working on a book that examines the privacy implications of the Internet.

Foreword

by the Hon Mr Justice Mortimer

By 1989 Hong Kong's transition to a service-based economy was well advanced. Leaders in privacy law and information technology recognised an increasing need for the regulation of personal data. Those conscious of Hong Kong's international status as a financial service provider saw 'a little cloud ... like a man's hand' on the horizon. The European Union had issued its first draft directive indicating the aim of member states to limit the transfer of personal data to jurisdictions without appropriate legal protection.

This perceived commercial threat was an additional factor which led to the establishment of the privacy sub-committee of the Law Reform Commission in 1990 to consider data protection law as its first task. The sub-committee's recommendations led to the passing of the *Personal Data (Privacy) Ordinance* on 3 August 1995. In consequence, Hong Kong has in place an extremely advanced and comprehensive law relating to data protection.

The authors of this work are uniquely qualified. Professor Raymond Wacks, Professor of Law and Legal Theory at the University of Hong Kong, and internationally recognised as an authority on privacy law, was, and is, a member of the privacy sub-committee. Mark Berthold – until recently legal adviser to the Privacy Commissioner for Personal Data – was secretary to the sub-committee charged with the necessary research. He was also concerned with briefing the Law Draftsman for the Bill and has a unique knowledge of the Ordinance.

The result of their joint labour is a comprehensive and scholarly work of unquestionable authority. It deals with an unfamiliar and often difficult subject in practical, clear, and readable terms. Not only will this become a standard text for lawyers but it will be the preferred handbook for all data holders who seek to comply with the law. I would advise anyone – lawyer or layman – not to wrestle with the text of this Ordinance without this book at his elbow. It deserves success. I expect it will go into many editions.

Court of Appeal
Hong Kong
14 July 1997

Barry Mortimer
Justice of Appeal
Chairman of the privacy sub-committee of the Law Reform Commission of Hong Kong

Preface

Reform of the law is inevitably a lengthy process, particularly when the issues are complex. The speed with which Hong Kong has addressed the difficult subject of the protection of personal records is therefore a tribute to the dedication and stamina of several individuals and bodies: the Law Reform Commission's privacy sub-committee that formulated the original proposals, the Commission itself, the Home Affairs Branch which oversaw the framing into law of these recommendations, and the members of the Legislative Council Bills Committee.

As members of the privacy sub-committee, we found the experience both stimulating and rewarding. Hong Kong now has what may be the most comprehensive legislation on this subject anywhere in the world. The Ordinance, moreover, was drafted with due regard to the requirements of the European Directive on Data Protection. This provides a powerful bolster to Hong Kong's status as an international financial and commercial centre.

Long before the bill was passed, we made the rash decision to write a book that would explain and analyse the new law, providing guidance for all who are affected and protected by it, including employers and employees, banks and customers, doctors and patients, law enforcement authorities and citizens. Indeed, it is no exaggeration to say that the lives of every member of our community is directly affected by the Ordinance.

In the course of writing this book, we have incurred many debts. We are grateful, in particular, to the former Australian Privacy Commissioner, Kevin O'Connor who was kind enough to read the manuscript and offer helpful comments. The text also reflects the contributions of Robert Stevens and Blair Stewart of the Office of the New Zealand Privacy Commissioner. Responsibility for remaining errors must of course be laid at our door.

Our analysis of the Ordinance has benefited from many discussions with Mark Berthold's former colleagues in the Law Reform

Commission Secretariat headed by Stuart Stoker and the Office of the Privacy Commissioner for Personal Data. Robin McLeish, Deputy Privacy Commissioner, will recognise a number of his insights.

A number of individuals lent a helping hand along the way. Special thanks go to Nigel Waters of the Australian Privacy Commission and Graham Greenleaf of the University of New South Wales. Magdalen Spooner, Diana Chow, and Douglas Kwok also assisted the project in a variety of ways. Linda Tan of Pearson Professional has been a friendly and helpful editor, struggling valiantly against ever tighter deadlines.

We are happy to express our appreciation to Mr Justice Barry Mortimer, long serving chairman of the privacy sub-committee, for his gracious foreword.

We would also like to acknowledge the University of Hong Kong's Committee on Conference and Research Grants which kindly provided financial assistance to support our work.

The Ordinance is merely the first step in the long march towards the effective legal protection of personal information. We hope that the pages that follow will make a small contribution to a better understanding and implementation of this important law.

Hong Kong, China
16 July 1997

Mark Berthold
Raymond Wacks

Contents

1 Introduction

The Personal Data (Privacy) Ordinance was enacted on 3 August 1995 heralding a comprehensive framework for the protection of the privacy of individuals' personal data. Apart from two sections (ss 30 and 33 which apply to 'matching procedures' and transferring data out of Hong Kong) the Ordinance came into force on 20 December 1996.

It is important to note at the outset that the concept 'personal data' means any representation of information relating to a living individual. The nature and scope of this definition is explored in Chapter 4, but a number of preliminary points need to be made at this stage:

- Only personal data that are recorded in a document are subject to regulation under the Ordinance. Purely oral communications or sign language, for example, are not covered;
- Any data relating to an individual are 'personal' data for these purposes. They may be apparently innocuous, such as a person's address, or they may pertain to his most intimate details, such as health; and
- Data not relating to individuals but to legal persons, such as corporations, are not covered.

The regulation of personal data so defined is achieved through the application of six principles of fair information practice which the Ordinance refers to as 'data protection principles'. These principles are set out in Schedule 1. A full exposition may be found in later chapters. In essence, however, they provide that personal data be:

- Collected only if they are relevant to the data user's activities and in a manner that is lawful and fair;
- Accurate and not retained longer than necessary;

- Used only for the purpose(s) for which the data were to be used at the time of collection, unless the data subject expressly consents; and
- Held securely.

The data subject should be able to ascertain:

- A data user's policies and practices and the kinds, and main purposes, of personal data held; and
- Whether data are held relating to that individual and have the right to access and correct such data.

Protecting Data Privacy

The long title to the Ordinance states that it is 'an Ordinance to protect the *privacy* of individuals in relation to personal data'.[1] This facilitates a purposive interpretation of the Ordinance's occasionally enigmatic provisions. Section 19 of the *Interpretation and General Clauses Ordinance* provides that an ordinance shall be deemed remedial and shall receive such 'fair, large and liberal interpretation as will best ensure the attainment of the object of the Ordinance'.

The concept of 'privacy' has a long and complex legal history. It is worth summarising the manner in which the common law has attempted to grapple with it. The problems generated by the widespread collection and use of personal data have only recently been brought under the ever-expanding umbrella of privacy. Yet it has quickly become the dominant concern of those who lament the failure of the law to protect the individual against the increasing inroads upon his personal privacy.

The genesis of the legal notion of privacy is the famous Warren and Brandeis essay which found that the common law implicitly recognised the 'right to privacy'.[2] Drawing upon English cases of, in particular, breach of confidence, property, copyright and defamation, they argued that these cases were merely instances and applications of a general right to privacy. The common law, they claimed, albeit under different names and forms, protected an individual whose privacy was invaded by the likes of snooping journalists. In so doing, the law acknowledged the importance of the spiritual and intellectual needs of man.

The law, they contended, developed from the protection of the physical person and corporeal property to the protection of the individual's '[t]houghts, emotions and sensations'.[3] But as a result of threats to privacy from recent inventions and business methods and from the press, the common law needed to go further. An individual's right to determine the extent to which his thoughts, emotions and sensations were communicated to others was already legally protected, but only in respect of authors of literary and artistic compositions and letters who could forbid their unauthorised publication. And though English cases recognising this right were based on protection of property, in reality they were an acknowledgement of 'privacy', of 'inviolate personality'.[4]

In 1902, the New York Court of Appeals was given an opportunity to consider the Warren and Brandeis thesis, in a case where the plaintiff complained that her picture had been used without her consent to advertise flour.[5] The majority rejected the privacy argument as it had 'not as yet an abiding place in our jurisprudence, and 'cannot now be incorporated without doing violence to settled principles of law'.[6] Three years later, in a case involving similar facts, the Supreme Court of Georgia explicitly adopted the Warren and Brandeis thesis.[7]

The new cause of action spawned a huge body of case law and academic comment. Almost every American state has incorporated the right to privacy into its law. Yet, despite the authors' almost exclusive reliance on English decisions, no similar development has occurred in England, or Hong Kong.

The American common law, following Prosser, recognises not one tort, 'but a complex of four'.[8] The four relatively discrete torts are described by Prosser as:

- Intrusion upon the plaintiff's seclusion or solitude, or into his private affairs;
- Public disclosure of embarrassing private facts about the plaintiff;
- Publicity which places the plaintiff in a false light in the public eye; and
- Appropriation, for the defendant's advantage, of the plaintiff's name or likeness.

These torts conveniently (though perhaps inaccurately)[9] capture the principal dimensions of the law of privacy. But to them must be added a fifth: the use of personal data in a manner that offends the individual's right of control over it – the chief mischief that the Ordinance is designed to address. The origin and nature of this aspect of privacy is discussed below.

American Constitutional Law

Until the Supreme Court's controversial decision in *Griswold v Connecticut* [10] declaring unconstitutional a Connecticut statute which prohibited the use of contraceptives on the ground that it violated the right of marital privacy – a right 'older than the Bill of Rights' – the constitutional protection of privacy did not significantly extend beyond the four torts mentioned above. Though the US Constitution is silent on whether there is a 'right of privacy', through several of its amendments (particularly the First, Third, Fourth, Fifth and Ninth), the court has recognised that such a right indeed exists. The incremental development of Supreme Court privacy doctrine is reflected in decisions such as *Roe v Wade*[11] and *Planned Parenthood v Casey*[12] invalidating abortion statutes on the ground of invading a constitutional right of privacy. In *Bowers v Hardwick*,[13] however, the court held (by 5 to 4) that the privacy protection of the due process clause does not extend to homosexual acts between consenting adults in private.

In the light of these decisions, it is not surprising that privacy discourse has expanded well beyond Warren and Brandeis's limited concern to establish a legal means of containing unwanted publicity.

English Law

In its recognition of the general failure of the common law to mirror American developments the legislature has, on several occasions, sought, without success, to create a statutory 'right of privacy'. The most comprehensive bill, introduced in 1969, was the result of an investigation by a Committee of Justice into the inadequacies of the common law. Rejecting mere tinkering with the laws of, for instance, trespass and nuisance, to provide remedies for invasions of privacy, and the enactment of piecemeal legislation, it recommended instead a bill to create a general right of privacy.

The matter was referred to a Home Office committee appointed on 13 May 1970 under the chairmanship of Kenneth Younger. It rejected, by a majority, the creation of a general right of privacy, preferring instead a piecemeal approach. It took the view that the best way to ensure regard for privacy was to provide specific and effective sanctions against clearly defined activities. It concluded that a general right would create uncertainty, and recommended instead:

- The creation of a new crime and a new tort of unlawful surveillance;
- The creation of a new tort of disclosure or other use of information unlawfully acquired; and
- Reference to the Law Commissions of the law relating to breach of confidence with a view to its clarification and statement in legislative form.

Other attempts to introduce legislation have followed, but the pressure for statutory measures to control the press grew in 1990. A committee chaired by Mr David Calcutt QC was formed to consider the conduct of the press in publishing intimate facts about the lives of members of the royal family and certain politicians. Its report of June 1990 recommended (not for the first time) that the press be given a 'last chance' to regulate itself; a new Press Complaints Commission (PCC) would replace the largely discredited Press Council. It decided that a statutory civil right of 'infringement of privacy' was inappropriate because reform should only fill existing gaps in protection. Door-stepping, bugging and the use of long-range cameras should be unlawful. Reporting restrictions in respect of children and victims of sex offences should be enhanced. If these proposals proved ineffectual, a statutory press tribunal, presided over by a judge, should be established.

The press took some steps to put its house in order. In his 1993 report on the effectiveness or otherwise of the new dispensation,[14] Sir David Calcutt was, however, unimpressed, and proposed activating the measures suggested in the earlier report which had been kept on ice. Self-regulation, he concluded, had failed. A legal framework was required. Its main feature was a statutory tribunal, the Press Complaints Tribunal (PCT) with jurisdiction over all newspapers, magazines and journals. It would enforce a code of practice and have the power to award damages and impose fines. It could also require publishers to apologise in a form specified by the tribunal.

He recommended the creation of a crime and tort of unlawful entry into private property or placing a surveillance device there, or the taking of a photograph or recording the voice of anyone with the intention of obtaining personal information with a view to its publication. It would be a defence if the act were done to prevent, detect or expose a crime or other seriously antisocial conduct, to protect public health or safety, to prevent the public being misled by a public statement or action or done under lawful authority. Sir David also recommended that the government consider (again) the enactment of a general tort of invasion of privacy.

In March 1993, the National Heritage Select Committee rejected the establishment of a statutory tribunal, preferring instead the creation of yet another self-regulatory organ, the Press Commission, to enforce a new Press Code.[15] The committee went further than Calcutt and urged the introduction of a new statutory tort of infringement of privacy.

These proposals have generated considerable debate, not to say anxiety, especially within the press.But the prospect of English law re-inventing such a privacy tort, revealed to exist in the law of England by two Americans, remains doubtful.

Surveillance and Interception of Communications

After completing its 1994 report on the protection of personal data, the Law Reform Commission of Hong Kong, following a consultation paper, *Privacy: Regulating Surveillance and the Interception of Communications* published on 16 April 1996, issued its *Report on Privacy: Regulating the Interception of Communications* in December 1996. While the consultation paper contains proposals relating both to surveillance and interception, the Commission decided to pursue only the latter in its report in the hope that this (less complex and less controversial) question might be the subject of legislation. The matter of surveillance will be dealt with in the next report which is imminent.

The Interception of Communications Bill incorporates many of the Law Reform Commission's recommendations, though they are weakened in a number of respects; in particular, the bill does not appear to cover the interception of e-mail messages. The bill establishes a new regime of control by judicial warrant of interception of communication, and creates new criminal offences of intentional interception of communications without a warrant and unauthorised disclosure of intercepted messages. A judge shall not issue a warrant (valid for six months) unless he is satisfied that the information sought cannot reasonably be acquired by means other than interception. He may issue a warrant only for the specific purpose of preventing, investigating, or detecting serious crime where there is reasonable cause to believe that the interception is likely to uncover useful information leading to a suspect or an arrest in respect of serious crime, or for the security of Hong Kong where the interception is likely to be of substantial value in furthering the purpose. Provision is made for the granting of *ex post facto* warrants in urgent cases. Warrants may be renewed for a further period of up to six months. Arrangements are to be made to limit to a minimum the extent to which intercepted material is disclosed or copied.

The bill provides that intercepted material shall not generally be admissible in evidence in any proceedings before a court or tribunal, and any evidence that tends to suggest that a warrant has been or is to be issued shall not be adduced; nor shall any question be asked that tends to suggest that a warrant has been issued.

The bill establishes a Supervisory Authority to review the issue of warrants and their proper execution, and the adequacy of arrangements in respect of the use of intercepted material. The authority shall be a Justice of Appeal.

The bill was gazetted on 28 February 1997 and the government announced that there would be a brief consultation period – a decision difficult to justify in view of the fact that the Law Reform Commission's sub-committee's consultation paper was available for public consultation for two months, and attracted over 30 submissions, including the Security Branch, ICAC, the legal profession, and several political bodies and media organisations. Frustration with the administration's apparent lack of will (exhibited in the Governor's statement that it raised technical and policy problems that required resolution) generated the publication of a Private Member's Bill by Mr James To. It was passed at the final sitting of the Legislative Council on 26 June 1997.

The sub-committee's tentative proposals in respect of the legal control of surveillance may be found in the consultation paper mentioned above. The main recommendations include the creation of three criminal offences:

- Entering private premises as a trespasser with intent to observe, overhear or obtain personal information therein;
- Placing, using or servicing in, or removing from, private premises a sense-enhancing, transmitting or recording device without the consent of the lawful occupier; and
- Placing or using such device outside private premises with the intention of monitoring either the activities of the occupant or data held on the premises relating directly or indirectly to the occupant without the consent of the lawful occupier.

The definition of 'private premises' includes hotel bedrooms and those parts of a hospital where patients accommodate or are treated, school premises, commercial premises, aircraft, vessels and vehicles from which the public is excluded.

The International Dimension

A fairly broad right to privacy is an acknowledged human right and is recognised in several international instruments. So, for example, Article 12 of the *United Nations Declaration of Human Rights* and Article 17 of the *International Covenant on Civil and Political Rights* (ICCPR) both provide:

> No one shall be subjected to arbitrary or unlawful interference with his privacy, family, home or correspondence, nor to unlawful attacks on his honour and reputation; and everyone has the right to the protection of the law against such interference or attacks.

Article 8 of the European Convention on Human Rights (ECHR) declares that:

> Everyone has the right to respect for his private and family life, his home and his correspondence. There shall be no interference by a public authority with the exercise of this right except such as is in accordance with the law and is necessary in a democratic society in the interests of national security, public safety or the economic well-being of the country, for the prevention of disorder or crime, for the protection of health or morals, or for the protection of the rights and freedoms of others.

Data Protection and Privacy

The relationship of the data protection principles set out in Schedule 1 and the substantive provisions in the body of the Ordinance (ie in Parts I-X) is defined by s 4, which provides that:

> A data user shall not do an act, or engage in a practice, that contravenes a data protection principle unless the act or practice, as the case may be, is required or permitted under this Ordinance.

This establishes the proposition that specific provisions should prevail over the rather general terms of the principles. However, as the principles effectively represent an operational definition of privacy in relation to personal data, it follows that the specific provisions should nonetheless be interpreted in a manner that accords with the principles.

In seeking to interpret the Ordinance, reference is inevitably made to the decisions made and guidelines formulated by data protection authorities in other jurisdictions. In the absence of legal precedents, they provide extremely useful guidance, particularly where the legislation in question is similar to our own. For this reason, we draw, where appropriate, upon the opinions, directives and guidelines of privacy commissioners in Australia and New Zealand, and of the United Kingdom Data Protection Registrar.

A New Approach to Personal Data

Although enactments addressing data privacy are popularly known as 'data protection laws', the term is misleading. The essential purpose of such laws is the protection of the individual ('the data subject') to whom the data relates. The 'protection' in the sense of the safeguarding of such data is but one aspect. As Bennett puts it, 'If you protect the data on which . . . decisions are made, you also protect the integrity, fairness and effectiveness of the decision-making process'.[16]

The Ordinance effects this aim by providing the individual with a degree of control over such data. Restricting the use of data to the purpose for which they are obtained is the linchpin of these controls. It is buttressed by providing the individual with the right to access and correct data relating to him. This vesting in the individual of relative control over data about him[17] represents a significant shift from the traditional approach adopted in Hong Kong. Organisations have tended to assume that they have exclusive control of personal data held by them. Attempts by the data subject to share this control have often been resisted on the ground that the organisation 'owns' the data. The converse argument that a data subject had a right of ownership, providing a proprietary basis for a right of access, was recently rejected by the Australian High Court.[18]

A corollary of this assertion of control by the individual over his data is that the data user becomes accountable for their accuracy and use. This is underlined by the Ordinance's providing the data subject with the right to compensation for a breach of its requirements causing damage or injured feelings (see Chapter 13).

While the Ordinance provides the individual with control over his personal data, such control is relative and not absolute. The data subject is not accorded general veto rights on the collection or use of data that are relevant to the functions of the organisation in question. The rights of the individual are balanced against the exigencies of both government and business, the functioning of which are dependent upon the processing of personal data.

This balancing exercise is expressly required by the Ordinance. It is expressed through its several references to compliance with requirements being 'practicable', a term which is defined in s 2 as meaning 'reasonably practicable'. This reasonableness test envisages a balancing exercise which takes into account such diverse factors as the resources of the data user and the impact of the data on the data subject.

An Ordinance to Regulate Organisations

While the focus of the protections afforded by the Ordinance is the individual, that is the data subject, the regulatory regime is directed at organisations such as companies and public bodies, that is the 'data user'. 'Data user' is defined in s 2 as 'a person who, either alone or jointly or in common with other persons, controls the collection, holding, or use of the data'. Such control is unlikely to be exercised by low-level employees. Nor are regulatory efforts likely to effect organisational change unless their primary target is the organisation which is responsible for the contraventions of employees committed in the course of their employment (see Chapter 13).

Relationship with Other Legislation

The relationship between the Ordinance and other Hong Kong enactments is defined by s 3(2), which provides:

> Where there is any conflict or inconsistency between the provisions of this Ordinance and the provisions of any other Ordinance, then the provisions of this Ordinance shall, to the extent of that conflict or inconsistency, as the case may be, prevail over the provisions of that Ordinance.

This essentially expresses the common law principle of statutory interpretation according precedence to a later provision which is 'so inconsistent with, or repugnant to, the provisions of an earlier enactment that the two cannot stand together'.[19] This canon of construction, including its restatement in s 3(2), applies only to existing ordinances. It does not extend to legislation enacted after the Ordinance. This is because the legislature is presumed to be aware of earlier legislation. However, s 8(1)(a) provides the Commissioner with the opportunity to comment on any proposed legislation that may affect privacy interests. On 23 February 1997 the Standing Committee of China's National People's Congress passed a decision to repeal or amend 14 ordinances under article 160 of the Basic Law. The decision refers to 'the provisions relating to the superior status' of the Ordinance in s 3(2).

There are several provisions in the statute book that relate to the transfer of personal data. Their interaction with the Ordinance is accordingly a matter of practical importance, especially because data protection principle 3 of the Ordinance requires that personal data shall not be used (including transferred or disclosed) for a purpose other than those for which they were collected. In determining the relationship between this principle and provisions found elsewhere, a distinction needs to be drawn between a transfer or disclosure which is required by such a provision and a transfer which is merely permitted. Where data are collected pursuant to a statutory requirement of their transfer to other data users, compliance with the statutory requirement may be considered to be a purpose of collection. A transfer in these circumstances would accordingly comply with principle 3. An example would be a doctor notifying the Health Department that a patient was suffering from a notifiable disease as required by the *Infectious Diseases Ordinance*.

Most legislative provisions do not, however, require the transfer of personal data but merely permit it. Unlike the Ordinance, however, such provisions inevitably lack a systematic reconciliation of the privacy principles with carefully circumscribed circumstances where their waiver is permissible on policy grounds. Nonetheless, the provision may identify the specific public interest grounds justifying such disclosure in terms that correspond with the exemptions under the Ordinance. One example is the provision of the *Dangerous Drugs Ordinance* providing for the disclosure of personal data contained in the dangerous drugs register to the Attorney-General when required for the purposes of preventing or detecting serious crime. The exercise of such provisions also accords with the exemption contained in s 58 of the Ordinance and no conflict between the two arises.

The remaining class of provisions permitting transfers of personal data are those that are not expressly conditioned by limitations on their use. Such provisions should, however, be exercised in a manner that is compatible with the Ordinance and accords with the principles as qualified by the exemptions. A particular application of this approach relates to court orders authorising the disclosure or transfer of personal data. Court orders are generally made pursuant to permissive statutory powers which specify or envisage specific public interest grounds justifying their exercise. Provided disclosure or transfer of such data is for purposes contained in the exemptions under the Ordinance, no conflict will occur.

No Opting Out of Compliance with the Ordinance

The Ordinance imposes a regulatory framework to protect personal data. As with other legislation imposing mandatory standards, the statutory scheme does not accommodate parties who purport to opt out of the protection afforded. To permit this would be to undermine the safeguards contained in the law. Thus, an employer may not hire an individual on the condition that he not exercise his statutory rights of access to and correction of his personal data. Such an attempt to limit the employee's rights would be ineffective. However, as regards those provisions that specifically provide for the data subject's consent, such consent, if it conforms to the statutory requirements that govern it, will be effective. For example, principle 3 permits a data user to use data for a purpose other than that for which they were collected if the data subject provides his 'prescribed consent', namely the express consent of the individual given voluntarily [s 2(3)].

The Role of the Commissioner

Part II of the Ordinance establishes the office of the Privacy Commissioner ('the Commissioner'). The government accepted that this complex area of regulation requires a body with the sole task of administering it. An important feature is the statutory protection of the Commissioner's independence. This is a crucial requirement since the Commissioner's role has an inherent potential to bring it into conflict with the administration.

The Commissioner has a central role in applying the Ordinance. His functions and powers (which are more fully examined in later chapters) enable him to oversee the application of the data protection principles. He may investigate possible contraventions, either upon receiving a complaint or on his own initiative. His rulings will provide essential guidance, especially to data users. More systematic guidance on the application of the principles will derive from guidelines he may issue and the formulation and promotion of the codes of practice.

The first Privacy Commissioner is Stephen Lau. He assumed duties on 1 August 1996 and his office reached its full establishment of 32 staff six months later. The office is divided into divisions handling enquiries, complaints and investigation, legal, finance, translation, administration and promotion and education. The Commission's budget is modest, currently running at less than half that allocated such bodies as the Consumer Council and the Equal Opportunities Commission.[20]

In his study of data protection authorities, David Flaherty cautions against the complacency that may result from the establishment of such a body.[21] To avoid the community being lulled into a false sense of security about their data privacy, it is plainly important that the regulatory authority should be provided with adequate resources. Now that the new office has commenced operation (and the scale of enquiries, complaints and other aspects of its work are becoming evident), its needs can be assessed more accurately.

The Ordinance does not, however, either assume or require that aggrieved data subjects should approach the Commissioner for assistance. Should the data subject seek monetary compensation, he is entitled to sue in court or the Small Claims Tribunal (s 66). There is no requirement that he should first refer the matter to the Commissioner. In addition, it is a criminal offence to contravene of any requirement of the Ordinance other than the principles contained in Schedule 1. Accordingly, the courts can be expected to play a significant role in the enforcement of the Ordinance. This provides a useful backstop to the role of the Commissioner.

The Structure of this Book

Broadly speaking, the arrangement of the text corresponds to the Ordinance. The Ordinance is structured in a manner that is novel for a Hong Kong statute. The body of the Ordinance's substantive provisions are divided into ten parts addressing matters in the following sequence:

- Preliminary, including definitions, relationship with other legislation and relationship of Parts I-X with the data protection principles set out in Schedule 1;
- Administration, detailing the setting up of the office of the Privacy Commissioner;
- Codes of Practice;
- Data User Returns;
- Access and Correction of Personal Data;
- Matching Procedures and Transfers to Places out of Hong Kong;
- Inspections, Complaints and Investigations;
- Exemptions;
- Offences and Compensation; and
- Miscellaneous.

After Part II, our analysis departs from this order and we follow instead the sequence that applies to the data processing cycle. Accordingly, we address data collection, data quality, use and disclosure and data security. We recognise that there is a degree of artificiality in dividing the data processing cycle in this manner and the different phases will in reality overlap. Nonetheless, we think it provides a more helpful basis on which to pursue our discussion of the new data protection regime. We then deal with access and correction rights.

Next we examine the Office of the Privacy Commissioner and the Commissioner's powers to investigate complaints and conduct inspections. We then examine the various exemptions provided under the Ordinance. Finally, we describe the offences created by the legislation, the provision of compensation and appeals.

Notes

1 Stress supplied.

2 'The Right to Privacy' (1890) 4 *Harvard Law Rev* 193.

3 At p 195.

4 At p 205

5 *Roberson v Rochester Folding Box Co* 171 NY 538; 64 NE 442 (1902).

6 At p 450.

7 *Pavesich v New England Life Insurance Co* 122 Ga 190; 50 SE 68 (1905).

8 William Prosser, 'Privacy' (1960) Calif Law Rev 383. Adopted by the *Restatement of Torts* Para 867.

9 It is not easy to see how the last two categories are properly described as wrongs offending the plaintiff's right to privacy. See R Wacks, (1989) *Personal Information: Privacy and the Law,* Clarendon Press, Oxford, chap 1.

10 381 US 479 (1965).

11 410 US 113 (1973).

12 112 S Ct (1992).

13 478 US 186 (1986). For an account of the New Zealand Act see E Longworth and T McBride, (1994) *The Privacy Act: A Guide*, GP Publications, Wellington.

14 David Calcutt QC, *Review of Press Self-Regulation*, Cm 2135.

15 National Heritage Select Committee, Fourth Report: *Privacy and Media Intrusion*, 294-1, 1993.

16 Colin Bennett, *Regulating Privacy: Data Protection and Public Policy in Europe and the United States* (Ithaca: Cornell University Press, 1992) p 37.

17 The use of the male person pronoun throughout this book is dictated by considerations of simplicity and grammatical elegance only.

18 *Breen v Williams* (1996) Unreported, FC 96/205, 6 September: A patient sought access to personal records held by a private practitioner. The other grounds for the claimed right rejected by the court relate to whether there was an implied contractual term allowing access, a right to one's records based on fiduciary duty or a more general right to know. See John Gaudin, 'Unrewarded in the High Court' (1996) 3 *Privacy Law & Policy Reporter*, 6 September.

19 *West Ham Church Wardens and Overseers v Fourth City Mutual Building Society* [1892] 1 QB 654 at 658 per AL Smith J.

20 Pressure on the Commission is (at the time of writing) high. The Ordinance came into force on 20 December; by 15 July 1997, the Office had received 108 complaints and 4,366 enquiries. For information on the PCO on the World Wide Web see www.pco.org.hk.

21 David Flaherty, (1989) *Protecting Privacy in Surveillance Societies: The Federal Republic of Germany, Sweden, France, Canada and the United States* Chapel Hill: University of North Carolina Press.

2 Background to the Ordinance

Introduction

The *Personal Data (Privacy) Ordinance* provides individuals with comprehensive safeguards against the misuse of personal information and a right of access to that information. The scope of the statute is plain once it is realised that personal data is broadly defined to mean any data relating to a living individual from which it is practicable for his or her identity to be ascertained. Even though this is restricted to data in a form in which access to or processing of the data is 'practicable', the reach of the law is long.

The protection of personal data is a delicate and difficult subject that touches on almost every aspect of our lives.[1] Not only does it represent a classic instance of the law's struggle to keep abreast of science, but the rapid advances in information technology have spawned problems that test the ability of the law to provide adequate protection against abuse. Data protection is merely one. The routine functions of government and private institutions require a continual supply of data about us in order to effectively administer the many services that are an integral part of modern life. The provision of health services, social security, credit, insurance and the prevention and detection of crime assume the availability of a considerable quantity of personal data and, hence, a willingness by individuals to supply it.

The new technology facilitates, in particular:

- The acquisition and retention of vast amounts of personal data;
- The rapid retrievability and transfer of data from any number of different points; and
- The combination and comparison of data in novel and complex ways.

The result of these developments has been an actual, as well as perceived, loss of control of personal information by the individual.

This often engenders a sense of powerlessness. On a practical level, decisions are continually made in reliance on the data affecting that person's vital interests. The dissemination of such data to parties not personally acquainted with the individual increasingly means that such data are the sole basis upon which such decisions are made.

The extent of this dissemination is indicated by a recent Swedish estimate that every Swede is the subject of between 50 and 300 files.[2] The rapid increase in the dissemination of personal data is achieved by technical advances. The need for such data, particularly in the private sector, is generated by its growing commercial value.[3]

The widespread use of computers and computer networks facilitates, of course, almost instant storage, retrieval and transfer of data, a far cry from the flat-footed world of manual filing systems. These developments are sometimes decried as the death of whatever vestiges of privacy still survive. In respect of the future of privacy at least, there can be little doubt that the questions are changing before our eyes. And if, in the domain of atoms, we have achieved only limited success in protecting individuals against the assaults on their privacy, how much better are the prospects in our binary universe?[4]

Hong Kong has at last caught up with over 30 other jurisdictions that have introduced data protection legislation in an effort to regain some of this lost ground. Most of these statutes draw on the provisions of the OECD guidelines of 1981 and those formulated by the Council of Europe in 1980. In 1995, the European Union adopted the *European Directive on Data Protection* which provides a comprehensive framework binding on member states which have until October 1998 to implement its provisions.[5]

Article 14 of the *Bill of Rights Ordinance* gives effect to Article 17 of the *International Covenant on Civil and Political Rights*, which provides for the protection against 'arbitrary or unlawful interference with . . . privacy . . . ' This article has been interpreted by the United Nations Human Rights Committee to include the protection of personal data. The United Nations General Assembly has also adopted guidelines for the regulation of computerised personal data files.

Articles 29 and 30 of *the Basic Law of the Hong Kong SAR* contain general declarations of support for privacy that might be construed as embracing the protection of personal data. Article 29 declares:

> The homes and other premises of Hong Kong residents shall be inviolable. Arbitrary or unlawful search of, or intrusion into, a resident's home or other premises shall be prohibited.

Article 30 provides:

> The freedom and privacy of communication of Hong Kong residents shall be protected by law. No department or individual may, on any grounds, infringe upon the freedom and privacy of communication of residents except that the relevant authorities may inspect communication [sic] in accordance with legal procedures to meet the needs of public security or of investigation into criminal offences.

These provisions (which, in extending their protection against intrusions by private individuals, as opposed to merely against public authorities, are wider than the *Bill of Rights*) impose a clear duty upon the SAR government to enact laws against 'intrusion'.

These articles are (perhaps inevitably) fairly broadly couched. In 1989, the Law Reform Commission of Hong Kong established a subcommittee to examine whether the law required reform. The subcommittee reported in August 1994.[6] Two months later the governor announced that legislation would be introduced. The Ordinance adopts most of the recommendations of the Law Reform Commission.

As with many – but by no means all – data privacy statutes elsewhere, the Ordinance applies both to computerised and manually held data. It is increasingly recognised that the distinction between computerised and manually held data is breaking down. This blurring of the difference is illustrated by the use of optical scanners (which speedily convert paper files into computer-readable disks) and the tagging of data. There is also evidence that data privacy laws which restrict their purview to computerised data encourage organisations to avoid regulation simply by retaining the data in manual form. This is not only unsatisfactory for the data subject, but is also inimical to the development of modern record keeping systems. Also, some classes of particularly sensitive data are usually held in manual files, such as social welfare and medical data. Most fundamentally of all, to restrict the application of the regulatory framework according to the medium in which the data are held is to allow policy to be dictated by form rather than principle.

In keeping with data privacy statutes in other unitary (as opposed to federal jurisdictions), the Ordinance extends both to the public and private sectors (another distinction that is increasingly difficult to draw).

At the heart of the new data protection regime is the concept of fair information practice, in particular, the proposition that data relating to an identifiable individual should not be collected in the absence of a genuine purpose and the consent of the individual concerned. At a slightly higher level of abstraction, it encapsulates the principle of what the German Constitutional Court has called 'informational self-determination'[7] – a postulate that expresses a fundamental democratic ideal. It is hard to overstate the importance of the 'use limitation' principle as a canon of fair information practice.

Adherence to, or more precisely, enforcement of, this idea (and the associated rights of access to one's personal data and correction of errors) has been mixed in those jurisdictions that have enacted data protection legislation. They share, however, a concern to establish an environment in which the collection and use of personal data is conducted fairly and openly.

One major problem resulting from the widespread dissemination of personal data is that such data are often inaccurate. An American study of state criminal records, for example, found that summaries of criminal histories that were complete, accurate and unambiguous ranged from 49.5 per cent downwards to only 12.2 per cent.[8]

Decisions based on inaccurate personal data are obviously flawed. This affects the interests not only of the data subject, but also those of the data user. These problems are common to all industrialised societies. They have been systematically addressed in several international instruments. These instruments first developed the data protection principles which form the core of the Ordinance.

The OECD Guidelines

The Organization for Economic Cooperation and Development ('the OECD') comprises member states from around the globe. Hong Kong is an associate member. The OECD is primarily concerned with fostering the economic development of its member states rather than human rights. The OECD has acknowledged that the economic interests of its members involve 'reconciling fundamental but competing values such as privacy and the free flow of information'. To this end, it issued a set of data protection guidelines to help member states adopt common standards. The objective was the promotion of trans-border data exchanges between member states unhindered by obstacles not justified on privacy grounds.

The OECD Guidelines represent an international consensus on what principles should govern the collection and processing of personal data. A number of member states have enacted laws giving effect to the eight data protection principles set out in the guidelines, including such Pacific Rim states as Japan, Taiwan, Australia and New Zealand. The content of the data protection principles set out in Schedule 1 of the Ordinance similarly are based on the OECD Guidelines.

The scope of the Ordinance is also similar to that of the guidelines. The data protection principles are applied to both the public and private sectors without differentiation. Nor is a distinction drawn between computerised and manual data. The OECD principles apply to all personal data 'which, because of the manner in which they are processed, or because of their nature or the context in which they are used, pose a danger to privacy and individual liberties'.[9] The Ordinance proceeds on the basis that all readily retrievable personal data pose such dangers and require regulation.

The Council of Europe Convention

The other two most influential data protection charters are European. The earlier of the two is the *Council of Europe Convention for the Protection of Individuals with regard to Automatic Processing of Personal Data*. Adopted in 1980 by the Committee of Ministers, its scope differs from the OECD Guidelines in only one major respect – unlike the guidelines, it focuses on the regulation of computerised data.

Whereas the OECD Guidelines are advisory, the convention is legally binding. It has provided the impetus for most of the council's member states enacting domestic legislation giving effect to its provisions, including the United Kingdom.

The European Directive

The more recent and, from Hong Kong's perspective more relevant, European charter on data protection is the *1995 European Directive on the Protection of Individuals with regard to the Processing of Personal Data and on the Free Movement of Such Data*. The Directive is important for several reasons. First, it represents a distillation of current thinking about data protection issues by that region in the world which has the greatest experience in this sphere of regulation. Several of the Ordinance's provisions were formulated with the

Directive in mind. For instance, s 34 requires that the data subject be offered the opportunity to opt out from the use of his data for direct marketing purposes.

Nor did the Directive influence only the content of the Ordinance. Rather, it provided a pressing economic reason why Hong Kong should legislate on data protection. There are a number of reasons why legislation is desirable in principle and these are set out above. But in its promotion of the need for legislation, the government emphasised also the risk to Hong Kong's trade position should adequate data protection not be implemented without delay. These concerns focused specifically on art 25(1) of the Directive. This provides that member states shall provide that the transfer to a third country of personal data that are undergoing or are intended for processing after transfer may take place *only if* [10] the third country in question ensures an adequate level of protection. Various exceptions are specified. 'Adequate level of protection' is defined to include a consideration of 'the rules of law – both general and sectoral – in force in the third country in question'.[11]

The Directive was adopted on 25 July 1995, just days before the enactment of the Ordinance. However, the initial draft issued in 1990 gave notice that restrictions were envisaged regarding the transfer of personal data from member states. Nor was this a new development; Some members were already imposing restrictions. For example, the French data protection authority has a discretionary power to prohibit transfers of personal data out of the jurisdiction. In one well publicised case, Fiat wished to transfer data on their French employees to their headquarters in Italy – a jurisdiction then lacking a data protection law. The French authority required Fiat (Turin) to enter into a contract with its French counterpart undertaking to apply the data protection principles when processing the data.[12]

The United Kingdom has also halted transfers to jurisdictions lacking data protection pursuant to a specific provision of the *Data Protection Act* 1984. It issued its first prohibition order in 1990 in respect of the transfer of names and addresses to the United States for direct marketing purposes.[13]

While the Directive's stricture on transfers has precedents, it has a much broader application. It requires all member states to incorporate into their domestic legislation the restrictions specified in art 25 by October 1998. The Ordinance (assuming it is properly enforced) enables the territory to avoid restrictions that would otherwise seriously threaten its position as an international financial centre. Indeed, the Ordinance (in s 33) imposes its own controls on the transfer of personal data out of Hong Kong.[14]

Local Factors

The international developments described above strongly suggested that Hong Kong follow suit and legislate to protect personal data. As mentioned, art 14 of the *Bill of Rights Ordinance* 1991 is relevant here. This enactment incorporated into domestic law the provisions of the *International Covenant on Civil and Political Rights*. Unlike the Ordinance, it lacks administrative complaints mechanisms, requiring instead that claimants litigate in the ordinary courts. It will be seen that the Ordinance combines both features.

During the second reading of the Bill of Rights bill, the Chief Secretary stated that privacy was, along with anti-discrimination, an area where supplementary legislation was proposed to extend protections in the private sector.

In addition to these related developments, the administration was already studying the issue of data protection. In 1985, the Secretary for Home Affairs established a working party consisting mainly of data processing experts to consider the matter. Progress was slow, and no report had been released by 1989 when, in an unrelated development, the Attorney-General and Chief Justice signed the terms of reference tasking the Law Reform Commission to conduct a comprehensive study of whether reform was required of laws relating to the protection of privacy. A subcommittee was established under the chairmanship of the Hon Mr Justice Barry Mortimer. The membership of the committee was drawn from a wider spectrum than that of the working party. It comprised a social scientist, government records supervisor, social worker, telecommunications manager, banker, government lawyer, senior police officer, legal academic and journalist.

The process which culminated in the legislation is instructive. Subcommittees appointed by the Commission generally appear to represent a coalition of interests and expertise, and, as far as one can tell, an attempt is made to provide a 'cross-section' of the community. Serving as a member of a subcommittee is time-consuming, unpaid work. The group met 56 times and, despite the difficult nature of the subject matter, a consensus emerged on all major questions. The consultation paper was unanimous in its proposals.

The Commission is not an independent body; it resides within the Legal Department and its chairman is the Attorney-General (now the Secretary of Justice). Though this may suggest a conflict of interest, or at least a confusion of functions, it plainly enhances the prospects of the Commission's proposals being translated into law, as occurred with spectacular speed in this case.

Another feature of this experience was the extensive consultation exercise conducted by the subcommittee. This included numerous seminars held by interested organisations such as the Consumer Council, the Journalists Association, the Society of Accountants, the Association of Banks, and the Direct Marketing Association. During the consultation period some 80 submissions were received (and required the subcommittee to meet another 20 times for them to be considered). Only three of those submissions doubted the need for data privacy legislation. The remainder focused on specific operational concerns.

The consultation period was twice extended and lasted from 17 March to 1 August 1993. Published in August 1994, the report of the Law Reform Commission made various adjustments to a number of the subcommittee's proposals to accommodate a number of points made in the submissions received during the consultation exercise.

Once the Law Reform Commission has published its recommendations, it is a matter for the administration to decide whether it places the issue on its agenda. Compared with other jurisdictions, it is noteworthy that a high proportion of the Law Reform Commission's reports have been implemented in legislation. A key factor appears to be the fact, mentioned above, that the chairman of the Law Reform Commission has been also the Attorney-General. His membership of the key policy-making bodies is crucial. Legal initiatives are first considered by a committee chaired by the Chief Secretary, of which the Attorney-General is a member. If approved, it is then considered by Hong Kong's equivalent of a cabinet, the Executive Council, which is chaired by the Governor (now the Chief Executive). Again, the Attorney-General was a member of this body and is well placed to argue the cause.

While the role of the Attorney-General may have been crucial in promoting this reform initiative, in the case of data protection, additional factors were at work. The key one was the role of the policy branch responsible for data protection, namely the Secretary for Home Affairs. Reference has already been made to his working group on data protection. This was established in 1985 – four years before the signing of the Law Reform Commission's terms of reference. The branch was therefore acutely conscious that data protection was a question that required attention. Thus, when the Law Reform Commission released its report the policy branch was already primed, enabling it – with considerable speed – to publish the first draft of the bill. This facilitated the commencement of an internal government consultation process. The main concern of government departments and other public authorities at this stage was to ensure that the exemptions were adequate to protect their operational requirements. The Bill was gazetted on 7 April 1995.

The Role of the Hong Kong Government

By the time the Bill was introduced in the Legislative Council (Legco), time was short. The Bill ran to 129 pages and Legco was due to be dissolved in early July prior to elections being held. The schedule was further tightened as a result of a delay in establishing a Bills Committee. Legco can service only 14 bills committees at any one time and no slot was available for some time. The first meeting of the committee examining the bill was on 16 May 1995. Emily Lau was elected chairman while other members contributed to a diverse span of alliances. All the political parties were represented.

Compounding the problem of the tight schedule was the generally heavy workload of Legco. Under these circumstances it is hardly surprising that the committee examining the bill sometimes wondered aloud whether they had undertaken 'Mission Impossible'. A major crisis occurred at the seventh meeting. There was no quorum and the meeting was abandoned. The chairman required all members subsequently to indicate whether they wished to continue their consideration of the bill. A majority voted to continue and as a result of the final push, the committee had its committee stage amendments ready by July.

Pure grit was a factor enabling the Bills Committee to complete its examination of this complex bill in less than two months. The composition of the Bills Committee was a significant factor. Three of its members were also members of the Legco Panel on Information Policy and this too was chaired by Emily Lau (the other two were Christine Loh and Anna Wu). In another departure from its usual practice, the Law Reform Commission's subcommittee had twice briefed the panel. As a result, three members of the Bills Committee already had a basic grasp of data protection issues even before the committee convened. This could have been crucial, given the restricted time available to brief members. In any event, it was a close call.

Data Protection and the Private Sector

Compliance with the Ordinance will require far-reaching changes in current attitudes and practices of information management. This is bound to generate expense and irritation. For most data users the law will intrude upon virtually all stages in the collection and use of personal data. The right of data subjects to obtain access to and correct erroneous data about them is having a profound effect on record keeping and confidentiality.

What are the costs of implementing data protection? It is clear that there are costs to the data user. These include those relating to the access and correction of data, fees for which must not be 'excessive' [s 28(3)]. Costs associated with compliance with the other provisions of the Ordinance must be met by the data user. These are difficult to quantify. It is important, however, to distinguish short-term and long-term costs and benefits. Whatever the short-term costs, compliance with the data protection principles is increasingly becoming a commercial necessity as privacy becomes a consumer issue.

A recent study,[15] based on interviews with executives in the banking, insurance and credit card industries, found that in the absence of legal regulation, executives are afraid to confront privacy issues and policy 'drift' results. This wandering and reactive policy-making process is attributed to the following factors:

- *Corporate culture:* Managerial attention tends to focus on items benefiting the company in the short term, whereas the information privacy principles are more likely to reap organisational benefits in the longer term;
- *Corporate organisation:* In the frequent absence of leadership from the top, middle managers are left to develop their own localised and often divergent policies; such fragmentation reduces the legitimacy of such policies and hence their influence;
- *Corporate coyness:* The reluctance of executives to be at the forefront of privacy policies delays the development of the consensus; and

- *Ambiguity:* This is the most serious obstacle identified by the author.

Since information privacy is not an area with clear-cut boundaries of appropriate and inappropriate behaviour, organisations are often left to plot their own courses through a thicket of conflicting views. A major achievement of the Ordinance is to dispel this ambiguity.

Notes

1 See R Wacks, (1993) *Personal Information: Privacy and the Law*, Clarendon Press, Oxford, pp 178-245; R Wacks (1996) 'Data Privacy: Reforming the Law' 26 HKLJ 149.

2 C Bennett, (1992) *Regulating Privacy: Data Protection and Public Policy in Europe and the United States,* Cornell, p 62.

3 See J Rothfeder, (1992) *Privacy for Sale: How Computerization has Made Everyone's Private Life an Open Secret*, Simon & Schuster, New York.

4 See R Wacks, (1997) 'Privacy in Cyberspace: Personal Information, Free Speech, and the Internet' in Peter Birks (ed), *Privacy and Loyalty*, Clarendon Press, Oxford.

5 See below.

6 *Report on Reform of the Law Relating to the Protection of Personal Data,* Topic 27 (1994) The Law Reform Commission of Hong Kong.

7 *Volkszahlungsurteil* [National Census Case] 1983 65 *BVerfGE* 1, 68-9, cited in S Simitis, 'Reviewing Privacy in an Information Society' (1987) 135 University of Pennsylvania Law Review 707, 734.

8 D Burnham, (1983) *The Rise of the Computer State*, Vintage Books, New York, p 73.

9 Organization for Economic Cooperation and Development (1981), *Guidelines on the Protection of Privacy and Transborder Flows of Personal Data*, OECD, Paris, para 35.

10 Emphasis supplied.

11 Art 26(2). See G Greenleaf, (1995) 'European Privacy Directive and Data Exports' 2 *Privacy Law and Policy Reporter*, p 205.

12 A Nugter, (1990), *Transborder Flow of Personal Data within the EC*, Kluwer, Deventer, p 204.

13 See S Dresner, 'First UK Ban', *Privacy Laws & Business*, Winter 1990/91, p 5.

14 At the time of writing, this provision is not yet in force.

15 H J Smith, (1994) *Managing Privacy*, The University of North Carolina Press, Chapel Hill.

3 Data Privacy and the Common Law

The Ordinance does not sweep away the existing remedies at common law. There is nothing to prevent an aggrieved data subject from seeking redress in the courts where, for example, a data user has wrongfully disclosed information imparted to him in confidence or whose publication is defamatory of the data subject. This chapter provides an outline of the principal common law actions that are most likely to assist data subjects whose personal data have been unlawfully collected or used.

A key consideration is whether personal data have been collected for a lawful purpose and by lawful means. By incorporating the concept of lawfulness, the Ordinance also incorporates a number of common law rules and principles, some of which are discussed in this chapter.

Lawfulness

Principle 1(1) of the Data Protection Principles declares that:

> Personal data shall not be collected unless (a) the data are collected for *a lawful purpose* directly related to a function or activity of the data user who is to use the data... (emphasis added).

Principle 1(2) provides that 'personal data shall be collected by means which are (a) *lawful* ...' (emphasis added).

What is meant by 'a lawful purpose', and 'means which are lawful'? The term 'lawful' is not defined in the Ordinance, but, unless the context suggests otherwise, may be taken to have its ordinary, natural meaning of 'not contrary to law'.[1] That is to say that Principle 1 will be breached when the collection of data or the means of their collection constitute a criminal offence, amount to a breach of contract, or a breach of a statutory or equitable duty. It may also constitute an unlawful use where a public body uses or discloses personal data *ultra vires*. In other words, a data user will be liable at common law where it fails to honour the ordinary legal rights of the data subject.

In practice, a data subject's most useful remedy in the field of personal information is likely to be the equitable remedy of breach of confidence, and the law is therefore examined at some length below. The tort of intentionally inflicting emotional distress on the defendant has recently attracted the interest of courts in England and, especially, Australia and New Zealand. The action may provide a means by which a data subject could obtain redress in circumstances where the misuse of personal data causes injury to feelings, and its scope therefore warrants discussion.

In addition, the collection, use or transfer of personal data may give rise to other wrongs at common law. Such activities may, for example, be in breach of a contract between the data subject and the data user or a third party. The disclosure of the data may, in certain circumstances, result in the data subject being defamed, or its collection or use may, as a consequence of the data user's negligence, cause the data subject to suffer damage. The following are also briefly considered:

- Breach of confidence;
- Intentional infliction of emotional distress;
- Defamation;
- Negligence;
- Breach of contract;
- Inducement of breach of contract;
- Breach of statutory duty;
- Trespass;
- Nuisance;
- Conversion; and
- Breach of copyright.

Breach of Confidence

Individuals may be willing to impart the most sensitive information on the basis that it will not be given to anyone save the recipient or, perhaps, those who have an obvious and explicit interest in receiving it.[2] In many cases, the individual himself is unaware that the ostensible confidentiality of 'personal information' about him has been breached, and this poses special difficulties in respect of its protection. Thus, for example, job applicants may have legitimate fears concerning the confidentiality of their personal data. A consequence of the apparent growth in the democratisation in the procedures of employment and promotion is the extent to which information concerning the applicant – revealed either by himself (in documents, in response to questionnaires or during an interview) or in testimonials by others – is circulated to persons other than his prospective employer. An applicant for appointment or promotion may be taken to have consented to such data (some of which may be sensitive) being known to those whom have a direct interest in them.

A similar expectation is shared by authors of references who will normally assume that the applicant himself will be denied access to such materials. While those who are privy to this information will generally be under an express or implied obligation of confidence, there can be little doubt that there is an increased risk in the unauthorised disclosure of personal data of which the applicant is unlikely himself to learn.

The law has long recognised the rights of A who imparts information in confidence to B and who then discovers that this information has been revealed (or is about to be revealed) by B to C. Not only may A be able to claim compensation against B for his loss (and to prevent its disclosure by injunction if he learns of it soon enough) but he may also be able to recover damages from C who knows – or ought reasonably to know – that the information is confidential. The overlap between breach of confidence and the Ordinance is immediately evident, both in respect of the general law under which A is protected, but also in the determination of whether B or C (assuming they are data users) have behaved unlawfully.

This is a complex branch of the law, but it may be summarised under the following headings:[3]

The Elements of the Action

The leading cases[4] provide some guidance as to when recipients of confidential information (either direct or indirect) may be restrained from using or disclosing it. Recent decisions recognise a wider equitable principle of 'good faith' or conscience on which to base the jurisdiction[5] but its scope remains uncertain. What is clear is that in order to found a cause of action, three general requirements must be satisfied:

- The information itself must 'have the necessary quality of confidence about it'.[6] (This requirement is normally satisfied by demonstrating that the information is 'not...public property and public knowledge');[7]
- The information must have been imparted in circumstances imposing an obligation of confidence. Such an obligation will normally arise when information is imparted – either explicitly or implicitly – for a limited purpose, and extends to any third parties to whom the information is disclosed, in breach of confidence, by the original confidant;[8] and
- There must have been an unauthorised use of the information by the party who was under an obligation of confidence.

Each of these requirements will be briefly examined with particular reference to the protection of personal data.

The information

Although the vast majority of decisions involve cases concerning trade secrets (including business and technical secrets), government secrets, artistic and literary confidences and personal information have all been the subject of litigation. The main concern here is of course with personal data (as defined in the Ordinance) and it is clear that there is a considerable overlap between such data and 'confidential information' for the purposes of protection by the action for breach of confidence.

There are several instances in which the courts have been required to examine the extent to which personal information (as opposed to trade secrets or commercial information which is anonymous or does not identify a living individual) may be used or disclosed in breach of confidence. So, for example, in *Duchess of Argyll v Duke of Argyll*[9] the Duchess successfully sought an injunction to prohibit the Duke and a newspaper from publishing confidences she had reposed in her husband in the course of their marriage. Ungoed-Thomas J held that such communications between spouses were protected against breach of confidence – notwithstanding the Duchess's subsequent adultery and divorce from the Duke. He declared, 'There could hardly be anything more intimate or confidential than is involved in [the relationship of marriage], or than in the mutual trust and confidence which are shared between husband and wife.'[10] Similarly, in *Stephens v Avery*,[11] the information concerned the plaintiff's lesbian affair. On the facts, the disclosure of intimate details regarding someone's sexual life was held by the vice-chancellor not to be trivial: 'I have the greatest doubt whether wholesale revelation of the sexual conduct of an individual can properly be described as "trivial" tittle-tattle'.[12] He added, 'I can see no reason why information relating to that most private sector of everybody's life, namely sexual conduct, cannot be the subject maker of a legally enforceable duty of confidentiality'.[13]

In *Woodward v Hutchins*,[14] the exploits of pop stars were the subject of the action. There were no submissions in respect of the actual quality of the information revealed, and Lord Denning MR proceeded on the basis that it was *prima facie* susceptible to the protection of a duty of confidentiality. Similarly, in *Lennon v News Group Newspapers Ltd*[15] the former wife of John Lennon sold the 'story' of her marriage to the ex-Beatle to the *News of the World* which commenced a serialisation of it. The articles disclosed intimate details of the relationship between the plaintiff and his ex-wife. The Court of Appeal denied an injunction on the ground that 'the relationship of these parties has ceased to be their own private affair...'. In *Khashoggi v Smith* [16] the former housekeeper of the plaintiff, an affluent socialite who had attracted considerable publicity, disclosed intimate facts to the *Daily Mirror* concerning the plaintiff. As there was an investigation proceeding into the alleged commission of an offence by the plaintiff, the Court of Appeal, on an interlocutory motion, refused to enjoin publication on the principal ground that there could be no confidence where it was sought to exploit information for investigation into the commission of alleged offences.

Many disclosures assume the form of a photograph taken or used without the subject's consent. It is a problem that, though its contemporary form assumes rather different proportions, began in the early days of photography. In *Pollard v Photographic Co*,[17] Mrs Pollard had her picture taken at the defendant's shop. An employee of the defendant used it in the shop window in the form of a Christmas card. There was some evidence that the employee may have been selling the cards for commercial gain (rather than using the card to advertise the services of the photographic company). North J held that a breach of confidence had occurred, declaring that '[w]here a person obtains information in the course of a confidential employment, the law does not permit him to make any improper use of the information so obtained'.[18]

The same principle was recently held to apply to the use by police of 'mug shots'. In *Hellewell v Chief Constable of Derbyshire,*[19] in order to assist and promote a local shop watch scheme to prevent crime, the police used photographs of the plaintiff taken when he was a police suspect three years before. His argument that this use was in breach of confidence was rejected by the court on the ground that it was in the public interest because it constituted reasonable use for the purpose of the prevention and detection of crime, the investigation of alleged offences and the apprehension of suspects.[20]

The obligation of confidence

The recipient of information normally incurs an obligation of confidence by virtue of the relationship in the course of which the information is imparted. Such an obligation may arise, with or without a contract, in a variety of circumstances ranging from marriage[21] to cabinet meetings.[22]

Notwithstanding the absence of an explicit undertaking by the recipient of information to maintain its confidentiality, an obligation of confidence will generally be imposed upon him if the circumstances are such as to indicate that he knew or ought to have known that the information is to be treated as confidential.[23] Even where a third party receives confidential information, and at the time he receives it is unaware that he has acquired it as a result of a breach of confidence, he will, on being given notice of the breach, be prima facie subject to a duty of confidence. This is clear from the following dictum by Sir Robert Megarry VC in *Malone v Commissioner of Police of the Metropolis (No 2)*:[24]

> If A makes a confidential communication to B, then A may not only restrain B from divulging or using the confidence, but also may restrain C from divulging or using it if C has acquired it from B, even if he acquired it without notice of any impropriety.... In such cases it seems plain that, however innocent the acquisition of the knowledge, what will be restrained is the use or disclosure of it after notice of the impropriety.

An important question is whether an obligation of confidence can arise in the absence of some pre-existing confidential relationship in which the plaintiff imparts confidential information to another. In the majority of instances where personal data is provided by a data subject to a data user (for instance where I provide personal data to my bank, my doctor or my employer), such a relationship will be present. Moreover, it will be suggested below that such an obligation may arise when a third party ought reasonably to have known that the data he has received must have been imparted in confidence. If this reading of the law is correct, the remedy for breach of confidence may offer data subjects a helpful weapon with which to protect their interests.

Unauthorised use

For the plaintiff in a breach of confidence action to establish that the defendant has actually used or disclosed the confidential information, he must prove that the information was 'directly or indirectly obtained from (the) plaintiff, without the consent, express or implied, of the plaintiff'.[25] He does not have to show that the defendant has acted dishonestly or even consciously in using the information.[26] Whether the plaintiff need establish that he has suffered (or will suffer) detriment as a result of the breach of confidence is unclear. While Megarry J (as he then was) in *Coco v A N Clark (Engineers) Ltd*[27] suggested that this might be a requirement of the action, the better view would seem to be that this factor ought to be conceived as relevant only to the determination of the appropriate remedy. In the context of the use or disclosure of personal data, the plaintiff may not have suffered any detriment in the strict sense of material disadvantage, though he almost certainly will have suffered injured feelings, embarrassment or distress.[28] The Ordinance provides in section 66(2) that damages may be awarded for injury to feelings (see Chapter 13).

A Relationship of Confidence?

As already mentioned, one of the most troublesome features of the law of confidence is whether there is a requirement of a relationship of confidence between the person who confides the information and the person to whom it is confided. A number of decisions may suggest that the action is not predicated upon a prior relationship between the parties but is based upon the principle of unconscionability, in particular, *Stephens v Avery*,[29] *Francome v Mirror Group Newspapers Ltd*,[30] *Attorney-General v Guardian Newspapers Ltd (Nos 1 and 2)* (the *Spycatcher* cases)[31] and *Franklin v Giddens*.[32]

In *Stephens*, the Vice-Chancellor, in response to the defendant's submission that there must be such a relationship for the duty of confidence to be imposed, stated that 'the basis of intervention...is that it is unconscionable for a person who has received information on the basis that it is confidential subsequently to reveal that information'.[33] This view was strongly endorsed in the second *Spycatcher* decision by Lord Goff:

> [A] duty of confidence arises when confidential information comes to the knowledge of a person (the confidant) in circumstances where he has notice, or is held to have agreed, that the information is confidential, with the effect that it would be just in all the circumstances that he should be precluded from disclosing the information to others.[34]

In *Francome*[35] the defendant newspaper sought an interlocutory application to discharge an injunction restraining it from publishing until trial extracts from the recordings of the conversations between the plaintiff and his wife. The information was such that both sides were conscious of its value: the plaintiff in destroying his reputation, the newspaper in profiting from a scoop concerning alleged illicit activities by one of Britain's leading jockeys. Even though the confidant (the plaintiff's wife) had committed no breach of confidence, the Court of Appeal nevertheless held that a third party (the tapper) could be held liable – for his conscience was pricked. The only basis upon which such a conclusion could have been reached was the tacit assumption that a person who unlawfully listens to another's telephone conversation acquires information that was intended to be received by no one other than the person on the end of the line. A tapper is, by definition, on notice, either explicitly or implicitly.

The trial court's willingness (at the interlocutory stage) to recognise a duty of confidence imposed by virtue merely of receipt of confidential information is significant. Indeed, *Francome* demonstrates that the traditional distinction between the obligation on a confidant within a relationship of confidence with the confider, and on a third party whose conscience may be pricked simply by notice, is, at least on certain facts, difficult to sustain. It looks like a straightforward acceptance of a duty based on unconscionable behaviour *per se*.

The limitations of the decision must, however, be acknowledged. First, it was an interlocutory hearing, and secondly, the court appears to condemn the manner in which the information was obtained, rather than its nature.[36]

While the force of *Francome* may be reduced by its interlocutory setting, the court was nevertheless faced with clear authority that in the case of telephone-tapping, no cause of action would lie. And while one presumes that in awarding an injunction, it was influenced by the fact that the plaintiff's remedy of damages if the article were published before trial was a fairly hollow one, the court explicitly addressed the conflicting authority on the point. It was obviously persuaded that there was a reasonable prospect of the plaintiff's substantive claim succeeding at trial.

In *Malone v Commissioner of Police of the Metropolis (No 2),*[37] on the other hand, the Vice-Chancellor declined an injunction to protect an individual whose telephone had been tapped by the police who had acted according to law under directions from the Home Secretary. In his view, 'however secret and confidential the information, there can be no binding obligation of confidence if that information is blurted out in public or is communicated in other circumstances which negative any duty of holding it confidential'.[38] He added, 'it seems to me that a person who utters confidential information must accept the risk of any unknown overhearing that is inherent in the circumstances of communication'.[39]

This reasoning was, however, distinguished by the Court in *Francome*. Fox L J observed:

> The [Vice-Chancellor] was only dealing with a case of authorised tapping by the police.... Illegal tapping by private persons is quite another matter since it must be questionable whether the user of a telephone can be regarded as accepting the risk of that in the same way as, for example, he accepts the risk that his conversation may be overheard in consequence of the accidents and imperfections of the telephone system itself.[40]

In *Spycatcher (No. 2)* Lord Goff observed that the duty of confidentiality, as currently defined, embraced the situation 'where an obviously confidential document is wafted by an electric fan out of a window into a crowded street, or when an obviously confidential document, such as a private diary, is dropped in a public place, and is then picked up by a passer-by'.[41] He then, rather cryptically, continued:

> I have...deliberately avoided the fundamental question whether, contract apart, the duty [of confidentiality] lies

> simply 'in the notion of an obligation of conscience arising from the circumstances in or through which the information was communicated or obtained'.[42]

The first statement is important for it plainly contemplates attaching a duty of confidence to a person who receives information that is obviously confidential by virtue only of the nature of the information. Hence, the reasonable man who stumbles across a private diary would clearly apprehend that the information unintentionally imparted to him should not be passed on to others.

In *Franklin v Giddens,* the defendant occasionally lent a hand at the plaintiff's orchard, subsequently set up his own rival orchard and then, surreptitiously, stole budwood cuttings from the plaintiff's premises. The cuttings provided the defendant with information regarding a new strain of nectarines that the plaintiff had cross-bred. Dunn J did not consider the obligation of confidence to be predicated upon a relationship between the parties during the course of which the information was divulged from confider to confidant. He found himself 'quite unable to accept that a thief who steals a trade secret, with the intention of using it in commercial competition with its owner, to the detriment of the latter and so uses it, is less unconscionable than a traitorous servant'.[43]

The limitations of the decision must, however, be acknowledged. The information was of a wholly commercial nature and, more importantly, the cutting – the carrier of the information – was obtained unlawfully from the plaintiff's orchard. The result could well have been very different if the defendant had stumbled upon the cutting lying on a road near the plaintiff's orchard.[44]

In *Kaye v Robertson,*[45] the plaintiff's photograph, taken by newspaper reporters while he was convalescing in a private room of a hospital from which they were expressly barred, was published in the defendant newspaper. Breach of confidence was not pleaded, but, apart from the question of prior relationship between the parties, the case has much in common with *Pollard*[46] and *Hellewell,*[47] which concern the unauthorised use of the plaintiff's likeness.

In *Koo and Chiu v Lam,*[48] the Hong Kong Court of Appeal held that a medical researcher was under a duty of confidence in respect of a questionnaire that had been prepared by a 'rival' research team and which, by the appellant's admission, he had used formulating his own questionnaire. The absence of a relationship between the parties did not prevent the court from imposing liability for breach of confidence. Unfortunately, however, there is no clear evidence as to how the appellant obtained access to the respondents' questionnaire. Penlington JA, commenting upon the trial judge's finding that the appellant had obtained the information 'surreptitiously', remarked:

> [H]e did somehow come into possession of the document, and he must have known it was confidential because of the amount of work which had gone into its preparation. It had not been given to him by the persons whose information it was and again he must have realised he was not entitled to use it.[49]

This dictum takes the law considerably further than both *Franklin* and *Francome* for in those decisions the 'surreptitious taker' acted contrary to law (theft and an offence contrary to the UK *Wireless Telegraphy Act* 1949, respectively). In *Koo*, Penlington JA emphasised that the finding of 'surreptitious obtaining' did not extend as far as theft which, he said 'cannot be supported by the evidence'.[50] But if surreptitious taking extends to the mere fact that the appellant 'did somehow come into possession' of the questionnaire with the knowledge that it was confidential, the Court of Appeal appears to have adopted the notion of receipt-based liability, albeit under cover of surreptitiousness rather than unconscionability.

The decision must, however, be confined to its facts. The actual finding, at first instance, that the information was imparted in circumstances imposing an obligation of confidence was not challenged upon appeal.[51] Secondly, the rival teams of researchers worked at the same university which implied a 'course of dealing' between the parties during which the appellant arguably became aware that the questionnaire was confidential. This could, to some extent, approximate to a relationship of confidence on orthodox principles.

While the judgment does not impose a duty of confidence on the stranger who finds a diary in the street, it does demonstrate the utility of the breach of confidence action where the strict requirement of a prior relationship is relaxed. It does not, however, remove all the obstacles in the path of the protection of personal information, for the finding that the appellant knew that the information contained in the questionnaire was confidential was derived less from the nature of the information than from his personal experience and the limited relationship between the parties.

Constructive Knowledge

If the principle of unconscionability is indeed at the heart of the action, the insistence on the need for a prior relationship between confider and confidant may be explained as the threshold of circumstantial evidence the plaintiff must establish in order to show that the recipient's conscience has been pricked by the confidential nature of the information. The question therefore becomes one of standard of proof: under what circumstances will constructive knowledge be attributed to a confidant – that he has received information he is expected to keep secret – when such knowledge cannot be said to exist in fact?

The existence of a relationship therefore becomes a sufficient but not a necessary condition of liability. It is, in other words, an important factor in determining whether the evidence supports the inference that the recipient of the information either knew or ought reasonably to have known that the information was subject to a duty of confidence, but it is not a requirement of the action.

How is constructive knowledge to be fixed? In *Coco,* Megarry J said:

> It seems to me that if the circumstances are such that any reasonable man standing in the shoes of the recipient of the information would have realised that upon reasonable grounds the information was being given to him in confidence, then this should suffice to impose upon him the equitable obligation of confidence.[52]

This statement pertains both to the confidant and to third party recipients.

In *Li Yau-wai v Genesis Films Ltd,*[53] the plaintiff, an insurance salesman, allowed his photograph to be taken by the defendant film company upon the understanding it would facilitate his being considered for casting in a future film. Instead, the defendant used the photograph as a prop in a film – a ribald comedy — causing the plaintiff considerable embarrassment. The court held that, in addition to liability in defamation, the defendant owed the plaintiff an obligation of confidence in respect of the photograph and, accordingly, the unauthorised use constituted breach of that obligation. Rhind J applied the reasoning of North J in *Pollard* to find that the photograph had the necessary quality of confidence about it, adding that '[w]here a person makes himself accessible to be photographed by another in circumstances where one would expect confidentiality to be respected, a duty of confidence on the part of the person taking the photograph will arise'.[54]

The court applied Megarry J's objective test to determine the second limb of the traditional test of actionability: was the information imparted in circumstances importing an obligation of confidence? It was satisfied that 'any officious bystander would emphatically pronounce that when Genesis took Mr Li's photograph, [it] knew full well that it was only supposed to use it for casting purposes'.[55] The plaintiff was able also to recover damages for defamation (see below).

In the case of a third party, his obligation to keep information secret is parasitic upon there being an obligation owed to the confider by a confidant.[56] The law attaches such a duty in respect of the confidences of a person whom the third party may never even have met because a duty of confidence has arisen at the primary level between confidant and confider.

The effect of *Francome* and *Franklin* may be that the court will not condone the improper or unlawful obtaining of information.[57] It is tempting to distinguish between such conduct and the innocent finding of a diary or, indeed, lawful telephone tapping. In any event, the distinction drawn by Fox LJ in *Francome* rests on the quality of the information. The information in *Malone* was information in the public domain; the conversations in *Francome* were not. Moreover, in *Francome* there was no breach of duty apart from the eavesdropping of a 'third party'. On what other ground could the telephone conversations be protected than that the conscience of the recipient was pricked by the confidentiality of the information? If that is an acceptable category of confidential information it requires, of course, only a limited exercise of the legal imagination to extend protection to the victim of the zoom lens for, 'in principle, there cannot be any distinction between eavesdropping on telephone conversations and intruding on private occasions by the use of long-range cameras or binoculars'.[58]

Public Domain

The availability or accessibility of information is better regarded as a factor initially negating the obligation of confidence than as a defence to an action for breach of confidence. In the commercial context, the classic formulation of the test is, as expounded in *Saltman*, that the information is public property and public knowledge. This has been refined by concepts like the so-called 'springboard doctrine'. Hence, in a typical trade case, *O Mustad v Dosen*,[59] the defendant, allegedly in breach of confidence, informed a rival company about details of the plaintiff's process for making fish hooks (the defendant having formerly worked for the plaintiff company). The details had to some extent been revealed by the plaintiff in their patent. In Lord Buckmaster's view,

> Of course, the important point about the patent is not whether it was valid or invalid, but what it was that it disclosed, because after the disclosure had been made by the plaintiff to the world, it was impossible for them to get an injunction restraining the defendant from disclosing what was common knowledge.[60]

In the case of personal data, the test works less successfully, though much of the confusion has arisen as a consequence of an incomplete analysis of the commercial doctrines or of the factual circumstances of the particular decisions in issue.[61] Thus in *Schering Chemicals Ltd v Falkman Ltd*[62] the court, in effect, imposed on the second defendant a blanket duty not to disclose matters which he had learned as an interviewer for a course that Schering had provided to counteract adverse publicity which had surrounded their pregnancy-testing drug. The court appeared to annihilate the public domain test to determine of liability and instead treated it as one of the factors to be taken into account in the 'public interest' balancing exercise.

The decision may, however, be read as an application of the springboard doctrine, that is that someone who acquires confidential information may not take advantage of that information even if it subsequently enters the public domain.

The Springboard Doctrine

The scope of the principle is well expressed by Roxburgh J in *Terrapin Ltd v Builders Supply Co (Hayes) Ltd*[63] where he states that 'springboard it remains even when all the features have been published or can be ascertained by actual inspection by any member of the public'.[64] But the obvious problem with this expression of the doctrine is that it appears to nullify the public domain test, ie that information obtained prima facie under an obligation of confidentiality can never be used even if it is subsequently published. This places the recipient of the information in a worse position than anyone else, and it contradicts *Mustad* which specifically acknowledges the inability of the courts to enforce a duty of confidence in respect of information available to the public at large. Attempts to reconcile *Mustad* and *Terrapin* have not been especially successful.[65]

There is much to be said for Gurry's view that emphasis be placed on the 'inaccessibility of the information to the public':

> What the courts are protecting, therefore, is essentially an original process of mind which produces inaccessible information, and the protection operates against anyone, who, by taking unfair advantage of the information which has been disclosed to him, saves himself the time, trouble and expense of going through the same process.[66]

In other words, although the information in *Schering* had, at some time, been accessible in the press and on television, the defendant, by virtue of his position 'inside the story', had a permanent advantage over all others since, even though the public could rekindle and augment their knowledge from existing media sources, the defendant was one step ahead in terms of the time, money and effort required to perform the requisite investigation.

It may be useful to consider some common examples of the operation of the equitable remedy in practice.

Solicitor and client

The clearest instance of the application of the principle of confidentiality described above, arises in the case of the relationship of solicitor and client, a privilege which is recognised by the law[67] in order to facilitate the obtaining and preparation of evidence by a party to an action in support of his case.[68] This privilege is narrower in scope than the solicitor's general duty of confidence to his client. The former prevents a solicitor from disclosing in any legal proceedings communications between his client and himself without the consent of the client.[69] The latter extends to any confidential information which he has obtained in his capacity as legal adviser: he may not use such information except in the interests of his client.[70] Depending on the circumstances this principle may operate to preclude a solicitor from acting for a former client's opponent.[71]

The special privilege attaching to the solicitor-client relationship is, of course, a function of the position of legal advisers in the administration of justice[72] and its extension to other relationships which rely equally on trust and candour has been resisted: the courts have refused to recognise its application to the relationship with priest,[73] doctor,[74] accountant,[75] banker[76] or to the claimed right of journalists not to disclose their sources.[77]

Legal professional privilege is recognised in s 60 of the Ordinance; it exempts data that 'consist of information in respect of which a claim to legal professional privilege could be maintained in law' from the access provisions of data protection principle 6 and s 18(1)(b). The draft bill restricted the exemption to circumstances where the privilege 'could be maintained in legal proceedings'. The formulation in the Ordinance, however, indicates that the exemption extends to confidential data held by a solicitor (see Chapter 12).

Doctor and patient

One of the most pervasive collectors of personal data is the medical profession and hospital authority. Patients routinely divulge the most intimate information to their doctors who, according to the Hippocratic oath,[78] the ethics of the profession[79] and the law,[80] are under a general duty to maintain the confidentiality of such information. This duty is occasionally overridden by the competing public interest in, for example, the protection of others against contagious diseases[81] or the administration of justice.[82]

In the particular context of AIDS, a number of arguments have been raised to justify the violation of medical confidentiality.[83] In particular it is urged that in order to contain the spread of the disease it may be necessary for doctors to report cases of AIDS to public health authorities.[84] The need for accurate information is obviously vital if research into the aetiology and spread of AIDS is to be properly conducted. Yet there is no compelling reason why such data cannot be anonymous. In view of the traumatic consequences that their disclosure will cause, the onus should be on the authorities to demonstrate that the benefits outweigh carriers' rights to have their medical histories kept confidential. Similarly, there is a considerable risk that a person who is rejected for individually screened small group coverage because he has been tested positive may find that the insurance company has passed on this information to his employer, resulting in discrimination.

Failure to enforce a strong duty of medical confidentiality is likely to prove counterproductive. Many individuals will simply be deterred from being tested for the virus. This will have the obvious consequence of drying up sources of information and, at the same time, contributing indirectly to the further spread of the disease. What, it is often asked, should a doctor do when his patient is tested positive for AIDS and the doctor knows or suspects that the patient is likely to continue engaging in sex with his (uninfected) partner? He has failed to persuade the patient to inform his partner or to desist or even to take precautions. Should the doctor breach his patient's confidence and inform the partner? It is difficult to see how an absolute duty of confidence could be maintained in such circumstances,[85] but it does not follow from this somewhat extreme and rather unlikely example that we should readily allow exceptions to the general duty. It merely suggests that, while maintaining a strict duty of confidence, doctors may, on rare occasions, have to consider breaching it.

In *Gillick v West Norfolk and Wisbech Area Health Authority and the DHSS*,[86] the House of Lords held, by a majority, that parental rights were not necessarily infringed where a doctor, in exceptional circumstances, gave contraceptive advice and treatment to a girl under 16 without her parents' knowledge or consent. The judgment which has become something of a *cause célèbre*, turned in part on the confidential relationship between doctor and patient, Lord Fraser declaring that 'to abandon the principle of confidentiality for contraceptive advice to girls under 16 might cause some not to seek professional advice at all, thus exposing them to 'the immediate risks of pregnancy and sexually transmitted diseases'.[87]

The confidentiality of medical records may be protected by the action for breach of confidence. But should a doctor, hospital or other holder of medical information disclose it without the patient's consent to a party who has no legitimate interest in receiving it, this is a rather hollow remedy, not only because the plaintiff will not generally know that the information has been disclosed, but also because even if he does know, the damage will have been done.[88] His objection would be to any unauthorised disclosure, and an injunction is likely to be the most effective remedy – but this, of course, presupposes that he is aware that a disclosure is about to take place, an unlikely eventuality. An injunction may, of course, enable him to prevent the information – if he is aware of its disclosure – being given wider circulation. Even if he is awarded damages for distress and embarrassment, it is improbable that this will satisfy a plaintiff whose objection is to the disclosure itself.

Section 59 of the Ordinance exempts 'personal data relating to the physical or mental health of the data subject' from either or both the access provisions of data protection principle 6 and s 18(1)(b) and data protection principle 3 where the application of these provisions 'would be likely to cause serious harm to the physical or mental health of the data subject or any other individual'.[89]

Banker and customer

The use of personal data held by banks is exemplified by the leading decision of the Court of Appeal in *Tournier v National Provincial and Union Bank of England*.[90] T's account with N Bank was overdrawn. He agreed with N to attempt to reduce his overdraft, but failed to do so. X, another of N's customers, drew a cheque in T's favour, which T endorsed to Y. On receiving the cheque for payment, N learned from Y's bank that Y was a bookmaker. N subsequently informed T's employers that T had endorsed X's cheque to a bookmaker, whereupon T's contract of employment was terminated. The majority of the Court of Appeal held that disclosure of this information, since it was acquired by N in their 'character as the plaintiff's banker',[91] was in breach of the bank's obligation of confidence. All three members of the court accepted that no information received from the customer himself, from the state of his account, and from the transactions that go through his account or securities, if any, given in respect of the account could be disclosed by the bank, except under compulsion of law.[92] This power was described by Lord Widgery CJ as 'a very serious interference with the liberty of the subject' and 'a gross invasion of privacy'.[93]

Information acquired under statute

Governments have a tendency to transfer data between departments, despite the absence of consent by the data subject. In *Hall v Commissioner of ICAC,*[94] a jockey had been investigated by the ICAC. He was, in the event, not prosecuted, but the ICAC forwarded a file of the evidence obtained to the Royal Hong Kong Jockey Club which informed Hall that he would face disciplinary proceedings. Hall sought declarations that the ICAC had acted unlawfully in passing on the evidence to the Jockey Club. The Court of Appeal denied relief. Cons VP held that although the *ICAC Ordinance* contained no express statutory basis for the passing on of the evidence, the legislature must have intended that the Commissioner of the ICAC should have the power to refer such information to the appropriate body in order to permit it to pursue such action as is necessary to reduce or eliminate corruption.[95]

Fuad JA went further. He held that in the absence of an explicit prohibition against such disclosure (to be found, for instance, in section 4 of the *Inland Revenue Ordinance*), there was nothing to prevent it.[96]

A different approach was adopted by the Court of Appeal in England in *Marcel v Commissioner of Police*[97] and *Morris v Director of the Serious Fraud Office*.[98] *Marcel* concerned an application for injunctions restraining the police from disclosing to third parties information obtained without a search warrant pursuant to statutory search and seizure powers. The police acquired the evidence in the course of investigating alleged criminal offences, but prior to any charges being laid, were served a subpoena to produce the documents in a civil action involving different parties. Since there was nothing in the legislation to prohibit disclosure, the *Malone* principle was prayed in aid. It received short shrift from the Court of Appeal, however, which declared:[99]

> [D]ocuments seized by a public authority from a private citizen in exercise of a statutory power can properly be used only for those purposes for which the relevant legislation contemplated that they might be used. *The user for any other purpose of documents seized in exercise of a draconian power of this nature, without the consent of the person from whom they were seized, would be an improper exercise of the power.* Any such person would be entitled to expect that the authority would treat the documents and their contents as confidential, save to the extent that it might use them for purposes contemplated by the relevant legislation.

This is plainly in line with data protection principle 3 and marks an important shift towards a recognition of an equitable duty of confidence arising in circumstances where information is provided under statutory requirements.

Breach of Confidence and the Ordinance Compared

The action for breach of confidence plainly affords substantial adventitious protection for the misuse of personal data. There will be situations in which a data subject's rights will be protected both by the action and by the Ordinance, but there are distinctions between the two (see Table 1). Most of these differences flow from the differing purposes of the two regimes. The purpose of the Ordinance is to prevent the misuse of data by formulating standards for their collection and use. The law of confidence, on the other hand, has as its main purpose the preservation of the relationship of trust between confider and confidant of personal information which is confidential. So, for example, where A provides confidential information to his insurance company, B, and learns that B is about to reveal this information to C, under the equitable remedy for breach of confidence, he may seek an urgent interlocutory injunction to prevent the use or disclosure of the information to C. In order to succeed he will need to satisfy the court that the information was imparted in confidence. The information need not relate to him provided it was imparted in confidence. Should the use or disclosure already have occurred, A may seek damages to compensate him for the breach.

Under the Ordinance, however, there is no requirement that the personal data were imparted in confidence, but the data must relate to A, the data subject. Nor does the legislation provide for injunctive relief, and though one of the main purposes of the Ordinance is to prevent the misuse of personal information, it does so by the enforcement of the data protection principles and other measures.

The main differences between the two regimes are summarised in Table 1.

Table 1: Breach of Confidence and the Ordinance Compared

Breach of Confidence	Personal Data (Privacy) Ordinance
Legal persons protected.	Only 'living individuals' protected.
Information must 'have the necessary quality of confidence about it', ie it is 'not public property and public knowledge' (*Saltman*).	Data need only be 'personal', ie relating directly or indirectly to a living individual from which it is practicable for his identity to be ascertained in a form in which access to or processing of the data is practicable.
The information must have been imparted in circumstances imposing an obligation of confidence.	Not required, but data may be collected only for a lawful purpose, such collection being necessary or directly related to that purpose, and the purpose must be specified to the data subject on or before collection (DPP 1).

Table 1 – *continued*

Breach of Confidence	Personal Data (Privacy) Ordinance
Extends to any information.	The data must be 'represented', ie recorded in some form.
The obligation of confidence normally arises when information is imparted for a limited purpose and extends to a third party to whom it is disclosed in breach of confidence by the original confidant or who ought reasonably to know that the information is confidential.	The obligation imposed on the data user is confined to observing the data protection principles; the duty is attached to each data user.
Remedy available only when there has been unauthorised use of the information (or such use is imminent).	Use of personal data in breach of data protection principle 3 may give rise to remedy.
Not required.	Law applies only where personal data is 'in a form in which access to or processing of the data is practicable'.
Would undermine duty of confidence.	Right of access to certain classes of personal data.
Any confidential relationship included.	Exemptions specified in legislation.
Purely civil remedy.	Certain criminal offences created.
Damages unlikely to be awarded for mental distress.	Section 66(2) provides for the award of damages for injury to feelings.
The plaintiff may need to show 'detriment' and this may result only in the award of an injunction, rather than damages.	Damages recoverable without need to show 'detriment', but no injunctive relief available.
Defendant may be required to make an account of profits obtained as a consequence of the breach.	Not available.

Conflicts

As indicated in Table 1, the duty of confidence is undermined by the very concept of a right of access to certain classes of personal data (see Chapter 9). Where such conflicts do occur, the Ordinance would take precedence. For example, in the context of the relationship of banker and customer discussed above, any conflict between the so-called *Tournier* exceptions[100] and the Ordinance would be resolved by the general legal principle that, in the event of any such conflict, a statute overrides the common law to the extent of that inconsistency. Thus where a data user is compelled by statute to disclose confidential information that constitutes 'personal data' under s 2, it must do so despite the fact that the data were provided pursuant to a duty of confidence.

Such compulsion may arise from the Ordinance's conferring a statutory right of access on the data subject. For example, X may provide personal data in confidence about a data subject to a bank. By compelling the bank to provide the data subject with access to the data, the Ordinance effectively overrides the application of the banker's duty of confidence in respect of X. The *Tournier* exceptions must therefore succumb to the Ordinance.

The exemptions to the Ordinance's access provisions (see Chapter 12) overlap to a considerable extent with the *Tournier* exceptions. Nevertheless, it is the terms of the statutory exemptions that are decisive in fixing the limits of access to personal data under the Ordinance whether or not they were provided in confidence. Where the confidential information does not satisfy the Ordinance's definition of 'personal data' it will, of course, continue to be governed by the law of confidence and the *Tournier* exceptions will remain relevant.

Intentional Infliction of Emotional Distress

In *Wilkinson v Downton*,[101] the defendant, as a practical joke, told the plaintiff that her husband had been injured whilst returning from a day at the races and was lying in a pub with broken legs. The plaintiff fell seriously ill as a result, and sought damages for, *inter alia*, mental anguish and for her consequent illness. The jury found that the defendant meant the words to be acted upon, that they were acted upon and that he knew the words to be false, and a sum of £100 was awarded to compensate the plaintiff for her loss and damage. Wright J held,

> The defendant has...wilfully done an act calculated to cause physical harm to the plaintiff – that is to say, to infringe her legal right to personal safety, and has in fact thereby caused physical harm to her. That proposition without more appears to me to state a good cause of action, there being no justification alleged for the act. This wilful injury is in law malicious, although no malicious purpose to cause the harm which was caused nor any motive of spite is imputed to the defendant.[102]

The decision therefore establishes that 'doing an act calculated to cause physical harm is actionable if physical harm results'.[103] The plaintiff must, of course, show that the defendant's act would cause harm to a person of ordinary firmness, and that the act caused the harm, and is not too remote. Liability will attach even if the act would not affect a person of ordinary sensibilities if the plaintiff can prove that the defendant was aware of the plaintiff's susceptibility.[104] As to remoteness of damage, Wright J explicitly recognised that recovery for nervous shock at that time was 'without precedent'.[105]

Might this action assist a data subject? Could the principle be applied in circumstances where a data user transfers data that causes the plaintiff physical harm?

In order to answer these questions, a number of preliminary issues need to be considered. How far can the general proposition put forward in *Wilkinson* be extended beyond false statements? What is meant by 'wilfully done an act calculated to cause physical harm'? What are the other elements of the action? Each of these questions is briefly addressed.

Conduct other than false statements

Judgments following *Wilkinson v Downton* reveal that the broad principle there enunciated is applicable not merely to false statements but to threats[106] and other conduct.[107] In *Bradley v Wingnut Films Ltd*,[108] for instance, the plaintiff, the holder of an exclusive right to burial in a plot in a certain cemetery, sought an injunction against the defendant film company to prevent the plot being shown as a backdrop to a particular scene of a comedy horror. The burial plot appeared in the film for a total of only 14 seconds and it was not possible to read the words on the tombstone marking the site. The plaintiff pleaded, *inter alia*, the intentional infliction of emotional distress as a cause of action having been 'shocked and upset' by the association of the burial site with the film. Although the plaintiff's claim on this ground was rejected (for reasons considered below) Gallen J clearly proceeded on the basis that the film's depiction of the cemetery plot constituted conduct sufficient to found an action under *Wilkinson v Downton*.[109]

The importance of the distinction between false statements and other conduct is that it is far easier to establish the defendant's requisite state of mind for the former than for the latter. In *Bradley*, the court specifically adverted to the relative unimportance of the burial plot in the scene in question and considered that the conduct of the defendant could not therefore be taken to have been calculated to produce harm to the plaintiff. Thus, the issue of how the defendant caused the plaintiff's harm directly affects the ease with which the plaintiff can prove that the emotional distress was 'intentionally' inflicted as a matter of law.[110]

The defendant's state of mind

The defendant's act must be wilful; that is to say either intentional or reckless.[111] Recklessness lies between that standard and negligence.[112] The second requirement is that the defendant's act, in the words of Wright J, be 'so plainly calculated to produce some effect of the kind which was produced that an intention to produce it ought to be imputed'.[113] The ease with which the plaintiff is able to prove that the defendant's conduct was 'plainly calculated' to cause physical harm depends on the nature of the act. As suggested above, this will be more difficult in the case of conduct other than overt, direct statements. In *Bradley*, Gallen J took the view that:

> There is no evidence in this case to suggest that the defendant intended in the ordinary sense of that word, to cause any distress to the plaintiff or his family in filming the sequence under consideration and in context I do not think that the consequences were so foreseeable in terms of the plaintiff's distress bearing in mind the position occupied by the tombstone in the film and its lack of relation to the action, that the damage even if proven could be said to have been intentional.[114]

Though the meaning of the term 'calculated' is far from clear, the boundaries of liability are reasonably plain. 'Calculated' cannot be restricted to intention, because in *Wilkinson* itself, the defendant's intention was to play a prank and presumably neither desired the harm nor considered it certain or substantially certain to follow from his statement. Moreover, in order to preserve the distinction between the intentional infliction of 'physical harm' and the corresponding action in negligence (see below), it should not be sufficient for the consequences of the defendant's conduct merely to be reasonably foreseen. The defendant must intend, or at least be reckless as to, the consequences. 'Calculated' seems to mean something between 'intended' and 'foreseeably likely'.[115]

The nature of the harm

As a matter of principle there is nothing to prevent a plaintiff recovering under *Wilkinson v Downton* simply for injury to the person, though, in fact, the decisions have all concerned 'nervous shock'.[116] There is a vital distinction between a transient shock, however severe, which is called 'emotional distress', on the one hand, and the subsequent development of physical symptoms as a result of the initial shock. Only in the latter event is recovery allowed.[117] As Lord Wilberforce has stated, 'nervous shock' is a 'hallowed expression',[118] but modern usage prefers 'recognisable psychiatric illness'.[119] In *Bradley*,[120] Gallen J said,

> I accept that on the authorities to which I was referred, it is necessary for the plaintiff to establish something more than a transient reaction, however initially severe. This must translate itself into something physical and having a duration which is more than merely transient.[121]

What of secondary victims? There is authority for the view that the principle in *Wilkinson v Downton* may be extended to compensate those who suffer shock but who were not the primary victim of the defendant's act. In the New Zealand decision of *Stevenson v Basham*,[122] Herdman J applied *Wilkinson* to allow the plaintiff to recover for nervous shock caused when she overheard somebody threatening to burn her husband out of his home. This case must, however, be approached with caution; the court found as a fact that the defendant knew that his primary victim's wife was in the house. But there is the possibility that proceeding under *Wilkinson* allows recovery by a wider number of people than for the strictly regulated negligence action.[123] In the words of Bray CJ in *Battista v Cooper*:[124]

> [T]here is no reason for restricting the category of plaintiffs who can recover for physical injury from an intentional tort to those who can recover in the same circumstances if the tort were a negligent one, and every reason, in my opinion, for widening it.[125]

If this is to occur, it would remove a significant hurdle mentioned above in respect of the equitable remedy for breach of confidence. The plaintiff's right in such actions is *in personam*. This normally means that the obligation may be enforced only by the person to whom it is owed.[126] A liberal approach to the range of persons qualifying as 'secondary victims' would enable a plaintiff to restrain the publication of a newspaper article that discloses intimate information about his girlfriend or grandmother.[127]

The future of the cause of action

It has been suggested in the light of the paucity of cases decided upon the *Wilkinson* principle, that it 'may well be a dying cause of action'.[128] At the time that view was expressed, *Wilkinson* had been followed in only one English decision: *Janvier v Sweeney*.[129] In that case, in order to gather information that the plaintiff might have about 'certain letters purporting to be written by Major X,' a private detective visited the plaintiff and announced, 'I am a detective inspector from Scotland Yard, and represent the military authorities. You are the woman we want, as you have been corresponding with a German spy'. This statement caused the plaintiff to suffer a severe shock leading to physical incapacity for which she successfully recovered. Bankes L J was in no doubt that *Wilkinson v Downton* was good law.[130]

Whatever the true relevance of *Wilkinson* in modern times, it is clear that, since *Dulieu v White & Sons*,[131] the action for the negligent infliction of nervous shock has gone from strength to strength. As already mentioned, it is not easy to categorise rigidly the varying degrees of foresight into negligence or recklessness, and this has engendered the view that *Wilkinson* should be, and has been, subsumed within the ever-expanding tort of negligence. In *Wilkinson* itself 'the physical harm was intended "only in a limited sense" – "the acts were intentional, [but] there was no evidence that the defendant intended the plaintiff to become ill" '.[132] The facts of *Wilkinson* certainly fall within current negligence principles, but at the time of the decision, recovery upon the basis of mere foreseeability of nervous shock was precluded by the Privy Council's decision in *Coultas*.[133]

The Court of Appeal rejuvenated *Wilkinson* in *Khorasandjian v Bush*.[134] The defendant launched a campaign of harassment against the plaintiff after their relationship broke down. Persistent unsolicited telephone calls were accompanied by threats of violence. The plaintiff was faced with the difficulty that, although the experience caused her considerable stress, she was not suffering from a recognisable psychiatric illness. Acknowledging the fact of her suffering, and that it was not in law sufficient to found an action under *Wilkinson v Downton*, Dillon LJ[135] stated:

> But there is, in my judgment, an obvious risk that the cumulative effect of continued and unrestrained further harassment such as [the plaintiff] has undergone would cause such an illness. The law expects the ordinary person to bear the mishaps of life with fortitude and...customary phlegm; but it does not expect ordinary young women to bear indefinitely such a campaign of persecution as that to which the defendant has subjected the plaintiff. Therefore, in my judgement, on the facts of the case and in line with the law as laid down in *Janvier v Sweeney*, the court is entitled to look at the defendant's conduct as a whole and restrain those aspects on a *quia timet* basis also of his campaign of harassment which cannot strictly be classified as threats.

This suggests that the court would protect the plaintiff in circumstances where there is only a risk, albeit an obvious one, of nervous shock later resulting from the cumulative effect of the defendant's conduct.[136] It might be possible to reconcile *Khorasandjian* with existing authority; the principle merely being applied to the special concerns of *quia timet* injunctions[137] rather than the usual action for damages. But it also possible to take the view that the Court of Appeal, in 'practical reality',[138] extended *Wilkinson* to cases of purely emotional distress in situations where an injunction is being sought.[139]

But this creative enlargement of the tort of nuisance has recently received a setback in the House of Lords. In *Hunter v Canary Wharf Ltd*[140] it held that an action in private nuisance could generally only be brought by a person with an interest in the land and persons with no proprietary interest with whom householders shared their homes could not sue. The Law Lords held (by 4 to 1, Lord Cooke dissenting) that the extension to nuisance by the Court of Appeal in *Khorasandjian v Bush* would transform it from a tort to land into a tort to the person, in which damages could be recovered in respect of something less serious than personal injury and the criteria for liability were founded not on negligence but on striking a balance between the interests of neighbours in the use of their land. *Khorasandjian* was therefore overruled in so far as it held that a mere licensee could sue in private nuisance.

As to the desirability of maintaining an action for the intentional infliction of emotional distress distinct from negligence liability, the policy arguments which have led the courts to reject recovery for mental distress in negligence cases are less persuasive when applied to the intentional tort.

It is hard to see why a plaintiff should be denied recovery where the defendant deliberately inflicts mental distress on him. If this were accepted, the action for the intentional infliction of emotional distress would closely resemble the American tort of 'extreme outrage'.[141] This action ordinarily compensates the plaintiff for 'nervous shock', though the *Restatement* makes it clear that it is not limited to 'bodily harm', and where the conduct is sufficiently extreme and outrageous, recovery may be allowed for emotional distress alone.[142]

Protecting privacy

The greatest obstacle to the application of *Wilkinson v Downton* is the need to prove that the act in question is calculated to cause physical harm. The plaintiff may, at most, be able to show that the defendant's conduct is negligent, and it is clear is that the courts will not allow recovery for mental distress in a negligence action.[143]

The Ordinance does provide for damages for injury to feelings caused by a data user (see Chapter 13) but the availability of a common law remedy for the use of personal data which occasions distress would provide plaintiffs with an additional means by which their damage might be compensated, and as against persons not confined to a data user, such as the Commissioner.

There is the possibility, as yet unsupported by authority, that for the intentional tort under *Wilkinson* the court will be prepared to award damages for purely emotional distress. But what constitutes a meritorious case? Perhaps only where there is distress caused by a course of conduct by the defendant or where the mental distress is serious.[144] There are difficulties, however, with both. In the former, isolated instances of extreme behaviour would not be caught by the action. In the latter, limiting recovery to objective states of mind would overlook different subjective reactions of individuals to the same stimulus. There is merit in the suggestion, albeit in a slightly different context, that:

> [T]he very vagueness of the applicability of a molestation tort could be seen as one of its strengths, for the focus is clearly on the actual parties to the action and their relationship. In assessing whether the acts done by the defendant were calculated to cause harm to the plaintiff and whether such harm did, or was likely, to ensue, the defendant's knowledge of his victim will be highly material... Flexibility enables the court to make common-sense judgments based on a determination of when intrusive and unpleasant conduct exceeds the bounds of what society will tolerate poses a risk of damage to an individual's fundamental right to freedom from injury.[145]

Similar considerations apply to the infliction of emotional distress.

Defamation

The tort of defamation consists in publishing a false statement about the plaintiff which tends to lower him or her in the estimation of right-thinking members of the community generally or which tends to cause him or her to be shunned or which bring him or her into hatred, ridicule or contempt or which tend to discredit him or her in his or her trade or profession.[146]

An imputation which, say, tends to injure a person's reputation in any business, trade, profession, or office held by him is defamatory. But it is inadequate that the statement merely tends to injure the plaintiff in his business, trade, profession or office; they must involve a reflection upon his personal character or his official, professional or trading reputation.[147] The test is an objective one; the fact that the defendant did not intend to defame the plaintiff is not a relevant consideration. Nor does it matter that he was unaware of the circumstances which rendered an apparently innocuous statement defamatory,[148] or that the statement is not believed to be true by anyone who reads it.[149] Previous decisions of the courts are only partially helpful; the facts are inevitably critical. Moreover, in any libel suit the court will consider the defendant's statement in their Hong Kong context (see below).

The defendant's words must refer to the plaintiff, though not necessarily expressly. Thus, if special facts are known only to some who read the statement which enable them to identify the plaintiff, these facts are admissible in evidence.[150]

It is irrelevant that the defendant did not intend to refer to the plaintiff,[151] or that the statement is true of a person other than the plaintiff; they may still be defamatory of the plaintiff if they could reasonably be understood to refer to him.[152]

The *Defamation Ordinance* provides in s 25, a special statutory defence in the case of unintentional and non-negligent defamation where the statement is published 'innocently'. He may make an 'offer of amends' to the party aggrieved which, if accepted, amounts to a bar to legal proceedings. If it is not accepted, it acts as a defence in any proceedings for libel to prove that the words were published innocently and that the offer was made as soon as practicable after the defendant received notice that they were or might be defamatory of the plaintiff.

The defendant may be held liable for the repetition of defamatory statements where he authorises or intends such repetition, but, as a general rule, he is not liable for unauthorised repetition unless the person to whom it was published was under a duty to repeat it.[153] So, in the case of a book, several publications normally occur: the author to the publisher, the author and publisher jointly to the printer, by the author, publisher and printer jointly to the distributor, and so on. Each repetition is a new publication which gives rise to a new cause of action.[154] The law does, however, distinguish between those who are mere distributors, on the one hand, and those who take an active part in the production of the work, on the other. Similar questions may arise in respect of the publishing a libel on the Internet.

Defences

There are four main defences to an action for defamation. First, the defence of justification (or 'truth'). In recognising the importance of free speech, the law provides that it is a complete answer to an action for defamation for the defendant to prove that the statement he published is substantially true. The *Defamation Ordinance*, s 26, declares that where the imputation consists in several allegations, the defendant, to succeed, need not prove the truth of every charge.[155]

Secondly, the defence of absolute privilege protects defamatory statements when made in the course of legislative, judicial and other official proceedings.

Thirdly, the defence of qualified privilege obtains in circumstances where the defendant has a duty (legal, social or moral) to make a statement to a person who has a corresponding interest or duty to receive it, ie where the publisher and those to whom the publication is made have a common interest in the data concerned.[156] The defence extends to fair and accurate reports of legislative and judicial proceedings.[157]

Fourthly, there is the defence of fair comment which, in practice, tends to be the most important. This defence protects honest expressions of opinion on matters of public interest and is particularly relevant to the protection of free speech, a fact recognised by the courts.[158] The comment must be on a matter of public interest. Such matters 'are very numerous and they should not be confined within narrow limits'.[159] In *London Artists v Littler,*[160] Lord Denning MR cast the net widely:

> Whenever a matter is such as to affect people at large, so that they may be legitimately interested in, or concerned at, what is going on; or what may happen to them or to others; then it is a matter of public interest on which everyone is entitled to make fair comment.

Matters of public interest have been held to include the public conduct of persons who hold or seek a public office or position of public trust, the administration of justice, political and state matters, the management of public institutions, works of art, public performances and 'anything which may fairly be said to invite comment'[161] or 'challenge public attention'.[162]

The statement must be one of opinion not fact. This is a distinction that is easier to draw in theory than in practice. It must be 'fair', that is it must be based on facts, and supported by those facts; there must be a basis of fact sufficient to warrant the comment made. The facts upon which the comment is based must be true.[163] If they are true and the defendant is 'an honest man expressing his genuine opinion on a subject of public interest',[164] then it does not matter whether a reasonable person would hold such an opinion.

Section 27 of the *Defamation Ordinance* provides that where the statement consists partly of allegations of fact and partly of expression of opinion, a defence of fair comment shall not fail merely because the truth of every allegation of fact is not proved, if the expression of opinion is fair comment having regard to such of the facts alleged or referred to in the words complained of as are proved.

The plaintiff may defeat the defence by proving that the defendant was actuated by malice. It is for the plaintiff to prove malice. Malice defeats also the defence of qualified privilege (mentioned above). In respect of fair comment, malice denotes any improper motive which may have caused the defendant to make his comment. In this sense, then, his comment is not an honest expression of his view. As a general rule, the test is: did the defendant believe the statement to be true?

An exception may arise in circumstances where the defendant's comment imputes corrupt, dishonest or wicked motives,[165] though it has been held that the defendant would not be liable if the comment was in the opinion of the jury warranted by the facts, in the sense that a fair-minded man might upon these facts hold that opinion in good faith.

Defamation and privacy

Among the four privacy torts recognised in the United States is 'publicity which places the defendant in a false light in the public eye'. Whether or not this is properly conceived as a matter of privacy, it underlines the association between defamation and privacy. Indeed, the argument is not infrequently heard that an action in defamation provides a means of protecting the plaintiff's privacy.

It has been said that 'the fundamental difference between a right to privacy and a right to freedom from defamation is that the former directly concerns one's own peace of mind, while the latter concerns primarily one's reputation'.[166] This, however, is not a distinction that has ever been a sharp one, and not only has the jurisdiction of defamation been enlarged, but (more to the point) recovery has been allowed for invasion of privacy in several American decisions where the plaintiff has been depicted in a 'false light' and it is the plaintiff's reputation, rather than his privacy, that would appear to be affected. The rationale behind the tort of public disclosure is not merely 'to prevent inaccurate portrayal of private life, but to prevent its being depicted at all'.[167] Moreover, even though the disclosure of sensitive information actually portrays the plaintiff in a favourable light, there is no reason why he should in principle be barred from recovery.[168]

Under the regime of data subject consent created by the Ordinance, it is possible that the use of personal data could carry the defamatory innuendo that the plaintiff consented to its use. This might be analogous to the facts of *Tolley v J S Fry and Sons Ltd*,[169] in which a caricature of the well-known amateur golfer, Cyril Tolley, was used without his permission to promote the defendant's chocolates. The House of Lords held that readers would assume that he had prostituted his amateur status in the cause of advertising. Such an innuendo is rarely present, and Greer L J in the Court of Appeal acknowledged the limitation of the law,

> I have no hesitation in saying that in my judgment the defendants in publishing the advertisement in question, without first obtaining Mr Tolley's consent, acted in a manner inconsistent with the decencies of life and in doing so they were guilty of an act for which there ought to be a legal remedy.[170]

Liability for defamatory statements published on the Internet raise a host of questions that extend well beyond the frontiers of data protection.

Defamation and data protection

The routine collection, storage, and especially the transfer, of personal data by computer obviously increases the risk (and the scope) of publication of defamatory matter. Moreover, in exercising his right of access under s 18 of the Ordinance, a data subject may discover information that is defamatory of him. This may be personal data about him held by the data user and compiled by the data user (say his employer) or by a third party (in a reference). In the case of employment, the exemptions contained in ss 53, 54 and 55 may be invoked to preclude access, and that provided for in s 56 means that access to a personal reference by its subject will be denied unless its author consents or until the post in question is filled, whichever first occurs. Nevertheless, the exercise of the right of access may well reveal false or incorrect personal data relating to the subject – indeed, that is one of the main objects of the creation of the right.

In such circumstances it is likely that the defence of qualified privilege will avail a data user who, in transferring personal data (which turn out to be defamatory) does so in accordance with principle 3. That is to say, if my bank, for example, transfers, with my consent, defamatory personal data to my employer, it will be open to the bank to show that it did so to a party with an interest in receiving such data. If, however, the bank should transfer the data to a party who has no interest in or duty to receive them, the data subject ought to be able to defeat the defence by establishing 'malice', ie that the defendant was not in fact using the occasion to perform the duty or protect the interest, which rendered the occasion a privileged one, but was instead abusing it for an extraneous or improper purpose.

There is therefore an interesting connection between the concept of qualified privilege (which clothes certain defamatory publications in lawfulness) and data protection principle 3 (which limits the purposes for which the data may be used, transferred or disclosed to purposes for which they were to be used when they were collected or a directly related purpose).[171]

Negligence

The requirements of the tort of negligence may conveniently be considered under the following three headings:

- Does the defendant owe the plaintiff a 'duty of care'?
- If so, has the defendant breached this duty?
- Has this breach caused the damage of which the plaintiff complains?

An action in negligence may be met by one or more of several recognised defences. The most likely defence to be raised in the present context is that of contributory negligence, which is briefly considered below.

Duty of Care

It is ultimately a matter of policy: The court must decide whether the factual circumstances in issue give rise to a duty. The classic statement of the nature and scope of this duty is to be found in the judgment of Lord Atkin in *Donoghue v Stevenson*:[172]

> The rule that you are to love your neighbour becomes in law: You must not injure your neighbour, and the lawyer's question 'who is my neighbour?' receives a restricted reply. You must take reasonable care to avoid acts or omissions which you can reasonably foresee would be likely to injure

> your neighbour. Who then, in law, is my neighbour? The answer seems to be persons who are so closely and directly affected by my acts or omissions that I ought reasonably to have them in contemplation as being so affected when I am directing my mind to the acts or omissions which are called in question.

This 'neighbour principle' (which has, more or less, stood the test of time) provides a useful means by which to determine whether a given plaintiff falls within the figurative circle that is drawn around the defendant. Hundreds of cases have been considered by the courts of common law jurisdictions;[173] each presents a slightly novel factual situation to which the plaintiff argues the duty be applied. The law also draws a distinction between physical and economic loss, and between loss caused by acts and those caused by words.

In respect of the former distinction, a victim of economic loss is unable to recover any damages for financial (or what is generally called 'pure economic') loss. Only where such loss is a consequence of some physical damage to the plaintiff can he recover compensation.[174]

In respect of the second distinction (acts versus words) a data subject is most likely to suffer loss where information relating to him is negligently used or transferred. In the leading case of *Hedley Byrne v Heller*[175] the House of Lords established the principle that (in the absence of a disclaimer) a duty of care is owed where the defendant has a special skill and undertakes to give advice knowing that the person to whom he gives advice is likely to rely on it. In this situation, a sufficiently close relationship exists between the parties so as to give rise to a duty of care. This principle has been extended to cover the situation in which a negative character reference about the plaintiff was given negligently by the defendant to a third party. As a result, the plaintiff was dismissed from his employment.[176] The question was whether a person who gives a negligently prepared reference to a third party is liable not to the recipient but to the subject of the reference. Lord Goff stated:

> [I]t is my opinion that an employer who provides a reference in respect of one of his employees to a prospective future employer will ordinarily owe a duty of care to his employee in respect of the preparation of the reference.... [T]he employee relies upon him to exercise due skill and care in the preparation of the reference before making it available

> to the third party. In these circumstances, it seems to me that all the elements requisite for the application of the *Hedley Byrne* principle are present.

He did not, however, wish to extend this duty owed by an employer to the recipient of a reference

Problems associated with references that are inaccurate or untrue (whether by accident or design) might be obviated by the right of access and correction. Permitting the subject of a reference to see, and if necessary, correct, the data contained therein would enable the subject to prevent the sort of consequence that occurred in *Spring*. The right of access, however, must be balanced against its effect on the candour that might be compromised were the subject able to read his referee's assessment of his ability. Moves in the United States to allow access to what would otherwise be confidential references have tended to result in many subjects waiving this right in the belief that this would facilitate a more honest (and hence more persuasive) statement of the subject's attributes and shortcomings.

Subject access inevitably encourages the hyperbolic or anodyne, and any prudent recipient is likely to adopt the simple device of telephoning the author in order to obtain the authentic version. Section 56 of the Ordinance attempts to strike something of a balance between the rights of recipient and subject. It exempts personal references from the access provisions of data protection principle 6 and s 18(1)(b) unless the referee informs the recipient in writing that the referee has no objection to the reference being seen by the subject, or, in the case of references given after the section has come into force, until the subject has been informed in writing that he has been accepted or rejected to fill the position or office in question, whichever occurs first. (See Chapter 9).[177]

The tort of negligence may be invoked to recover damages for what is called 'nervous shock' (a recognised psychiatric illness), though the House of Lords have, on explicitly policy grounds, fixed fairly narrow boundaries of recovery, and circumstances of sufficient gravity are unlikely to arise in the data protection context.[178] Nevertheless, the circumstances of the *Alcock* decision do have some relevance for the purveyor of news by electronic means. Several of the plaintiffs witnessed the disaster at Hillsborough Stadium on television and while the court rejected their claim, they did not entirely rule out such liability in a case in which such damage is reasonably foreseeable and there is a sufficiently proximate relationship between plaintiff and defendant. It is not inconceivable that a data user could be held responsible where data are negligently conveyed to a data subject and such data occasion nervous shock. Might it not be applied to, say, a hospital that negligently informs a person who has submitted to an HIV test that the test was positive when it was not?

In *Lai Hing-tong v Attorney General*[179] the plaintiff was wrongly recorded as having been convicted of an offence which he had not committed; his name had been confused with another's. His action for negligence was based on evidence that, as a consequence of this error, he had been dismissed from three positions in the nine years during which the inaccurate record had been in existence. He successfully claimed damages both for lost income and for injury to his feelings. Whether this case ought more properly to have been pleaded in libel,[180] it demonstrates the prospects of claiming damages, including those for injured feelings, where personal data are negligently transferred.

Breach of Duty

A plaintiff can recover damages in negligence only if the defendant's conduct has failed to measure up to the standard reasonably expected of someone in the defendant's position.[181] In the present context, this objective test will assume the form of enquiring how 'the reasonable data user' would have behaved in the circumstances presented to the court. This may call for evidence of what is 'common practice' among similar data users; expert witnesses may be called to testify to the standard commonly accepted among, say, banks.[182] In arriving at such a determination, the nature of the data held may be relevant; the more sensitive the data, the higher the standard of care to be exercised by the defendant.

In addition, the cost of the measures required to protect the data will be an important factor to be considered by the court. Thus, for example, should the data user, in breach of the security provisions of data protection principle 4, negligently allow unauthorised access to data under his control, the court will consider whether the cost or inconvenience of preventing such access were so high that it would be unreasonable to expect the data user to have adopted them

The fact that the Ordinance embodies standards to be applied in regulating the collection, transfer and use of personal data will also be an important factor in deciding whether a particular data user has fallen short of the reasonable standard of care.[183]

Causation

The data subject must prove that his loss was caused by the defendant's breach of duty owed to him. This is a matter of both fact and law.

Defence

It may be possible for the defendant data user to prove that the plaintiff data subject was itself negligent and hence contributed to his own damage. Suppose, for instance, that the data subject, after having obtained access to his file, fails to correct an error therein and the erroneous personal data are transferred negligently by the data user to a third party. In such circumstances the defendant may be able to demonstrate that the plaintiff contributed to his own damage. If so, this may result in the plaintiff's damages being reduced in proportion to the plaintiff's share of negligence 'to such extent as the court thinks just and equitable'.[184]

Breach of Contract

Contracts specifying duties of confidence are not uncommon. An employee, for instance, is frequently bound by his contract of employment not to divulge confidential information, such as customer lists, during or after the term of his employment.[185] Breach of this duty (which may, in some cases, be implied[186]) gives rise to an action for breach of contract or, in the circumstances described above, for breach of the equitable duty of confidence. Indeed, where the contract simply designates the information sought to be protected as 'confidential', without sufficient clarity, the equitable jurisdiction of breach of confidence may perforce need to be resorted to in order to provide relief, particularly where an injunction is sought to restrain the defendant from disclosing the information in question.[187]

Contractual relationships between data subject and data user exist in a number of situations: banker and customer, insurer and insured, accountant and client, and so on. The common law will therefore buttress the Ordinance in enforcing the obligations of the data user and protecting the rights of the data subject in respect of the use of personal data. Of course, in the absence of privity of contract (ie a contractual nexus between the parties) the common law is unable to assist. Thus, where personal data have been obtained by a third party without any breach of contract by the data user, the data subject will be deprived of a remedy.

The law of contract is also likely to play an important part in facilitating transfer of personal data to jurisdictions lacking legal protection similar to the Ordinance. Section 33 provides that a data user shall not transfer personal data to a place outside Hong Kong unless, *inter alia*, the data subject consents in writing to the transfer or there is in that place a similar law in force. Subsection (3) provides that the Commissioner may, by notice in the Gazette, specify places that meet these criteria. Subsection 2(d) declares that where there is no similar law, the transfer may nevertheless take place if the data user has exercised due diligence to ensure that the data will be dealt with in a manner consistent with the Ordinance. Contract provides an important means by which the data user can discharge this due diligence requirement (see Chapter 7).

Inducement of Breach of Contract

An action in tort will lie where the defendant intentionally interferes with the plaintiff's contractual rights thereby causing him damage.[188] It is possible to imagine circumstances in which a third party induces a data user to transfer personal data to him in breach of a contract between the data user and data subject. In such circumstances, a data subject who is able to prove that he has suffered damage may be able to recover compensation (including exemplary damages) from the third party or an injunction to prevent him from using the data.[189] This may extend to damages for 'nervous shock' (see above).

Breach of Statutory Duty

Where legislation stipulates that a party is under a duty to act in a particular way, a person who suffers damage by reason of a breach of this duty may be able to recover damages quite independently of the tort of negligence (see above) for his loss.[190] Everything turns on the intention of the legislature.[191] Should the legislation provide a regime for the determination of complaints and the awarding of compensation (as the Ordinance does in Parts VII and IX respectively) the pursuit of this common law remedy is likely to be of little utility to the plaintiff data subject – unless there are circumstances in which it might be argued that since s 66 establishes a right of compensation only against data users, any breach of his duties to members of a protected class (data subjects) by the Commissioner may give rise to a cause of action against his office by this tort.[192]

Trespass

An unauthorised interference with the plaintiff's enjoyment of land or goods constitutes the tort of trespass. Trespass to land, however, requires actual entry upon the land which the plaintiff possesses.[193] Thus, where a person enters the plaintiff's land in order to obtain personal data he may have an action in trespass, or if he interferes with the plaintiff's computer or other means by which personal data are held, he may be liable for trespass to goods.

The more difficult question is where the data are obtained without physical entry or contact with the computer or network. Though it is actionable *per se*,[194] trespass to goods is sometimes thought to require proof of damage. The view of almost all the textbooks is that it does not: mere touching of, say, a picture in a gallery, is almost certainly a trespass. But does a 'hacker' interfere with the plaintiff's interest in his goods?[195] It is arguable that the computer hardware and software constitute 'goods'. Nor should it matter that the plaintiff's equipment are physically unaffected by the hacking, for, as stated above, the tort of trespass to goods is actionable *per se*.[196]

Nuisance

The tort of private nuisance provides protection against 'interference with one's enjoyment, one's quiet, one's personal freedom, anything that discomposes or injuriously affects the senses or the nerves'.[197] But it will not generally avail a plaintiff who does not have an interest in the land.[198] Nor will he have a remedy unless the circumstances of the interference subsist for a sufficient period of time to constitute a 'state of affairs'.[199]

Despite these limitations, the action may perhaps assist a data subject who, following *Khorasandjian*,[200] is subjected to persistent harassment by a data user seeking to obtain personal data from him.

Conversion

The tort of conversion consists in the unauthorised intentional interference with or assumption of ownership over goods which is inconsistent with the owner's right of possession whereby that other is deprived of the use and possession of it. It is doubtful whether personal data could be characterised as 'goods',[201] and hence, unless one were to consider the subject matter of the action the plaintiff's computer or the disk or print out containing the data, the action's limitations in the data protection context seem limited. It may, however, provide a remedy against a person who gained access to personal data without regard to the rights of the owner of the hardware or software which held it.

Breach of Copyright

Copyright protects the form rather than the content of 'original' ideas.[202] It is at least arguable that the form in which personal data are held or transferred might attract protection.

Notes

1 See *R v R* [1991] 4 All ER at 488 where Lord Keith gives as the ordinary meaning of unlawful 'something contrary to some law or enactment or ... done without lawful justification or excuse'.

2 This section draws on R Wacks, (1989), *Personal Information: Privacy and the Law*, Clarendon Press, Oxford, pp 84-192.

3 We draw here on R Wacks, (1995) *Privacy and Press Freedom,* Blackstone, London, pp 48-80.

4 In particular, *Prince Albert v Strange* (1849) 1 H & Tw 1 47 ER 1302; 1 Mac & G 25; and *Morison v Moat* (1851) 9 Hare 241 68 ER 492.

5 *Seager v Copydex* ([1967] 2 All ER 415, 417 per Lord Denning MR; *Fraser v Evans* ([1969] 1 All ER 8, 11 *per* Lord Denning MR.

6 *Saltman Engineering Co Ltd v Campbell Engineering Co Ltd* (1948) 65 RPC 203, 215; [1963] 3 All ER 413, 415 per Lord Greene MR.

7 *Ibid.*

8 *Lord Ashburton v Pape* [1913] 2 Ch 469.

9 [1967] Ch 302.

10 *Ibid,* 322.

11 [1988] 2 All ER 477. See too *HRH Princess of Wales v MGN Newspapers Ltd* (1993) and *Shelley Films Ltd v Rex Features Ltd* (1993). Both decisions are as yet unreported, but are briefly considered by H Fenwick and G Phillipson in 'Confidence and Privacy: A Re-examination' (1996) 55 CLJ 447.

12 [1988] 1 Ch 449 at 454.

13 *Ibid* at 455.

14 [1977] 1 WLR 760.

15 [1978] FSR 573.

16 (1980) 130 NLJ 168.

17 (1889) 40 Ch 345.

18 *Ibid* at 349.

19 [1995] 4 All ER 473.

20 The court adopted the reasoning in *Marcel v Commissioner of Police of the Metropolis* [1992] 1 All ER 72, [1992] Ch 225, in which the Court of Appeal held that the police were subject to a duty of confidence in respect of seized documents, though in this instance they were under an

obligation to disclose such documents when served with a subpoena to produce them in civil proceedings. See the discussion of the defence of 'public interest' below.

21 *Duchess of Argyll v Duke of Argyll* [1967] Ch 302.

22 *Attorney-General v Jonathan Cape Ltd* [1976] 1 QB 752.

23 The objectivity of the test was suggested, *obiter,* by Megarry J in *Coco* [1969] RPC 41 at 48.

24 [1979] 2 All ER 620, 634.

25 *Saltman Engineering Co Ltd v Campbell Engineering Co Ltd* (1948) 65 RPC 203 at 213 per Lord Greene MR.

26 *Seager v Copydex Ltd* [1967] RPC 349.

27 [1969] RPC 41, 48; see also, *Dunford & Elliott Ltd v Johnson & Firth Brown Ltd* [1978] FSR 143 at 148 *per* Lord Denning MR.

28 See *Attorney-General v Guardian Newspapers Ltd* (No 2) [1988] 3 WLR 776 at 782 per Lord Keith, *obiter*. See, too, *X v Y* [1988] 2 All ER 648 at 657; *Li Yau-wai v Genesis Films Ltd* [1987] HKLR 711; and M Pendleton (1987) 17 HKLJ 36.

29 *Stephens v Avery* [1988] 2 WLR 1280.

30 *Francome v Mirror Group Newspapers Ltd* [1984] 1 WLR 892.

31 *Attorney-General v Guardian Newspapers (No 1)* [1987] 1 WLR 1248; and, *Attorney-General v Guardian Newspapers (No 2)* [1988] 3 All ER 545.

32 *Franklin v Giddins* [1978] 1 Qd R 72 . See W J Braithwaite 'The Secret of Life: A Fruity Trade Secret' (1979) 95 LQR 323.

33 [1988] 2 All ER 477, 482.

34 *Spycatcher (No 2)* [1988] 3 All ER 545, 658.

35 [1984] 1 WLR 892.

36 In respect of the first matter, the Master of the Rolls warned: 'It is of paramount importance that everyone should understand the exercise upon which . . . we are engaged. There is to be a speedy trial at which the rights of the parties will be determined . . . It is not our function to decide questions of law or fact which will be in issue at the trial'. (At 894-5).

37 For a discussion of the case, see Wacks, *Personal Information* (Note 2 above), pp 276-285.

38 [1979] Ch 344, 376.

39 *Ibid,* 376.

40 [1984] 1 WLR 892, 900.

41 [1988] 3 All ER 545, 658-9.

42 *Ibid,* 659.

43 [1978] 1 Qd R 72, 80.

44 The Law Reform Commission specifically reviewed *Franklin* under the heading 'Can information initially become impressed with an obligation of confidence by reason only of the reprehensible means by which it has been acquired?' (Part IV, Section C). As remarked above this unwillingness to discuss the case in relation to the wider issue may be a result of the terms of reference of the Commission's considerations.

45 [1991] FSR 62. See B S Markesinis 'Our Patchy Law of Privacy – Time to Do Something about It' (1990) 53 MLR 802; P Prescott '*Kaye v Robertson* – a Reply' (1991) 54 MLR 451; B S Markesinis, 'The Calcutt Report Must Not be Forgotten' (1992) 55 MLR 118; and, D Feldman, (1993) *Civil Liberties and Human Rights in England and Wales*, Clarendon Press, Oxford, pp 387-8.

46 (1889) 40 Ch 345.

47 [1995] 4 All ER 473.

48 Civil Transcript No 116 (1992).

49 *Ibid,* 30. Similar sentiments are evident in the dictum of Laws J in *Hellewell* where he says, *obiter*, 'If someone with a telephoto lens were to take from a distance and with no authority a picture of another engaged in some private act, his subsequent disclosure of the photograph would, in my judgment, as surely amount to a breach of confidence as if he had found or stolen a letter or diary in which the act was recounted and proceeded to publish it. In such a case the law would protect what might reasonably be called a right of privacy, although the name accorded to the cause of action would be breach of confidence'. (At 476). No direct authority for this bold extension of the action (which appears to conflate surreptitiousness and unconscionability) is cited.

50 *Ibid,* p 29.

51 One is bound to ask why not? The decision of the trial judge represented a significant divergence from existing authority.

52 [1969] RPC 41, 48.

53 [1987] HKLR 711. See note by M Pendleton (1987) 17 HKLJ 362.

54 *Ibid*, p 719

55 *Ibid.*

56 See F Gurry (1984) *Breach of Confidence*, Oxford, Clarendon Press, especially pp 269-276.

57 The Law Reform Commission's view on this matter was almost entirely based on *Malone* and is therefore questionable in the light of *Francome*. See paras 4.7-4.10 of the report (note 2 above).

58 P Milmo, 'Confidence and Privacy' (1993) 143 NLJ 1647.

59 (1963) RPC 41.

60 At 418.

61 The apparent difficulty of applying the test in a non-technical context emerges from *Spycatcher (No 1),* and in particular the comments of Sir John Donaldson MR in the Court of Appeal, especially at [1987] 1 WLR 1248 at 1275-6. See R Wacks, *Privacy and Press Freedom* (Note 3 above) 72-3.

62 [1981] 2 WLR 848.

63 [1967] RPC 375.

64 *Ibid*, 391. See Gurry (note 56 above), especially pp 245-9.

65 See Wacks, (note 3 above), 76-77.

66 Gurry, (note 56 above), p 247.

67 *Lord Ashburton v Pape* [1913] 2 Ch. 469; *Parry-Jones v Law Society* [1969] 1 Ch. 1; *Alfred Crompton Amusement Machines Ltd. V Commissioners of Customs and Excise* [No. 2] [1974] AC 405; *Waugh v British Railways Board* [1979] 2 All ER 1169.

68 Law Reform Committee, *Privilege in Civil Proceedings* Cmnd 3472 (1967) Wigmore, *Evidence*, para 2301.

69 In this respect the position of the solicitor and barrister (*Carter v Palmer* (1839) 1 Dr. & W. 72; (affirmed) (1842) 8 Cl. & F. 657, 8 ER 256 – is no different from that of other professional advisers such as accountants, surveyors, or financial advisers who are in a fiduciary relationship with their client: *Brown v Inland Revenue Commissioners* [1965] AC 244, 265 (per Lord Upjohn).

70 *Rakusen v Ellis, Munday & Clarke* [1912] 1 Ch. 831.

71 As it did in *Davies v Clough* (1837) 8 Sim. 262; 59 ER 105. Cf. Re *Flint Coppock v Vaughan* [1885] WN 163; *In re John Holmes (a solicitor); In re The Electric Power Co Ltd* (1977) 25 WR 603; *In re Sarah C. Getty Trust* [1985] 2 All ER 809.

72 *D. v National Society for the Prevention of Cruelty to Children* [1977] 1 All ER 589, 606 per Lord Simon.

73 *Wheeler v Le Marchant* (1881) 17 Ch. D. 675, 681; *Pais v Pais* [1971] P 119, 121.

74 *R v Duchess of Kingston* (1776) 20 How. St. Tr. 355, 373, *R v Gibbons* (1823) 1 Car. & P. 97 171 ER 1117, *Ho Yee Sup v Dr Chan Yuk May* [1991] 1 HKC 499.

75 *Chantrey Martin v Martin* [1953] 2 QB 286; *Clough v United States*, 425 US 322 (1973).

76 *Lloyd v Freshfield* (1826) 2 Car. & P. 325; *Foster v The Bank of London* (1862) 3 F. & F. 214; *Attorney-General v Mulholland* [1963] 2 QB 477, 489; *California Bankers Association v Schultz*, 416 US 21 (1974), *Ho Yee Sup v Dr Chan Yuk May* [1991] 1 HKC 499.

77 *Attorney-General v Mulholland*, note 76 above, at 489; *Attorney-General v Clough* [1963] 1 QB 773. On the newspaper rule in libel actions see *Sham John v Eastweek Publisher Ltd* [1995] 1 HKC 264. See s 44(2) of the Ordinance.

78 The modern form is: 'Whatever in connection with my professional practice, or not in connection with it, I see or hear, in the life of men, which ought not to be spoken of abroad, I will not divulge, as reckoning that all such should be kept secret.' The Medical Council of Hong's Professional Code and Conduct for the Guidance of Registered Medical Practitioners (Hong Kong, June 1996) appears to adopt the International Code of Medical Ethics which provides 'A doctor shall respect the rights of patients . . .and shall safeguard patient confidences', and 'A doctor shall preserve absolute confidentiality except where others are endangered on all he knows about his patient even after the patient has died', p 5. The MAHK Code specifies a number of 'forms of professional misconduct which may lead to disciplinary proceedings. Section 8 is entitled 'abuse of professional confidence' and includes the following two 'offences': '8.1 Where a medical practitioner has without proper justification disclosed information which was obtained in confidence from or about a patient. 8.2 Whatever the circumstances, a medical practitioner must always be prepared to justify his action if he has disclosed confidential information. If a medical practitioner is in doubt about disclosing information in a particular situation he will be wise to seek advice from a professional association or his legal adviser.'

79 See Medical Association of Hong Kong, Professional Code and Conduct, note 14 above, and Warning Notice of the Medical Council of Hong Kong: Professional Discipline for the Guidance of Registered Medical Practitioners (Hong Kong, 1982).

80 *Hunter v Mann* [1974] 1 QB 767. *Furniss v Fitchett* [1958] NZLR 396, 400. See generally JK Mason and RA McCall Smith, (1994) *Law and Medical Ethics*, 4th ed, Butterworths, London, Dublin, Edinburgh, Chapter 8.

81 *Quarantine and Prevention of Disease Ordinance* s 8(3)(a).

82 *Infectious Diseases Ordinance, Quarantine and Prevention of Disease Regulations.*

83 Though some have argued for an unqualified duty of confidentiality; see MH Kottow (1986) 'Medical Confidentiality: An Intransigent and Absolute Obligation', 12 *Journal of Medical Ethics* 117. Some of the central issues are usefully analysed by the court in *X v Y* [1988] 3 All ER 648 and *W v Egdell* [1990] 2 All ER 835. See too R Wacks, (1988) 'Controlling AIDS: Some Legal Issues' 138 NLJ 254.

84 In some jurisdictions AIDS is a notifiable disease and there is therefore a legal duty imposed on doctors to report cases to the authorities. This is not the case in Hong Kong. The *Venereal Disease Ordinance* and the Prevention of Spread of Infectious Diseases Regulations require reporting of certain infectious diseases do not extent to HIV or AIDS. Section 59 of the Ordinance exempts from the access provisions of s 18(1)(b) and data protection principles 3 and 6 personal data relating to the physical and mental health of a person were such access would be likely to cause serious harm to the physical or mental health of any person.

85 Though it has been argued that even in this sort of case the duty should not be breached for it is 'self-defeating': 'if physicians become known as confidence-violators, problem-ridden patients will try to lie to accommodate facts to their advantage or, if this does not work, avoid physicians altogether . . . It is better to treat and advise the syphilitic husband without informing the wife than not to have him come at all for fear of undesired revelations'. MH Kottow (note 83 above) 'Medical Confidentiality' pp 119-20. See M Brazier (1987) *Medicine, Patients and the Law* 36 ff. See also KM Boyd, 'HIV Infection and AIDS: The Ethics of Medical Confidentiality' 1992 18 *Journal of Medical Ethics* 173.

86 [1986] AC 112.

87 Phrase from DHSS circular. Following *Gillick*, the Medical Council advised general practitioners that the decision does not guarantee confidentiality for children whom the doctor believes to be inadequately mature to give consent. Cf. (1987) 17 Family Law 101.

88 See *W v Egdell* [1990] Ch 359, 1 All ER 835; *R v Crozier* (1990) 12 Cr App R (S) 206; *Duncan v Medical Practitioners' Disciplinary Committee* [1986] 1 NZLR 513.

89 See MLM Gilhooly and SM McGhee (1991) 'Medical Records: Practicalities and Principles of Patient Possession', 17 *Journal of Medical Ethics* 138. JK Mason and RA McCall Smith (note 80 above) observe that there is no hard evidence that the *United Kingdom Access to Health Records Act* of 1990 has affected medical practice adversely 'and such musings may be unduly pessimistic; certainly an impressive body of research can be quoted which stresses the practical advantages', p187.

90 [1924] 2 KB 461. Section 120 of the *Banking Ordinance* complements the common law protection of banking secrecy. See further below.

91 At 474 per Bankes LJ. See *Chase Manhattan Bank NA v FDC Co Ltd* [1985] 2 HKC 470, *R v Chang Chen Feng* [1977-79] HKC 511.

92 Several statutory provisions permit or require bankers to disclose information concerning bank records. For example, Section 67 of the *Police Force Ordinance* requires banks and deposit-taking companies to provide data about a customer whom the police reasonably suspects of having committed an indictable offence. Section 14(1)(f) of the *Prevention of Bribery Ordinance* empowers the ICAC to require a bank manager to provide the investigating officer copies of the accounts of such suspects at the bank or of his spouse, parents or children. Section 20 of the *Evidence Ordinance* compels, subject to a court order, the production of a banker's record as evidence where the bank is not a party to the proceedings. Section 13(2) of the *ICAC Ordinance* provides that the Commissioner, for the purpose of the performance of his functions 'shall have access to all records, books and documents relating to the work of any government department in the possession of any crown servant. The far-reaching provisions of the *Drug Trafficking (Recovery of Proceeds) Ordinance* undermine the duty of confidence by permitting the tracing of, confiscation, and recovery of the proceeds of drug trafficking. A court order may require that material be made available to investigating officers where it is satisfied that (a) a specified person has benefited from trafficking, (b) there are reasonable grounds for believing the material is substantially relevant, and (c) it is in the public interest that access to the material be granted.

93 *Williams v Summerfield* [1972] 2 QB 512 at 518.

94 [1987] HKLR 210.

95 At 216. *Hall* was followed in *Ho Shau-hong v Commissioner of Police* [1987] HKLR 945.

96 This echoes the proposition stated by Sir Robert Megarry in *Malone v Commissioner of Police* (No 2) [1979] 2 All ER 620 at 630 and 638, that 'England . . . is not a country where everything is forbidden except what

is expressly permitted: it is a country where everything is permitted except what is expressly forbidden.' This is hardly a congenial basis on which to rest the protection of civil liberties. 'A better approach might be simply to deny that the government has any power beyond what is expressly or impliedly given it in statute, or, narrowly conceived, the prerogative', P Wesley-Smith (1994) *Constitutional and Administrative Law in Hong Kong,* 2nd ed, Longman Asia Limited, Hong Kong, p 314.

97 [1992] Ch 225, [1992] 1 All ER 72.

98 [1993] 3 WLR 1.

99 [1992] 1 All ER 72 at 86 per Sir Christopher Slade. Stress supplied. A similar approach was adopted by the High Court of Australia in *Johns v Australian Securities Commission* (1993) 178 CLR 408, 67 ALJR 850, which held that a statute conferring power to obtain information by compulsion limits, expressly or impliedly, the purposes to which that information may be used or disclosed.

100 See *Tournier v National Provincial and Union Bank of England* [1924] 2 KB 461, discussed above.

101 [1897] 2 QB 57.

102 *Ibid*, 58-9.

103 NJ Mullany and PR Handford (1993) *Tort Liability for Psychiatric Damage*, Law Book Co, Sydney, p 284 and see, generally, Chapter 13.

104 Eg, *Timmermans v Buelow* (1984) 38 CCLT 136.

105 [1897] 2 QB 57, 61. Times have, of course, changed. The Privy Council's decision to refuse to allow recovery for the negligent infliction of nervous shock in *Victorian Railways Commissioner v Coultas* (1888) 13 App Cas 222 was not followed by the English Court of Appeal in *Dulieu v White & Sons* [1901] 2 KB 669.

106 *Khorasandjian v Bush* [1993] 3 WLR 476 and see below.

107 See Winfield and Jolowicz, *Tort,* (1994) 14 ed, Sweet & Maxwell, pp 74-5; F A Trindade 'The Intentional Infliction of Purely Mental Distress', (1986) 6 OJLS 219, 230-1. In *A v B's Trustees* (1906) 13 SLT 830, the plaintiff landlady suffered nervous shock when she came across a lodger who had committed suicide in her bathroom.

108 [1993] 1 NZLR 415.

109 *Ibid*, 420-2.

110 'As regards the conduct which precipitates the physical harm, it may take any form . . . What matters is not the kind of conduct but its likely effect on the plaintiff', Mullany and Handford (Note 103 above), p 289.

111 *The American Restatement (Second) of Torts*, para 8A, comments that conduct is intentional when the actor either desires to cause particular consequences or knows that they are certain or substantially certain to result from the act.

112 *Ibid*, §500. In *Abramzik v Brenner* (1968) 65 DLR (2d) 651, 654, Culliton CJS said, 'There can be no doubt that an action will lie for the wilful infliction of shock, or a reckless disregard as to whether or not shock will ensue from the act committed.'

113 *Wilkinson v Downton* [1897] 2 QB 57, 59.

114 [1993] 1 NZLR 415, 422.

115 Mullany and Handford (note 103 above), p 288. However, this view has been questioned. Winfield and Jolowicz (note 107 above) cite *Slatter v British Railways Board* (1966) 110 SJ 688 in support of the proposition that a negligent act could entail liability under *Wilkinson v Downton* (p 75). But negligence liability and the rule in *Wilkinson v Downton* should be distinguished, for many of the arguments which support a restrictive approach to compensation for the former are weak when applied to the latter. This is examined in greater detail below. The *American Restatement (Second) of Torts*, para 312, uses the formulation 'likely to result' in harm to the plaintiff.

116 See *Janvier v Sweeney* [1919] 2 KB 316; *Burnett v George* [1992] 1 FLR 525; *Khorasandjian v Bush* [1993] 3 WLR 476 and *Hunter v Canary Wharf Ltd* (1997) The Times, 25 April.

117 Lord Ackner recently reiterated that, 'mere mental suffering, although reasonably foreseeable, if unaccompanied by physical injury, is not a basis for a claim for damages', *Alcock v Chief Constable of South Yorkshire Police* [1992] 1 AC 310, 401.

118 *McLoughlin v O'Brian* [1983] 1 AC 410, 418.

119 *Hinz v Berry* [1970] 2 QB 40, 42 per Lord Denning MR.

120 [1993] 1 NZLR 415.

121 *Ibid*, 421.

122 [1922] NZLR 225. See also, eg, *Johnson v Commonwealth* (1927) 27 SR (NSW) 133.

123 The House of Lords in *Alcock* (Note 117 above) refused to extend the exceptions to the 'aftermath doctrine' beyond marital and filial ties.

124 (1976) 14 SASR 225.

125 *Ibid*, 230.

126 *Fraser v Evans* [1969] 1 All ER 8.

127 Or others, ie categories outside the recognised marital/filial exception to the 'aftermath doctrine' in negligence actions.

128 Mullany and Handford (note 103 above), p 290.

129 [1919] 2 KB 316.

130 *Ibid*, 324.

131 [1901] 2 KB 669.

132 AL Goodhart (1943) 7 MLR 86, 88. See Mullany and Handford (note 103 above), pp 290-2.

133 *Victorian Railways Commissioner v Coultas* (1888) 13 App Cas 222.

134 [1993] 3 WLR 476.

135 *Ibid,* 483

136 See J Bridgeman and MA Jones 1994, 'Harassing Conduct and Outrageous Acts: A Cause of Action for Intentionally Inflicted Mental Distress?' (1994) 14 Legal Studies 180.

137 Literally 'because he fears'. It is an injunction granted to prevent or restrain a threatened act which, if done, would cause the applicant substantial damage for which money would be an inadequate substitute.

138 *Ibid*, 196.

139 In *Burnett v George* [1992] 1 FLR 525, the Court of Appeal, on facts not dissimilar to those in *Khorasandjian*, refused to apply *Wilkinson v Downton*. Sir John Arnold P stated that molestation or interference is not an actionable wrong unless 'there be evidence that the health of the plaintiff is being impaired by [such conduct] calculated to create such impairment, in which case relief would be granted by way of an injunction to the extent that it would be necessary to avoid that impairment of health'. (527)

140 (1997) The Times, 25 April.

141 See *Restatement (Second) of Torts*, para 46.

142 See *Alcock* (note 185 above).

143 *Ibid*, comment K.

144 Bridgeman and Jones (note 136 above), 198-201. The concentration upon conduct would be in conformity with the American approach discussed above which distinguishes between mere insult and 'extreme and outrageous conduct'.

145 M Brazier 'Personal Injury by Molestation – An Emergent or Established Tort' (1992) Fam Law 346, 348.

146 See Lord Atkin in *Sim v Stretch* [1936] 2 All ER 1237 at 1240; *Yu Kwong Chiu v Consolidated Newspapers* A258 of 1968; *Kazim Wilson Tuet Wai Sin v Nurudeen Ma Kwong Ming A1537* of 1985; *Carter-Ruck on Libel and Slander*, 4th ed, 1992, 34, *Gatley on Libel and Slander* 8th ed, 1981, 31-420; J Cottrell, 'The Law of Defamation' in *Law Lectures for Practitioners* Hong Kong Law Journal Ltd 1992. For general observations on the relationship between the action and Article 16 of the *Bill of Rights Ordinance*, see *Hong Kong Polytechnic University v Next Magazine Publishing Ltd* (1996) HCt, HCA No A3238 of 1995 (reversed on appeal, Civil appeal 28/97). The so-called newspaper rule (which protects a defendant from disclosing his sources prior to a libel action) was adopted in *Sham John v Eastweek Publisher Ltd* [1995] 1 HKC 264. See too *Sham v Eastweek Publisher Ltd* [1994] 1 HKC 687; *Liu Yau-wai v Genesis Films Ltd* [1987] HKLR 711.

147 *Griffiths v Benn* (1911) 27 TLR 346 at 350.

148 *Cassidy v Daily Mirror Newspapers Ltd* [1929] 2 KB 331.

149 *Hough v London Express Newspaper Ltd* [1940] 2 KB 507; *Morgan v Odhams Press Ltd* [1971] 1 WLR 1239.

150 *Morgans v Odhams Press*, note 149 above; *Lok Kwai-fu v YC Chan* [1978] HKLR 225.

151 *E Hulton & Co v Jones* [1910] AC 20.

152 *Newstead v London Express Newspaper Ltd* [1940] 1 KB 377.

153 *Derry v Handley* (1867) 16 LT 263.

154 *Duke of Brunswick v Harmer* [1849] 14 QBD 185.

155 See *Kwing Shou Wendahl Ting v Parke Civ App No 2229* of 1985; *Khan v O'Dea* [1985] HKLR 237.

156 *Adam v Ward* [1917] AC 309 at 334; *Kazim Wilson Tuet Wai Sin v Nurudeen Ma Kwong Ming* A1537 of 1985.

157 *Defamation Ordinance*, Cap 21, s 14 and Schedule Part II.

158 See *Slim v Daily Telegraph* [1968] 2 QB 157 at 170.

159 *Gatley on Libel and Slander*, (1981) 8th ed, Sweet & Maxwell, London, 731.

160 [1969] 2 QB 375 at 391.

161 *Campbell v Spottiswoode* (1863) 3 B & S 769 at 781, 122 ER 288 at 292 per Blackburn J.

162 *Seymour v Butterworth* (1862) 3 F & F 372 at 386, 176 ER 166 at 172 per Cockburn CJ.

163 *Cohen v Daily Telegraph Ltd* [1968] 1 WLR 916.

164 *Slim v Daily Telegraph Ltd* [1968] 2 QB 157 at170.

165 *Campbell v Spottiswoode* (1863) 3 B & S 769 at 776, 122 ER 288 at 290 per Cockburn CJ.

166 *Themo v New England Newspaper Publishing Co* 27 NE 2d 753, 755 (1940).

167 SD Warren and LD Brandeis, 'The Right to Privacy' (1890) 4 *Harvard Law Rev* 193, 197.

168 The suggestion is sometimes made that by modifying the defence of justification many of the actions brought to vindicate the plaintiff's loss of privacy might be accommodated within the tort of defamation. The proposal is that in order for the defence to succeed, the defendant ought to be required to show not only that the statement is true, but that its publication is in the public interest – the position which obtains in several Australian and American jurisdictions and in the Roman-Dutch law in Sri Lanka and South Africa. Even if the law of defamation were to be so modified, many actions would still not succeed where the plaintiff's reputation has not, in fact, been affected by the private facts disclosed.

169 [1931] AC 333.

170 [1930] 1 KB 467, 478.

171 The Lindop Committee on Data Protection concluded that the defence of qualified privilege available to 'mutual' trade protection societies, was rightly denied to commercially motivated credit reference agencies by the Consumer Credit Act of 1974 (despite the view of both the Younger Committee on Privacy and the Faulks Committee on Defamation), and 'a Data Protection Act is not, in our view, the right place to make that kind of change in the law of defamation', *Report of the Committee on Data Protection* (Chairman: Sir Norman Lindop) Cmnd 7341, 1978, para 32.14. See *Report of the Committee on Privacy* (Chairman: Kenneth Younger) Cmnd 5012, 1972, para 275; *Report of the Committee on Defamation* (Chairman Mr Justice Faulks) Cmnd 5909, 1975.

172 [1932] All ER 1, 11.

173 For an analysis of the law of Hong Kong of the policy questions generated by the concept of 'duty of care' see *Yuen Kun Yeu v Attorney General of Hong Kong* [1988] AC 175 (PC).

174 This a complex and controversial question. For a recent analysis of some of the difficulties, see the House of Lords decision in *Caparo Industries plc v Dickman* [1990] 1 All ER 568.

175 [1963] 2 All ER 575.

176 *Spring v Guardian Assurance PLC* [1994] 3 All ER 129. Liability in defamation might also, of course, arise in these circumstances. See above.

177 The exemption in s 55 from access to data which are the subject of a 'relevant process' may also cover personal references. See Chapter 9.

178 *Alcock v Chief Constable of South Yorkshire Police* [1992] 1 AC 310.

179 [1990] 1 HKLR 56.

180 As argued by R Glofcheski in (1990) 20 HKLJ 393.

181 *Glasgow Corporation v Muir* [1943] AC 448.

182 See *Edward Wong Finance Co Ltd v Johnson, Stokes & Master* [1984] AC 296 (PC).

183 This arises independently of the question of whether there may be liability for the separate tort of breach of statutory duty. See below.

184 For an analysis of the guidelines adopted see *Leung Nai Wing v Hsing Kieng Shing* (1985) HCA 8451 of 1984.

185 Such restrictions are prima facie against public policy unless they are reasonable in respect of time and place. See the recent trilogy of cases on contracts in restraint of trade in Hong Kong: *Bridge v Deacons (A Firm)* [1984] 1 AC 705, *Kao Lee & Yip (A Firm) v Edwards* [1994] 1 HKLR 232 and Kao. *Lee & Yip (A Firm) v Koo Hoi Yan, Donald* [1994] 2 HKC 228. See A Carver 'Restraint of Trade in Hong Kong' (1995) 25 HKLJ 309.

186 The leading case is *The Moorcock* (1886-1890) All ER 530 at 534. In *Saltman Engineering Co v Campbell Engineering Co* (1948) 65 RPC 203, Lord Greene MR said (at 211) 'If two parties make a contract, under which one of them obtains for the purpose of the contract or in connection with it, some confidential matter, even though the contract is silent on the matter of confidence, the law will imply an obligation to treat that confidential matter in a confidential way as one of the implied terms of the contract'. The objective test applied, following Megarry J's dictum in *Coco v AN Clark (Engineers) Ltd* [1969] RPC 41 at 48, is discussed above.

187 See F Gurry (1984), (note 56 above), p 61. An exemption clause may purport to limit or even avoid liability for breach of a 'confidentiality clause', though it is doubtful whether this would be effective where the

party is under a fiduciary duty: GJ Treitel (1991) *The Law of Contract* 8th ed, Sweet & Maxwell, p 224.

188 The leading case is *Lumley v Gye* (1853) 2 EL & BL 216, 118 ER 749.

189 See *Tse's Forex Investment Co Ltd v Man Yuk Lan* [1995] 3 HKC 450.

190 *London Passenger Transport Board v Upson* [1949] AC 155 at 169.

191 See *Winfield & Jolowicz on Tort*t (note 107 above) pp 191-4.

192 Or perhaps the tort of misfeasance in a public office, should the officer have acted maliciously or in the knowledge that his act is invalid and would necessarily injure the plaintiff. See *Bourgoin SA v Ministry of Agriculture, Fisheries and Food* [1986] QB 716. An action law for judicial review in administrative law would also normally lie.

193 *Victoria Park Racing and Recreation Grounds Co Ltd v Taylor* (1937) 58 CLR 479 at 494; *Bernstein of Leigh (Baron) v Skyviews & General Ltd* [1978] 1 QB 479, discussed in R Wacks, 'No Castles in the Air', (1997) 93 LQR 491.

194 *Leitch v Riley* (1853) 22 LJMC 48.

195 See Andrew Charlesworth, 'Addiction and Hacking' (1993) 143 NLJ 540, David Bainbridge, 'Hacking: The Unauthorised Access of Computer Systems – The Legal Implications' (1989) 52 MLR 236. Hacking is partly dealt with by Section 27A of the *Telecommunication Ordinance*. In *R v McLaughlin* (1980) 53 CCC (2D) 417 the Canadian Supreme Court held that a similar provision would not catch unauthorised access to a computer that was not effected by *another* computer. This limitation appears to apply to Section 27A and has been addressed, to some extent, by Section 161(1) of the *Crimes Ordinance*.

196 Thus it was held to be a trespass to erase a tape recording, see *The Times* 1 October 1966, quoted by *Salmond & Heuston on the Law of Torts*, (1992) 20th ed, Sweet & Maxwell, London, p 98. Showing a letter to an unauthorised person has also been held to be a trespass: *Thurston v Charles* (1905) 21 TLR 659. The argument that overhearing a conversation was a trespass was, of course, rejected in *Malone v Metropolitan Police Commissioner* [1979] Ch 344 at 374-6. See above.

197 *St Helen's Smelting Co v Tipping* (1865) 11 HLC 642 at 650 11 ER 1483 at 1486. In the Victoria Park case (note 48 above) Latham CJ declared, 'The category of nuisance is not closed . . . and if some new method of interfering with the comfort of persons in the use of land emerges the law may provide a remedy'. (At p 493).

198 *Malone v Laskey* [1907] 2 KB 141 and the House of Lords decision in *Hunter v Canary Wharf Ltd* (1997) The Times, 25 April. See above.

199 *Cunard v Antifyre* [1933] 1 KB 551 at 556; *Bank of New Zealand v Greenwood* [1984] 1 NZLR 525 at 532; SCM *(United Kingdom) v WJ Whitall & Son Ltd* [1970] 2 All ER 417 at 430; *Miller v Jackson* ([1977] QB 966.

200 [1993] QB 727. Cf *Hunter v Canary Wharf Ltd* (1997) The Times, 25 April.

201 In *Oxford v Moss* [1978] 68 Cr App R 183 information was held not to be property for the purposes of theft. The dishonest use without due authority or the wasting or diverting of electricity is an offence under Section 15 of the *Theft Ordinance*. This would almost certainly be committed by a hacker.

202 For a comparison between copyright and confidence see *Fraser v Thames Television Ltd* [1983] 2 All ER 101 at 117.

4 Key Concepts

The Ordinance adopts rather specialised terminology, and familiarity with the basic concepts is essential to an understanding of the various provisions. While most of these key concepts are defined in s 2, several are not.

Personal Data

This is, of course, the subject matter of the Ordinance, which does not purport to regulate 'data' that are not 'personal data'. However, the definition of 'personal data' builds upon the definition of 'data' which are defined as:

> Any representation of information (including an expression of opinion) in any document, and includes a personal identifier.

This complex definition indicates that the following elements of 'data' exist:

A Representation of Information

The concept of 'data' does not extend to, and hence the law does not cover, information *unless it is represented.* Furthermore, it is this representation that is regulated and not the information it is intended to convey. This is an aspect which generates some misunderstanding. The Ordinance does not cover, for example, comments or conversations that are not recorded. In this respect, it is narrower than the common law duty of confidence, the application of which is not restricted to recorded confidences (see Chapter 3). It would appear, however, that oral disclosures *based* on recorded data are covered: s 2 provides that 'disclosing' in relation to personal data, includes disclosing information inferred from data.

Data are Regulated Only if They are Contained in a Document

'Document' is given the following inclusive (rather than exhaustive) definition. It:

> includes, in addition to a document in writing -
> (a) a disc [*sic*], tape or other device in which data other than visual images are embodied so as to be capable, with or without the aid of some other equipment, of being reproduced from the disc, tape or other device; and
> (b) a film, tape or other device in which visual images are embodied as to be capable, with or without the aid of some other equipment, of being reproduced from the film, tape or other device.

A 'document' is therefore essentially a recording medium.

Examples of data which are subject to the Ordinance include electronic mail (e-mail) stored on computers and networks during the course of transmission.

The Ordinance's exclusive concern with recorded information is directly related to the mischief it is concerned to address. Oral comments do not pose the same dangers as their recorded equivalents. It is a matter of degree, of course, but the Ordinance is concerned with assertions of fact or opinion which, because they subsist in a record, pose a continuing source of information about the data subject upon which decisions are based.

A related reason for regulating only recorded material is the nature of the data protection principles. They are expressed in terms that preclude their meaningful application to unrecorded information. This is most obviously the case with the principle according the individual access and correction rights.

The definition of 'personal data' builds on the above description of 'data' and:

> means any data-
> (a) relating directly or indirectly to a living individual;
> (b) from which it is practicable for the identity of the individual to be directly or indirectly ascertained; and
> (c) in a form in which access to or processing of the data is practicable.

These three requirements are conjunctive, and data not fulfilling all three criteria are excluded from the definition of 'personal' data and accordingly fall outside the Ordinance. We have characterised the three requirements as concerning:

- Attribution;
- Identification; and
- Retrievability.

Attribution

Only data 'relating' to the individual are covered. Data so relate if they purport to describe the individual, to attribute things to the individual, including relationships such as ownership. A virtually identical requirement of 'information which relates to a living individual' is contained in the UK *Data Protection Act* definition of 'personal data' [s 1(3)].

The UK Data Protection Tribunal has ruled that under this definition a description of the type of property a ratepayer lived in constituted personal data.[1]

If the data lack *any* nexus with the individual they do not so 'relate'. In particular, data do not 'relate' to the individual merely because they are applied to that individual. Thus, certain criteria are commonly applied to an individual. For instance, a bank may use lending criteria. The bank record may state that Mr Wong is ineligible for a loan because he earns less than $15,000 per month. In this example, the data attributing an income to Mr Wong are clearly data relating to him. But the data stating the bank's minimum lending criteria merely record the direct application of that criteria to Mr Wong.

Nor do opinion data 'relate' to an individual because they record or reflect his opinions. A research paper or book does not constitute personal data about the author unless it has autobiographical content. Similarly, A's evaluation of B does not sufficiently relate to A to constitute personal data about him. It does, however, relate to B.

As these examples indicate, a general term such as 'relate to' must be given a purposive interpretation which accords with the aims of the Ordinance. The Ordinance will become unworkable unless it is interpreted as applying in particular to data the use of which – at least potentially – have an impact upon the individual data subject.

Identification

Data about individuals may or may not need to be identifiable. A newspaper vendor, for example, will normally be interested only in the total number of newspapers sold. Such data will be anonymous. However, a multitude of official and business relationships require a continuing record regarding specific individuals for the provision of goods and services and monitoring the fulfilment of reciprocal duties and payments. Such data must be effectively and validly identified as relating to the individual in question. In other words, it is often essential that a data user can distinguish one individual from another. A large number of complaints reported in the annual reports of privacy commissioners elsewhere arise from mistaken identification whereby data relating to another individual are mistakenly attributed to the data subject.

The identification component of 'personal data' excludes from the application of the Ordinance anonymous data where the individual's identity cannot be practicably ascertained, whether 'directly or indirectly'. Where identification can be ascertained solely from the data in question such ascertainment is direct. 'Indirect' ascertainment extends the test to where identification can be practicably effected by recourse to other data held by the data user or readily obtainable by him. For example, if I find in the street a diary whose only identification is 'Mr Wong', there is little hope of my ever knowing to which Mr Wong the data relate. Should the diary provide his occupation this is similarly unlikely to suffice. However, the addition of a telephone number makes it practicable to establish the identity of the Mr Wong in question.

Another example is where the data user holds data indirectly linked to an individual's membership of a club. The data may criticise the attitude of club members generally, without singling out specific individuals. If, however, other data held by the data user lists the individual as a member, then the critical data would be identifiable.

It follows from these examples that whether or not data are 'personal data' is not determined solely by reference to the class of data such as name or occupation, but by their context. The relevant test requires a consideration of all the circumstances of the case.

Living individual

Section 2 of the Ordinance defines personal data as 'data relating directly or indirectly to a living individual'. Furthermore, the long title of the Ordinance is 'an Ordinance to protect the privacy of individuals in relation to personal data'.

The Ordinance therefore does not purport to regulate the confidentiality of business data as such. The difficulty is drawing the line between personal and business affairs. Certainly, data concerning an individual's ownership or other relationship *with* a business would constitute personal data, just as other data indicating an individual's financial position would. However, where the business has in law an existence which is independent of the individuals making it up then data concerning that business do not 'relate to' those individuals as such. This is clearly the case with a business conducted through an incorporated company. Such data relate to the company which has a separate legal personality. Nor may it be possible to identify the individual from the data.[2]

Partnerships can be viewed in similar terms to companies, although they do not constitute legal persons as such. The *Partnership Ordinance* distinguishes the partnership from its members, so that (for example) it refers to partners as 'agents' of the firm (s 7). Data relating to a partnership will not therefore relate to the constituent individuals and are not personal data under the Ordinance. Only data which relate an individual *to* the partnership would constitute personal data, such as profits earned.

Unlike a company or partnership, a sole proprietorship has no separate legal status so that there is no apparent basis on which data can be related to an entity other than the individual owning the business. Under the *Business Registration Ordinance* a sole proprietorship is, in law, merely an activity carried on by an individual and data relating to that activity must relate to that individual because they cannot be related to any other person or entity. Any qualification of this position could lead to problems of application where an individual was running a business as drawing the line would be difficult. Nonetheless, data relating to a sole proprietorship may not constitute personal data where it is not reasonably practicable to infer the identity of the individual from data relating to the proprietorship. For example, it may have a completely different name from that of its owner and require a business registration search to identify the individual.

Use of identifiers including ID card numbers

Record-keeping systems adopt a variety of methods of distinguishing one individual from another. Names and addresses may suffice, but computerised systems will usually allot a shorthand reference. In Hong

Kong, the tendency is to resort not only to the individual's name and/or address but also to an ID card number. Inaccurate reference to ID numbers occurs more frequently than might be supposed. A survey conducted at Queen Mary Hospital found an error factor of more than five per cent, and Hong Kong Telecom discovered an error rate of between five and ten per cent.[3]

The requirement of identifiability provides data users with a method short of purging which takes data outside the scope of the Ordinance, namely their anonymisation. The anonymisation must not, however, be reversible by reasonably practicable methods or it remains within the definition.

Retrievability

In addition to being attributable and identifiable, to constitute 'personal data', such data must be in a form in which access to or processing of the data is practicable. Many data will relate to identifiable individuals, but they may for practical purposes be unusable. For example, a long report may make scattered references to an individual and, depending on the nature of the report, it may be unduly onerous to locate them. Section 2 defines 'practicable' as 'reasonably practicable'. An objective standard of reasonableness is accordingly adopted, although the 'reasonable man' is displaced in this context by the 'reasonable data user'.

The reasonableness standard accommodates the myriad relevant factors ranging from the nature of the data to the functions of the data user. There are two main aspects:

- The form in which the data are held: automated data will necessarily be retrievable, as will adequately indexed records; and
- The nature and sensitivity of the data.

No absolute duty is imposed on data users to computerise their data. Nor does the Ordinance impose any obligation to organise such data as are retained in manual form in such a way as to facilitate its retrieval. But while the Ordinance acquiesces in disorganised records, the reasonableness test also attends to the nature of the data and the resources of the data user. Depending on these factors, the retrieval of data may be reasonably required notwithstanding that this requires greater effort than would be the case if they were properly organised.

A shopkeeper's old customer invoices may well not be reasonably retrievable, but old police records held in unindexed manual files will be subject to a more stringent test of reasonable retrievability. The application of the standard of reasonableness thus ensures that a data user cannot exclude the application of the Ordinance merely by resorting to poor record management of data.

The retrievability test qualifies the Ordinance's focus on personal data in recorded form. It recognises a harm test: recorded data may pose only negligible risks to the individual because their effective inaccessibility preclude them from being utilised. In practical terms they may not exist, but with this difference. So long as they do exist they possess the potential to be organised, thereby facilitating their subsequent retrieval. The dusty old file may be read by an optical scanner on to a disk which may then, with little effort, be searched for key words. Indeed, many large organisations are currently involved in transforming paper file to disk, including the Hong Kong Government. Immediately the personal data are converted into the new readily retrievable format they become subject to the Ordinance.

Data User and Data Subject

'Data user' and 'data subject' are derivative definitions, depending on the relationship with personal data. A 'data subject' is 'the individual who is the subject of the data'. We pointed out above that this must be a living individual. Legal persons are not included. On the other hand, a data user is defined as:

> a person who, either alone or jointly or in common with other persons, controls the collection, holding, processing or use of the data.

'Person' includes, but is not restricted to, an individual and is defined in s 2 of the *Interpretation and General Clauses Ordinance* as including 'any public body and any body of persons, corporate or unincorporate'. 'Public body' is defined in the same provision as including certain councils and boards and 'any department of government'. Accordingly, government departments are separate data users from the Hong Kong government. Similarly, subsidiary companies are separate data users from their parent company.

Collecting, Holding, Processing or Use

Collecting

This term is not defined. The concept is explored in Chapter 5. For present purposes, it is sufficient to note that it encompasses not only the acquisition of data from other sources but also the creation of personal data records.

Holding

This term is also not defined, and has its usual English meaning.

Processing

Section 2 provides that 'processing' includes amending, augmenting, deleting or rearranging the data, whether by automated means or otherwise.

Use

Section 2 provides that 'use' (the verb) 'includes disclose or transfer the data'.

Does 'use' encompass not only the deployment of data but also the simple searching and retrieval of data? We believe that the Australian Privacy Commissioner is correct in maintaining that the searching of data may constitute its 'use'[4], and prefer this approach to that adopted under the United Kingdom *Data Protection Act* 1984. In *R v Brown*,[5] the House of Lords considered the ambit of 'use' under s 5(2)(b) of the Act. Unlike the Ordinance, the UK Act requires all data users to register and it is a criminal offence to 'use' data other than for a registered purpose. The defendant, a police officer, had accessed and viewed data stored in a police computer directly relevant to a private debt collecting company with which he was personally associated. By a majority of 3 to 2, the House held that, under the *Data Protection Act*, 'use' did not extend to the simple retrieval of information from a computer and that the concept of 'using' required that the information should be subsequently used.[6]

This narrow approach would not appear to be sustainable under the different provisions of the Ordinance. As previously mentioned, the short title of the Ordinance provides that the legislation is 'to protect the privacy of individuals in relation to personal data'. It is significant that the minority decisions in *Brown* holding that 'use' did extend to simple retrieval emphasised the protection of privacy as requiring this broader interpretation. But the minority was unable to draw on a provision in the UK legislation similar to the short title of the Hong Kong Ordinance.

Control of the Data Cycle

For a person to be a data user, not only must one of the enumerated processes occur, but the person must 'control' that process.

'Control' is not defined. The concept is fundamental for in identifying the legal subjects of regulation, it also defines the territorial application of the Ordinance. It matters not where in the world the collection, processing, etc occurs as long as it is controlled by a person in Hong Kong. Any control over any aspect of the data cycle is sufficient to attract regulation under the Ordinance.

In Griffin[7] the High Court interpreted 'control' under section 5(1) of the UK *Data Protection Act* 1984. The defendant was a self-employed accountant. He received clients' accounting information in the form of invoices and other records and transferred it to a spreadsheet computer programme. The court held that the defendant 'controlled' the data as he had the power to manipulate the data according to his own professional judgement. He was not merely acting on instructions but determined what data should be recorded and how they should be manipulated. The court also held that this control existed notwithstanding the fact that the defendant had no right to use the data for his own purposes, but solely for the purposes of producing his clients' accounts.

Shared Control

Following gazetting of the Bill, various telecommunications organisations and internet service providers expressed the concern that they might be deemed to be data users in respect of electronic mail, data or files they merely transmit or store on behalf of a subscriber. Clearly the subscriber would be a data user in respect of data being transferred in this manner. Whether the carrier is a joint data user depends on whether it is exercising the requisite control.

Carriers do have a degree of control over the processing of the data. For example, they could stop the transfer of data if the situation warranted, but only to the extent necessary to effect transmission. Insofar as 'control' can be said to be exercised in such circumstances, it is nonetheless insufficient to warrant the application of the requirements of the Ordinance. Accordingly, s 2(3) provides that the Ordinance does not apply where the person is acting solely as an agent:

> A person is not a data user in relation to any personal data which the person holds, processes or uses solely on behalf of another person if, but only if, that first mentioned person does not hold, process or use, as the case may be, those data for any of his own purposes.

Application of the proviso would result in a telecommunications carrier being deemed a data user in respect of data it accessed for its *own* purposes. This might include an Internet provider that browses e-mail or an eavesdropping fax line operator. Such accessing would constitute 'processing' for its own purposes.

In s 2(2), the qualification of the control test is itself subject to a significant restriction by omitting reference to collection. Accordingly, a person will be a data user in relation to personal data which he collects, even if he does so solely on behalf of another person and not for any of his own purposes. However, as explained in Chapter 5, 'collection' means the active process of gathering or creating data and does not extend to the mere receipt of unsolicited data

Consent

As pointed out in Chapter 1, the Ordinance does not permit data users to contract out of the application of the Ordinance by obtaining the agreement of the individual. However, an individual's consent is relevant to the application of a number of the Ordinance's requirements. Under the Ordinance, the data subject's consent must be express, voluntary and informed.

There is more than one term of consent in the Ordinance. The principal usage is 'prescribed consent', although s 33 refers to 'written consent'. Section 2(3) defines 'prescribed consent' as follows:

Such consent –

(a) means the express consent of the person given voluntarily;

(b) does not include any consent which has been withdrawn by notice in writing served on the person to whom the consent has been given (but without prejudice to so much of that act that has been done pursuant to the consent at any time before notice is so served).

'Prescribed consent' is a key term because it is incorporated into principle 3 of the data protection principles. This principle governs the use of personal data and is addressed more fully in Chapter 7. Suffice it to say at this stage that data protection principle 3 requires the data subject's prescribed consent to the use of data for any purpose other than the purpose for which the data were to be used at the time of the collection of the data.

The basic principle is that parties cannot opt out of the application of the Ordinance. However, where a provision is subject to 'prescribed consent', the ambit of that expression requires determination. The requirement that consent be 'express' means it must be an affirmative act. This requirement is not fulfilled by simply advising a data subject of a proposed course of action and asking him to indicate if he objects (the so-called 'opt out' procedure). A bank would not, therefore, be entitled to send circulars to all its customers advising that, failing receiving instructions to the contrary, it will henceforth deploy account details for direct marketing purposes.

Secondly, 'consent' must mean informed consent. As the UK Data Protection Registrar has put it, 'S/he must be fully aware of what s/he is consenting to for it to constitute proper consent'.[8] The data subject must be advised in clear terms what the data user is proposing to do with his data. 'Consent' does not merely mean acquiescence in a vaguely formulated proposal.

While 'prescribed consent' must be 'express', the affirmative act need not be expressed in writing but may be given orally or even by a nod of the head. Written consent better ensures the avoidance of subsequent disputes.

Subject to this, whether consent is prescribed or written, it may extend to a series of transactions, such as disclosures, matching procedures or transfers out of Hong Kong. A new consent would not have to be obtained for each such transaction provided they clearly come within the terms of the earlier consent.

Notes

1 UK Data Protection Registrar (1989) 5th Annual Report, HMSO, London, pp 16-17.

2 This is not affected by the *Companies Amendment Ordinance of 1997*, s 5A of which provides: 'A company has the capacity and the rights, powers and privileges of a natural person'. The intention of the legislature cannot have been radically to amend the effect of statutes such as the *Personal Data (Privacy) Ordinance*.

3 The Law Reform Commission of Hong Kong (1994) *Reform of the Law Relating to the Protection of Personal Data* (Topic 27), p 131.

4 Australian Privacy Commissioner (1996) *Plain English Guidelines to Information Privacy Principles*, Human Rights Australia, Sydney 8-11, p 11.

5 [1996] 2 WLR 203.

6 Lord Hoffmann declared, 'Retrieving data from a computer seems to me a use of the computer rather than a use of the data' (at 219). Cf Lord Griffiths (dissenting): 'To read personal data about an individual displayed on a computer screen or in a printout is an invasion of that person's privacy, if there is no legitimate purpose for doing so' (at 213). The majority's view, while elegant in its logic, undermines the protection that it is not unreasonable to suppose the Act intended to afford to data subjects.

7 (1993) The Times, 5 March.

8 UK Data Protection Registrar (1994) 10th Annual Report, HMSO, London, p 63.

5 Data Collection

Introduction

Although the Ordinance makes frequent reference to the 'collection' of data, the term is undefined. It is clear, however, that it covers two situations:

- The gathering of existing data from data subjects (for example, from a completed questionnaire) or other data users; and
- The creation of data *about an individual* by *recording* information elicited from data subjects or other data users. For example, asking the data subject questions and noting the replies.

Both of these activities require the active involvement of the data user. However, persons may also be the recipients of unsolicited data. The Australian Privacy Commissioner has adopted the view that the acquisition of data by unsolicited receipt does not constitute 'collection' until the data user takes active steps to incorporate them into the official working material of the organisation. As explained below, the principle addressing data collection imposes requirements that assume that the data user has control over the collection process and is not merely the passive recipient of personal data.

Principle 1 of the data protection principles addresses the purpose and manner of collection of personal data. It has three aspects, namely that collection is necessary, that it is lawful and fair and that the collection from the data subject is genuinely consensual. These aspects are now examined in detail.

Collection is Necessary

Principle 1(1) provides:

> Personal data shall not be collected unless –
> (a) the data are collected for a lawful purpose directly related to a function or activity of the data user who is to use the data;
> (b) subject to paragraph (c), the collection of the data is necessary for or directly related to that purpose; and
> (c) the data are adequate but not excessive in relation to that purpose.

This requirement applies to the collection of data (in the sense explained above) from both data subjects and other data users.

Underpinning this principle is the notion of relevance. To ensure that only relevant data are collected, the statutory test requires that a data user should identify:

- Its functions or activities;
- All those lawful purposes directly related to those functions or activities; and
- The classes of data whose collection is necessary for or directly related to those purposes.

Functions or Activities of a Data User

In this context 'function or activity' must refer to the actual functions or activities being carried out by the data user, or those specifically contemplated.

In the public sector, an agency's functions are often specified by statute. In the private sector, it is common practice when incorporating a company to include every conceivable function or activity in the articles of association. However, these articles probably define what activities are permitted, not those which are actually carried out. To countenance collection for all such purposes would render this limitation imposed by principle 1 meaningless. Furthermore, the collection of data relevant to every conceivable function would grind the company to a halt! The clear intention of the Ordinance is to limit collection and this must be on the basis that the data user is engaging in identifiable functions and activities.

The 'function or activity' of a data user may be defined with varying degrees of precision. For example, a retailer may define its own function or activity as that of selling shoes or retailing. Going even further, it could be argued that the 'function or activity' of a shoe shop is the generation of profits.

A data user may be tempted to define its functions or activities as generally as possible so as to enlarge the corresponding scope for collecting data. Leaving aside the question of whether 'the generation of profits' indeed constitutes a function or activity as opposed to an objective or goal, such a broad statement would permit a multitude of data purposes that could be wholly irrelevant to the activities of a shoe shop, such as earning professional fees. This approach is hardly conducive to good records management.

More fundamentally, it overlooks the objective nature of the test. In practice, the Commissioner can be expected to make a sensible assessment of the actual functions or activities of the data user being investigated. Thus, for example, the Australian Privacy Commissioner does not allow a data user's definition of the situation to preclude him from making his own assessment of the actual position as regards the related issue of data purposes. The alternative approach here would enable the general scheme of the Ordinance to be subverted.

Lawful Purposes Directly Related to Those Functions or Activities

The ordinary meaning of 'lawful' means both compliance with any relevant statutory provisions and any applicable common law requirements (see Chapter 3). Thus, 'unlawful' has been held to mean 'something which is contrary to some law or enactment or is done without lawful justification or excuse'.[1] According to this approach, 'lawful' is not restricted to compliance with the criminal law. Nor is there anything in the Ordinance indicating that such a narrow approach is appropriate. On the contrary, the short title of the Ordinance states that the legislation is 'to protect the privacy of individuals in relation to personal data'. The statutory purpose therefore is protection from interference in a broad sense.

This approach accords with that adopted by the UK Data Protection Registrar in construing the requirement under the UK Act that data be obtained 'lawfully'. The Registrar considers 'unlawful' to include not only breaches of the criminal law, but also breaches of the private law.

Collection for an unlawful purpose would occur, for instance, where a data provider discloses data in breach of confidence. If the data collector has notice of the duty of confidence at the time of collection, or if he ought reasonably to know that the data have been imparted in confidence, he would be bound by the duty of confidence. If part of the purpose of collection is the unauthorised use or disclosure of that data, then this would constitute an unlawful purpose (see Chapter 3).

Necessary for or directly related lawful purposes
That 'function or activity' envisages a rather specific description is further indicated by the additional requirement that data purposes be 'directly related' to the function or activities. Such a reference would be redundant if very broad descriptions of function/activities were contemplated by the legislation. In respect of the collection of data by government departments, the Australian Privacy Commissioner, for example, does not normally accept the view that an agency collects personal information merely to administer an agency or a set of laws. The purpose of collection should be more specific than this and it should relate to the specific reason for collecting the information Some purposes that he would accept as regards government data users include:

- Allowing the agency to give someone a particular benefit or service; and
- Helping the agency to run a particular government programme.[2]

The classes of data whose collection is necessary for or directly related to those purposes
The Australian Privacy Commissioner adds that 'collecting information just because it may be useful in the future is generally not acceptable'.[3] In the example given above of the selling of shoes, compiling payment accounts would be so related, but obtaining detailed information relating to customers would not.

Avoiding the Collection of Irrelevant Information

Data which are not necessary for the primary or directly related purposes are irrelevant. The obtaining of irrelevant information includes the following activities:

- Collecting data when oral inquiries should suffice;
- Recording the identity of an individual unnecessarily. For example, a cash purchase will seldom require any details about the purchaser;
- Retaining a full copy of a document when the relevant data should be abstracted or the irrelevant data blacked out;
- Collecting data from an entire group when the data are relevant only to some members of the group; and
- Collecting more data from or about an individual than is required in the circumstances.

Credit checks on address-linked data

Relevant in this context is the practice of some credit bureaux to collect data about other individuals to assist credit providers to determine a data subject's creditworthiness. This practice has been considered by the UK Data Protection Tribunal in ruling on appeals from four credit reference bureaux (CCN, Infolink, Equifax and CDMS) against enforcement notices issued by the Registrar under the UK *Data Protection Act* 1984.[4] At the beginning of its decision, the Tribunal gave the following illustration which was accepted by counsel for both sides as representative of the type of complaint for consideration:

> In 1985, Mr Simon Jones, a chartered accountant, sold his house to Mr J Watson. In 1988, Mr Jones applied to a building society for a cheque guarantee card. He was refused a card and informed that a credit reference had been sought from CCN. Mr Jones applied to CCN (under consumer credit legislation) for a copy of his file. Among the information supplied was an entry showing a judgment awarded in 1987 against Mr Watson. The only link between Mr Jones and Mr Watson was that they were respectively vendor and purchaser of a house a few years earlier. Put in another way, the only link between them was that they had at different times lived at the same address. Mr Jones was distressed by this incident.

At the outset it should be emphasised that access was not provided under the *Data Protection Act*, but under consumer credit legislation which has no counterpart in Hong Kong. This is important because the data relating to another individual would not have been furnished under the access provisions of the UK *Data Protection Act* (nor under the Ordinance) precisely because it does not relate to the data subject. However, the issue for the Tribunal was whether the collection of the data put on the credit file contravened principle 1 of the *Data Protection Act* that provides, 'The information to be contained in personal data shall be obtained, and personal data shall be processed, fairly and lawfully'.

The essential issue was whether the collection of data by reference to address was fair in all the circumstances. This was thought to depend on whether the data were relevant. The Registrar argued that they were irrelevant in that they did not relate to the data subject. The credit bureau argued that they were relevant to the question of whether the data subject was a member of class of persons of whom a certain percentage would be likely to default. It argued that 'fairly' should balance any possible unfairness to the data subject against such competing interests as reducing default rates and hence the cost of loans generally.

The Tribunal preferred the Registrar's definition of 'fairly' and ruled that address-based searches as a matter of routine would be unfair. However, it was not unfair to collect data about persons who were believed on the basis of previous inquiries to be closely financially linked with the data subject as indicated by shared names.

Compliance programmes and data collection
To avoid collecting irrelevant data a data user should:

- Clearly identify all data purposes. Data users should also identify all categories of collection which are necessary for or directly related to those purposes; and
- Check all forms and interview questions against the above criteria. They should instruct and train their interviewers accordingly.

Relevance and the Other Data Protection Principles

While principle 1(1) will address new collections of irrelevant data, data users are likely to hold significant amounts of irrelevant data collected prior to the Ordinance being enacted. The requirement of principle 2(2) that data shall not be kept longer than necessary for the fulfilment of the data purpose is discussed below.

Collection by Lawful and Fair Means

Principle 1 requires also that collection must be by lawful and fair means:

> Personal data shall be collected by means which are –
> (a) lawful; and
> (b) fair in the circumstances of the case.

These two requirements are conjunctive.

We examined earlier the requirement that data be collected for lawful *purposes*. We saw that 'unlawful' encompasses both statutory and civil wrongs. This limb of principle 1 focuses not on purposes but on collection by lawful *means*. The Australian Privacy Commissioner has provided the following examples of unlawful collection:[5]

- The data collector commits an offence, such as intercepting mail without authority;
- The data collector is sued as a consequence of collecting data by trespassing on to property; and
- The data collector is established by statute and lacks statutory power to collect the information in question.

Collection from another party necessarily entails both a disclosure by a data provider and a collection by a data collector. Principle 1 focuses on the lawfulness of the collection from the standpoint of the data collector; the position of the data provider is addressed by principle 3 (see Chapter 7). The disclosure of the data may be an unlawful act on the part of the data provider, yet the collection of that data by the data collector may be lawful. For example:

- A number of statutes impose a secrecy requirement. Whereas an official disclosing the data will commit a criminal offence, the recipient data collector will not necessarily do so; or
- A data provider may disclose data in breach of contract. For example, it is an implied term of the contract between a bank and its customer that account details should not normally be disclosed to third parties. While disclosure would constitute a breach of contract by the bank, the data collector would not necessarily be in breach. For his collection to be unlawful, some tort would have to be committed, such as inducing a breach of contract.

Fair in the Circumstances of the Case

In addition to being lawful, the collection must be means that are 'fair in the circumstances of the case'.

In his guidelines,[6] the UK Registrar has taken the view that the standards of fairness must be objectively assessed and the test of the reasonable man applied. A data user may accordingly contravene the principle although it did not intend to do so. This approach was upheld by the Data Protection Tribunal in its ruling (discussed above) on the extraction for the purpose of credit references data on previous occupiers not financially linked to the data subject.[7] The data user argued that extracting such data was fair because:

- In determining fairness, regard should not be primarily for the interests of the data subject applying for credit, but to the interests of lenders and borrowers generally; and
- The processing was not inaccurate or misleading. On the contrary, the Tribunal accepted that such data were statistically predictive of credit risk.

The Tribunal rejected these arguments, holding that having regard in particular to the principles, the purpose of the *Data Protection Act* 'is to protect the rights of [the data subject] rather than those of the data user,' and 'In our view in deciding whether the processing is fair we must give the first and paramount consideration to the interests of the applicant for credit – the 'data subject' in the Act's terms'.[8]

The Ordinance uses the term 'fair in the circumstances of the case'. The term is derived from the New Zealand law. It is arguable, however, that these words make explicit, rather than widen, the need to consider what fairness requires in pursuing particular goals.

Intentional Unfairness

Fair means are straightforward and direct. Unfair means include deception and undue pressure.

Trickery or deception

Unfair means may involve deception or trickery, such as:

- Misrepresenting the identity of the data collector. For example, an investigator may pretend to a neighbour that he is a relative of the individual he is asking about;

- Misrepresenting what will be done to the data once they are collected, such as claiming they will be treated 'in confidence' when it is proposed to pass them on; or
- Misrepresenting the consequences of failing to provide data, such as asserting that a prosecution may result although there is no legal requirement to provide the data. Conversely, it would be unfair to misrepresent benefits that may accrue from furnishing the data.

It will be seen below that when data are collected directly from the data subject, there is a positive duty to inform the individual of the data purposes and data recipients, as well as whether furnishing the data is obligatory or voluntary. Accordingly, actively misleading the data subject would breach that duty as well as constituting unfair collection.

Undue pressure
The Australian Privacy Commissioner provides the following examples of data collections that are unfair because undue pressure has been applied to the data subject:

- Visiting people's homes at unreasonable hours;
- Persistently asking for information;
- Insulting or intimidating conduct by an interviewer; and
- Asking for information in ways that might unnecessarily embarrass a person.[9]

Notification to Data Subject

Principle 1(3) declares:

> Where the person from whom personal data are or are to be collected is the data subject, all practicable steps shall be taken to ensure that:
> (a) he is explicitly or implicitly informed, on or before collecting the data, of –
>   (i) whether it is obligatory or voluntary for him to supply the data; and
>   (ii) where it is obligatory for him to supply the data, the consequences for him if he fails to supply the data; and

(b) he is explicitly informed –
  (i) on or before collecting the data, of:
    (A) the purpose (in general or specific terms) for which the data are to be used; and
    (B) the classes of persons to whom the data may be transferred; and
  (ii) on or before the first use of the data for the purpose for which they were collected, of
    (A) his rights to request access to and to request the correction of the data; and
    (B) the name and address of the individual to whom any such request may be made unless to comply with the provisions of this subsection would be likely to prejudice the purpose for which the data were collected and that purpose is specified in Part VIII of this Ordinance as a purpose in relation to which personal data are exempt from the provisions of data protection principle 6.

Under this requirement, the person from whom the data are sought (or compiled from information supplied) must:

- On or before the collection of the data, be informed of –
  (i) Data purposes (although the Ordinance uses the singular 'purpose', as a matter of statutory interpretation, the singular is deemed to include the plural).[10] The statutory language is not an invitation 'to invent the vaguest, most abstract single-sentence purpose possible'.[11] Accordingly, if there is more than one purpose, it should be spelt out;
  (ii) Data recipients;
  (iii) Whether it is obligatory to supply the data and if so, the consequences of failing to do so. Where there is a legal requirement that data be provided, this should be specifically identified.

  In the case of (i) and (ii), but not (iii) this advice must be explicit.
- Before the first *use* of the data, be explicitly informed of this access/correction rights and relevant contact details.

The principle's differentiation between 'explicit' and 'implicit' notification acknowledges that, as regards the willingness to supply data, this will often be obvious from the situation. For example, it is obviously not obligatory to furnish personal data in response to a newspaper advertisement or promotional leaflet. Similarly, the consequences of failing to respond are also obvious, namely that no transaction will occur. Hence, there is no invariable requirement of explicit notification of these matters. The identification of data purposes and classes of transferees, however, will often be ambiguous and hence the requirement of explicit notification to avoid any misunderstandings.

Form of Notification

No form of notification is specified; it may therefore be oral or written. The manner in which data are collected often indicates the most suitable approach. The Australian Privacy Commissioner gives the following practical advice under similar legislation:

- If the data user collects personal data by asking a person to fill in a form, the notice can be printed on the form. It should not be hard to find nor in type too small to read. Alternatively, a supplementary notice can be provided;
- If the data are collected in a face-to-face interview, the individual can be given a notice and provided sufficient time for the reading of the notice and to clarify any queries;
- If the interview is conducted by telephone, the individual should be advised orally. The words used by the interviewer should preferably be written down and included in staff instructions; and
- Where providing some of the data is obligatory and the remainder is voluntary, the questions may be usefully segregated in the form or interview sheet.

Where standard forms are used for the collection of data, it will be necessary to bring them up to date in order to include reference to these matters.

The obligations imposed by principle 1(3) are not absolute but must be fulfilled wherever 'practicable', ie 'reasonably practicable' (s 2). For example, strict compliance will not be feasible if physical data is collected from an unconscious patient.

A decision of the UK Data Protection Tribunal[12] indicates that mere inconvenience, however, would not suffice to displace the obligation. The ruling related to a mail order business, Innovations, which advertised its goods in various ways including through catalogues and advertisements in the press, television and radio. Customers responded in writing or by telephone, and it was a business practice of the company to make lists of the customers' names and addresses. These lists were rented to other companies. On some occasions the customer did not learn of this practice of list rental until after providing the information. The Registrar issued an enforcement notice requiring the company to give a notification informing customers of its rental of lists not later than the collection of data in all cases.

Innovations argued that it was not practicable to give a notification in respect of all forms of media, in particular in relation to short radio or television advertisements. It argued that it was more realistic to give the notice after information had been obtained from the customer. It submitted also that this would be clearer to the customer because at the time of ordering he would be more concerned with the choice of goods than whether Innovations would trade the name and address supplied. The company further argued that a notification on the telephone would increase the cost of calls to the customer and that a later notification could be more detailed.

The Tribunal concluded that a warning must be given before the information is obtained. This accords with the statutory requirement contained in principle 1(3). Of particular relevance in the present context, however, was the Tribunal's rejection of the company's arguments that it was impracticable to provide a notification within any form of advertising currently available and was not prepared to exclude any of the media from its judgment.

Collection by Data User's Own Observations

Principle 1(3) applies only where data are collected from the data subject. On this view, where the data are collected solely through the data user's own observations, the data subject need not be advised of the matters specified. This is indicated by the reference to the data subject's *supplying* the data. However, the requirements would apply whether or not the data subject volunteered the data. Furthermore, the requirement would apply where the data subject supplies any data at all, even if it is significantly enhanced by data compiled as a result of the data user's observations, such as describing demeanour.

Collections from Families

The obligations imposed by principle 1 apply to the party collecting the data. However, some data users tend to treat a group of data subjects such as a family as a unit. The Ordinance does not recognise the concept of a unit and instead focuses on the privacy of individuals. It does not follow, however, that the notification requirement contained in principle 1(3) must be applied regardless of whether compliance will result in prejudice to the members of that unit. The notification requirements are not absolute but only require the taking of 'all (reasonably) practicable steps'. For example, the notification requirement could discourage battered spouses from seeking help if they had to consult their family members before disclosing family conditions to social workers. However, compliance with the notification requirements is not required if it is likely to prejudice the purpose for which the data are collected and that purpose is exempted under Part VIII, such as the prevention, preclusion or remedying of unlawful or seriously improper conduct under s 58(1)(d). Furthermore, the mere oral disclosure to the data user of information by a family member about others in the family does not involve their collecting personal data from those members. Accordingly, such disclosures can be made without consulting or notifying those other members. Similarly, where a family member records matters relating to another member that the former has known for some time, it becomes artificial to describe this process as involving the collection of data from the latter and principle 1(3) is accordingly not directly relevant in such situations.

Repeated Collections

The practical exigencies arising from repeated collections are explicitly accommodated by s 35. There are many situations where data are collected on a continuous basis in virtually identical circumstances, such as from a hospital patient. Here, it would be pointless to repeat ritually the requirements after the initial collection.

Accordingly, s 35 provides:

> (1) A data user who:
>
> (a) has complied with the provisions of data protection principle 1(3) in respect of the collection of any personal data from the data subject ('first collection'); and

(b) on any subsequent occasion again collects personal data from the data subject ('subsequent collection'),

is not required to comply with those provisions in respect of the subsequent collection if, but only if –

(i) to comply with those provisions in respect of that subsequent collection would be to repeat, without any material difference, what was done to comply with that principle in respect of the first collection; and

(ii) not more than 12 months have elapsed between the first collection and the subsequent collection.

The provision concludes by stating that the cycle can be repeated from year to year, on the basis that an annual reminder is desirable.

Collection and Consent

Principle 1(3) requires that the data subject be *informed*. Prescribed consent, with its corollary of withdrawal in writing [s 2(3)], is not required, although if the data subject disagrees with what is proposed, he can decline to furnish the data. The consequence, however, is that once furnished, there is no mechanism enabling the data subject to reverse the collection process.

Collections from Third Parties

Principle 1(3) provides robust protection to the data subject when personal data are solicited from him. They may be bypassed, however, by collecting the data from other sources. The Ordinance lacks any general duty requiring the collection of data from the data subject rather than secondary sources. The danger is that excessive reliance on other sources for data on the data subject tends to exclude the individual from the data processing cycle. This poses its own risks to data users. The data subject will often be the best source of accurate data about him. Undue reliance on other sources may well compromise data quality. This, in turn, exposes the data user to claims for compensation for the use of inaccurate data. The Ordinance's requirements on data quality are examined in Chapter 6.

Exemption from Obligation to Inform Data Subject

The proviso states that all reasonably practicable[13] steps should be taken to inform the data subject the above matters. This is addressed earlier. In addition, however, the proviso states that compliance is not required where this would be likely to prejudice the purpose for which the data were collected and that purpose is subject to an exemption under Part VIII from principle 6. A similar provision of the New Zealand *Privacy Act* has been considered by the New Zealand Privacy Commissioner:

> The complaint related to an employer's use of a surveillance camera in the locker area of the workplace. It had been installed after the employer became concerned at the amount of stock going missing from the warehouse. Following a period when the whole locker area had been monitored a camera was directed specifically at the complainant's locker. The commissioner concluded that the video surveillance was intended to film covert and unlawful behaviour. The employer was not required to inform the complainant that he was being filmed in advance because this would have prejudiced the purpose of collection, namely the prosecution of crime.[14]

Notes

1 *R v R* [1991] 4 All ER 481 at 488, per Lord Keith.

2 Australian Privacy Commissioner (1994) *Plain English Guidelines to Information Privacy Principles* 1-3, p 6, Human Rights Australia, Sydney.

3 See note 2 above, p 6.

4 UK Data Protection Registrar (1991) 7th Report, pp 18-21, HMSO, London.

5 See note 2 above, p 8-9.

6 *The Data Protection Act 1984, Guideline 4: The Data Protection Principles*, UK Data Protection Registrar (1989), Wilmslow.

7 See note 4 above.

8 See note 4 above.

9 See note 2 above, p 10.

10 See s 7, Interpretation and General Clauses Ordinance.

11 R Clarke and G Greenleaf, (1988) *Australian Proposals to Implement the OECD Data Protection Guidelines*, Canberra, Australian National University.

12 See note 4 above.UK 10th Annual Report, p 32, HMSO, London.

13 Cf s 2 – definition of 'practicable'.

14 New Zealand Privacy Commissioner (1994) Case note 0632.

6 Data Quality

Introduction

Decisions are increasingly made solely on the basis of personal data. Where such data are inaccurate, decisions will plainly be flawed. In general, therefore, where the quality of data is concerned, data user interests coincide with those of data subjects. For example, denying a loan because of a negative assessment of the applicant's financial position not only has an impact on the applicant's finances, but also denies the potential lender the prospect of a profitable relationship. On the other hand, extending credit to a poor risk may result in the loan having to be written off.

Accordingly, maintaining data quality is essential if an organisation is to ensure that its own decision-making is sound. It is also subject to principle 2:

> 'All practicable steps shall be taken to ensure that:
> (a) personal data are accurate having regard to the purpose (including any directly related purpose) for which the data are or are not to be used.'

Accuracy under the Ordinance is accordingly a relative concept and is determined by the data purpose. Data purposes are regulated by principle 3 and must accord (subject to data subject consent) with the purposes for which they were collected. Principle 1 restricts data collections to those relevant to the data user's functions or activities.

'Inaccurate' is defined as meaning the personal data are 'incorrect, misleading, incomplete or obsolete' (s 2). These concepts, although overlapping, are distinct.

Incorrect

This term is more appropriate in respect of factual misstatements than invalid opinions. The purposes for which the data are used will determine the precision required of the data.

Many data state a position as at a certain date. For example, a reference will provide a summary of an individual's attributes and achievements as at the date it was compiled. While the passage of time will not render such data 'incorrect', it may render them misleading or obsolete (see below).

Misleading

Misleading data include sweeping judgements, for instance describing a person who consumes three cans of beer a day as 'an alcoholic'. It also encompasses biased opinions and the selective use of facts. Compliance requires that:

- *Existing* data that are misleading should be corrected; and
- *New* data should endeavour to be objective, and generalisations should be supported by representative examples. For example, 'Paul is not punctual, averaging more than 30 minutes late to work twice weekly in the last month'.

Incomplete

Incomplete data means insufficient data from which to draw valid inferences. For example, data indicating that an individual is in arrears in payments are likely to lead to unreliable or mistaken conclusions if no mention is made of the fact that he is suing for non-delivery of the goods in question. 'Complete' should be distinguished from 'comprehensive', ie the compilation of *all* available data.

Obsolete

Obsolete data fail to represent the current position where currency is required by the data purpose. For example, in determining a credit application, the data should reflect the applicant's current financial position. On the other hand, the data purpose may be to maintain a historical record of transactions. Although not current, such data are not obsolete. Updating such records would be clearly inappropriate.

The additional requirement that the retention of such records is necessary is discussed below.

Principle 2 continues:

> Where there are reasonable grounds for believing that personal data are inaccurate having regard to the purpose (including any directly related purpose) for which the data are to be used –
>
> (a) the data are not used for that purpose unless and until those grounds cease to be applicable to the data, whether by the rectification of the data or otherwise; or
>
> (b) the data are erased;
>
> (c) where it is practicable in the circumstances of the case to know that –
>
> (i) personal data disclosed on or after the appointed day to a third party are materially inaccurate having regard to the purpose (including any directly related purpose) for which the data are or are to be used by the third party; and
>
> (ii) data were inaccurate at the time of that disclosure,
>
> that the third party–
>
> (A) is informed that the data are inaccurate; and
>
> (B) is provided with such particulars as will enable the third party to rectify the data having regard to that purpose.

The Scale of the Problem

Experience in other jurisdictions

Studies in countries lacking a data protection regime have produced alarming results. A study of United States police records is a case in point. Criminal history records held in official repositories were compared with the information in the original files of county courthouses. The results were disturbing, with the percentage of summaries found to be complete, accurate and unambiguous in the states surveyed ranging from 49.5 per cent down to a mere 12.2 per cent.[1]

Compensation for Inaccuracy

A breach of the accuracy principle will, as with other contraventions, expose the data user to a claim for compensation. However, in a claim for compensation for damage suffered by reason of inaccuracy, two defences and a transition period are relevant.

Section 66(3)(a) provides a defence where: 'The data user had taken such care as in all the circumstances was reasonably required to avoid the contravention'. This is a general defence to compensation claims, but is particularly relevant to claims arising from inaccuracy because of the propensity of data accurate upon inputting to be overtaken by subsequent events and changes in context. Indeed, data users will be largely dependent on the data subject to maintain its data in an up-to-date state. The Ordinance, however, declines to impose a positive duty on the data subject to regularly update his or her data. Such an obligation could deluge data users with access and correction requests. The defence of reasonable care will bar compensation for data the inaccuracy of which is attributable to the data subject's lack of input.

This highlights the role of data subject access and correction rights in improving data quality. The individual is often best equipped to correct data relating to himself.

Principle 5 of the UK *Data Protection Act* is similar and requires that 'personal data shall be accurate, and when necessary, kept up to date'. In his guideline[2] on the application of the corresponding principle of the UK *Data Protection Act*, the Registrar identifies the following matters as relevant to whether the data user has taken all reasonable steps to prevent the inaccuracy:

- *The source from which the inaccurate information was obtained.* Was it reasonable for the data user to rely on information received from that source?

- *Any steps taken to verify the information.* Did the data user attempt to check its accuracy with another source? Would it have been reasonable to ask the data subject, either at the time of collection or at another convenient opportunity, whether the information was accurate?

- *The procedures for (computerised) data entry and for ensuring the system itself does not introduce inaccuracies into the data.*

- *The procedures followed by the data user when the inaccuracy came to light.* Were the data corrected as soon as the inaccuracy became apparent? Was the correction passed on to any third parties to whom the inaccurate data may have already been disclosed? Did the inaccuracy have any other consequences in the period before it was corrected? If so, what has the data user done about those consequences?

In addition, a specific defence applying to claims regarding inaccurate data is that 'the data accurately record data received or obtained from the data subject or a third party' [s 66(3)(b)]. This qualification is also in the UK Act and has been described by the Data Protection Registrar as protecting a data user 'from having to act as a guarantor of the complete accuracy of everything other people tell him'.[3]

It should be noted that compensation for a breach of the accuracy principle is not payable for the first year that the Ordinance is in force [s 66(4)].

Principle 2 concludes:

> (2) Personal data shall not be kept longer than is necessary for the fulfilment of the purpose (including any directly related purpose) for which the data are or are to be used.

The UK Data Protection Registrar has provided the following guideline on the virtually identical provision of the UK Act:

> To comply with this principle, data users will need to review their personal data regularly and to delete the information which is no longer required for their purposes. Data users who hold more than a very small quantity of personal data may find it convenient to adopt a systematic policy of deleting data. This might involve setting a standard 'life' for records of a particular category. At the end of that life the record should be reviewed and deleted unless there is some special reason for keeping it. The length of the review period will depend upon the nature of the record. If the data have only a short-term value to the data user, it may be appropriate to delete them within days or months.

> If personal data have been recorded because of a relationship between the data user and the data subject, the need to keep the information should be considered when that relationship ceases to exist. For example, the data subject may be an employee who has left the data user's employment or a customer who no longer does business with the data user. The end of the relationship will not necessarily cause the data user to delete all the personal data. It may well be necessary to keep some of the information so that the data user will be able to defend legal claims which may be made in the future. However, even in such a case, it may be possible to delete some of the data which could not possibly be relevant to such a claim. Unless there is some reason for keeping them, the personal data should be deleted when the possibility of such a claim arising no longer exists, ie when the relevant statutory time limit has expired.[4]

This aspect of the principle is amplified by the positive duty imposed by s 26 on a data user to erase data held where they are no longer required for the purpose for which they were used. The only exceptions stipulated are:

- Such erasure is prohibited under any law. For example, the *Inland Revenue Ordinance* requires that tax records be kept for seven years; and
- It is in the public interest (including historical interest) for the data not to be erased.

Information To Be Generally Available

Principle 5 states:

> All practicable steps shall be taken to ensure that a person can:
> (a) ascertain a data user's policies and practices in relation to personal data;
> (b) be informed of the kinds of personal data held by a data user;
> (c) be informed of the main purposes for which personal data held by a data user are or are likely to be used.

This principle requires data users to answer reasonable questions not only from data subjects but from members of the public, ie 'persons'. It is derived from the OECD principle of openness. The OECD considered that for such access and correction rights to be effective, it must be possible in practice to acquire information about information systems. Such information could be disseminated in a number of ways, including notices and pamphlets.

Notes

1 D Burnham, (1983) *The Rise of the Computer State,* Vintage Books, New York, p 73.

2 *The Data Protection Act 1984, Guideline 4: The Data Protection Principles*, p 18-20, UK Data Protection Registrar (1989), Wilmslow.

3 UK Data Protection Registrar, (1989) 5th Report, HMSO, London, p 70.

4 See note 2 above, p 21.

7 Use and Disclosure of Data*

Introduction

Principle 3 imposes restrictions on data users changing the use of data following their collection. It provides:

> Use of personal data
> Personal data shall not, without the prescribed consent of the data subject, be used for any purpose other than –
> (a) the purpose for which the data were to be used at the time of the collection of the data; or
> (b) a purpose directly related to the purpose referred to in paragraph (a).

Use

'Use' is defined as including the transfer or disclosure of the data (s 2). The Australian Privacy Commissioner's guidelines[1] state that it also covers searching records for any reason and using personal information in a record to make a decision. We argued in Chapter 4 that this broad approach is more appropriate under our Ordinance than the narrower interpretation adopted in relation to the UK *Data Protection Act*.

Neither 'transfer' nor 'disclosure' are defined. Whereas 'use' covers what is done with personal data within the data user, 'transfer and disclosure' extend to the release of the data to a third party. However, if the data transferred or disclosed are only a copy then, of course, control will be retained by the transferor of the original data. 'Transfer' conveys the active process of transmission, whereas 'disclosure' may be set up automatically so that an authorised third party can log on whenever data are sought.

Disclosing

Section 2 provides:

> '"disclosing", in relation to personal data, includes disclosing information inferred from the data.'

Disclosing personal data would therefore cover the oral disclosure, ie reading out what is contained in the data whether by way of direct quotation or by summarising the contents. In addition, however, it would cover disclosing matters which are implicit in the data, even if they are not written down. For example, an individual's intention to change jobs is an obvious inference from his providing his employment data to an employment agency. Accordingly, by contacting a potential employer, the employment agency would be 'disclosing' this data and such use must comply with principle 3.

Collection

Though, as pointed out above, 'collection' is not defined, it encompasses both the creation of data and gathering pre-collected data from data subjects or third parties.

Departures from Principle 3 Permitted under the Ordinance

The Ordinance permits a data user to depart from principle 3 in only two situations, namely with the data subject's prescribed consent or if an exemption applies:

- *Prescribed consent*
  It will be recalled that such consent must be express and informed (see Chapter 4). It may not be possible to obtain the prescribed consent of a data subject because he cannot be contacted. The Ordinance makes no provision for the situation where it is not reasonably practicable to obtain the consent of the individual. Alternatively, the data subject may fail to respond affirmatively to the request for consent. However, the requirement that consent be express precludes a data user from inferring consent in the absence of a response. Section 2(3)(b) provides that where prescribed consent has been provided, it may be withdrawn in writing.

- *Exemptions from principle 3*
  Failing the obtaining of express consent, principle 3 may only be departed from if a relevant exemption applies. The exemptions are discussed in Chapter 12.

Scope of Principle 3

Principle 3 applies to the use of all personal data whether they have been collected from the data subject, collected from third parties, or are a mixture of both. Furthermore, it applies to all data regardless of whether they were compiled before the Ordinance came into force. Its application requires ascertaining 'the purpose for which the data were to be used at the time of collection' (referred to in the discussion as the 'prescribed purpose'). The data user may, however, have failed to specify or otherwise identify his data purposes when collecting personal data, particularly if the collection occurred before the Ordinance came into force. Nonetheless, the application of principle 3 requires in every case the determination of the prescribed purpose. This is a question of fact. An objective test is appropriate.

Purposes v Activities

Data purposes relate to objectives and are distinguishable from processes or activities. For example, data user A may use personal data to facilitate data user B (to whom it will transfer the data) subsequently making contact with the data subject for particular purposes. Facilitating the contacting of data subjects will not itself constitute a data purpose of A. The data purpose will be the reason for making contact, such as B conducting research or direct marketing. Accordingly, the contacting of data subjects will not constitute a separate data purpose but will merely constitute an activity instrumental in achieving the purpose in question.

Substitution of Data Users

The application of principle 3 is determined by purposes, not transferees. Provided the data purposes remain consistent, it matters not that a new data user steps into the shoes of an earlier data user. For example, if a company is taken over as an ongoing concern, no change of use will arise in respect of the personal data which are acquired by the new company. For example, data relating to staff will continue to be used to maintain the employment relationship assumed by the new company.

On the other hand, a change of use will arise if such continuity cannot be assured. For example, a company may engage in a due diligence exercise in respect of a company it is considering purchasing. While the would-be-purchaser would be entitled to data indicating the staff structure of the company it may purchase, providing it with the personal data of identifiable staff members would require their prescribed consent. The ordinary employee would not reasonably expect his personal data to be transferred to an organisation that may fail to step into the shoes of his employer.

The following factors are relevant in determining prescribed purposes.

The Data User's Functions and Activities

Personal data will often relate to the administration of a relationship, such as that of vendor and consumer and employer and employee. Personal data collected in the course of such relationships will be for the various purposes which are pertinent to maintaining the viability and integrity of the relationship in question. For example, maintaining the relationship between employer and employee requires that attention be paid to a range of data purposes encompassing such matters as training, promotion and discipline. Accordingly, the purposes for which data collected from an employee will be used include these purposes whether or not they were specified at the time of collection. Similarly, in commercial relationships providing goods and services, the purposes for which the customer data are to be used at the time of collection will extend to facilitating receiving payments and recovering any debts that may arise.

A more precise identification of the prescribed purpose requires a consideration of the matters set out below, including restrictions imposed by the party providing the data.

Restrictions Imposed by the Party Providing the Data

Whether data are collected from either a data subject or another data user, the terms on which they are provided will determine the purposes for which they are collected. Principle 3 does not entitle a data user to superimpose his own purposes on the data without regard for the purposes for which the data are provided.

Collecting data from the data subject

Data are generally provided to the collecting party subject to its abiding by the basis on which they are specifically provided. It will be recalled that principle 1(3) requires that upon collection from the data subject that individual must be explicitly informed of 'the purpose (in general or specific terms) for which the data are to be used'. He is also to be informed whether the provision of the data is voluntary or obligatory. Furthermore, he must be informed of these matters 'on or before' the collection of the data. This is to enable the data subject to make an informed decision whether to provide the data on the terms proposed by the data user. It follows that by voluntarily providing data about himself, the data subject is doing so on the basis that the specified purposes will be complied with.

Collecting data from another data user

Data users also collect data from other data users. Data may be sought from a third party *instead* of the data subject. For example, a bank may seek data regarding a loan applicant from a credit agency. Alternatively, it may seek from another data user data previously provided by the data subject. In neither situation is there an explicit requirement that a data user inform another data user from whom he is seeking data of the purposes he may use it for. Principle 1(3) only applies to collections directly from the data subject. Nonetheless, as the Australian Guidelines point out, if a data user collects personal data from another data user, 'then its purposes in obtaining the information is limited by any conditions the other organisation places on releasing the information'.[2] It is the transferor who determines the prescribed purpose. After all, it is the transferor who determines whether he shall transfer the data at all, and if so, on what terms. Transfers accordingly have a conditional character: receipt of the data implies acceptance of these purposes.

Collecting data from a data user previously supplied by the data subject

Where the data being transferred from one data user to another were collected from the data subject, the transferor will need to acquaint the collecting party of the data purposes previously specified to the data subject. Failure to do so will result in the transferor using (ie transferring) the data for a purpose other than the purpose for which they were collected: it is meaningless to inform the data subject that the data are collected for a specific purpose and then transfer them to another data user in circumstances where the latter cannot be expected to know what that purpose was. By the same token, once the transferee is advised of the prescribed purpose, alteration of that purpose without prescribed consent will also breach principle 3. This is so whether or not the transferor itself collected the data from the data subject.

For example, an employer may pay for an employee's medical consultations. Ordinarily this would be for the medical care of the employee. Upon examining the employee, the doctor (data user A) should inform him that he will use the personal data collected for the purpose of diagnosis and treatment of illness. In accordance with these data purposes he transfers to data user B, a diagnostic centre, blood samples for analysis. That employee's prescribed consent would be required for the doctor's report to be used for the different purpose of informing his employer of the results. On the other hand, the specific purpose of the consultation may be to determine a prospective or present employee's fitness for the position concerned. If so, one data purpose will be to disclose the results to the employer.

When transferring data, A must ensure that B is aware of the purposes which were specified to the data subject upon collection. As noted above, principle 1(3) requires that the data subject is explicitly informed of the purpose for which the data are to be used. Unless A ensures that B is aware of the data purposes he is countenancing B using it for different purposes. Transfer to B in such circumstances would contravene principle 3 which requires that A shall use data only for the prescribed purpose: a transfer in circumstances which do not alert the transferee to the relevant purposes cannot itself constitute a transfer for those purposes.

The same logic applies to subsequent transfers from B to C and so on. Each subsequent transfer entails a corresponding new collection. In each case the data user transferring the data should ensure that the data user collecting the data is aware of the purposes governing the transfer, namely the original purposes specified to the data subject by A. In this manner, the data purposes specified to the data subject at the outset continue to apply to the use of the data regardless of the number of subsequent transfers involved in pursuing those purposes. In the example given above, health data were collected from a patient by a doctor who then transfers them to the data subject's employer. However, following their collection, the employer may transfer them to an insurance company. Determining whether each such transfer is permitted by principle 3 depends on whether it accords with the prescribed purpose of the collection in question.

The Data Subject's Expectations

When the data subject has been advised of the data purposes upon collection of the data from him, his expectations will be determined accordingly. However, he may not have been advised of the data purposes as required by principle 1(3). This will often have been the case with data collected prior to the Ordinance coming into force on 20 December 1996. Even after that date, a data user may fail to comply with his obligations under principle 1(3). In either case it remains necessary to establish the purposes of collection to determine the application of principle 3. In such situations the reasonable expectations of the data subject are relevant. As the Australian Privacy Commissioner's Guidelines put it, 'the purpose for obtaining the information also should be what a reasonable person expects'.[3] If an individual provides data to his doctor, he expects them to be used in relation to his treatment. He would not expect them to be transferred to his insurer. The Australian Guidelines provide the following additional examples of what would be reasonably expected to be data purposes:

- Personal data obtained on an application form are collected for the purposes of assessing the application;
- Personal data obtained when making an enquiry are collected for the purpose of answering the enquiry;
- Personal data obtained in a survey are collected for the purpose of finding out statistical and not individual information; and
- Personal data collected in an audit are to assess compliance in the past and risk of non-compliance in the future.

Data may be collected about the subject but not obtained *from* him. For example, a social worker may compile observations on an individual as to whether intervention may be warranted. In these circumstances not only will principle 1(3) not apply, but also there is lacking the interaction which requires notifying the data subject of data purposes. In these circumstances, where the data subject does not advert to the collection of data, he will not have the opportunity to entertain any expectations about its use. In these cases the constraints on the data user's purposes will derive from another source of control, such as that imposed by its functions and activities.

Statutory Requirements

Numerous statutory provisions provide for the transfer of personal data. Usually, they do so only in broad permissive terms. However, some go further and *require* the transfer of data in specified circumstances. For example, the *Infectious Diseases Ordinance* imposes a statutory duty on a doctor to disclose data collected from a patient indicating an infectious disease.[4] A statutory requirement of disclosure will in effect define a purpose of collection for the recipient. Whereas some permissive powers may refer also to the purpose of collection, others do not.

Public Records

A number of ordinances require the disclosure of information to any person upon payment of a prescribed fee. For example, the *Companies Ordinance* provides for the inspection of annual returns stating directors' and shareholders' names, ID numbers, nationalities and addresses. Or data may be provided in the form of a public notice, such as a notice to be displayed for three months under the *Marriage Ordinance* specifying occupation, age and dwelling place.

The role of public registers is to record transactions or events that have broad community significance. Hence those managing the register are usually under a legal duty to provide access. Public registers pose particular challenges to data privacy because they countenance indiscriminate access. But it does not follow that the obtaining of access to a public register is unconstrained by the purposes of the register. Public disclosure is not a *purpose* of the data on the register. Public disclosure is merely a *means* by which data purposes are fulfilled. This makes it important that the purposes of a register are identified with as much precision as possible. Those administering the register should identify these and notify members of the public accordingly. It would suffice to state them in a wall notice. It will then be the responsibility of those accessing the register to abide by such purposes.

Directly Related Purposes

Principle 3(b) provides that data may be used for 'a purpose directly related to' prescribed purpose. The discussion above has focused on primary purposes of collection. A directly related purpose is accordingly different from the primary purpose. For example, using personal data to ascertain the efficiency of a service provider's activities (eg monitoring delivery delays) would be directly related to the primary purpose of administering specific customer relationships.

Prescribed Consent Requirement for All Changes of Use

Principle 3 accommodates also the situation where the purpose has changed between the time of the original collection and the time of collection by the new user. Under this scenario the change of use would have required the data subject's consent at that point. So too, however, do all subsequent modifications of the prescribed purpose. Accordingly, the duty applies regardless of how far down the chain the data have been transferred (provided they can be said to be the same data).

This interpretation accords also with the policy of the Ordinance. It is essentially that the data subject has a degree of control over data relating to him. Such a policy would be negated by an interpretation whereby once his consent has been obtained to an initial change of use, it can be further changed thereafter without reference to his wishes. While this is clearest where the data were originally supplied by the data subject, the statutory language invites the same interpretation where the data were originally supplied by a third party.

Under principle 3 the restriction on altered purposes is enforceable only by the data subject: other data users cannot invoke it. This underlines the point that the principal aim of the Ordinance is to confer on the data subject a degree of control regarding data relating to him. Other data users will have to resort to any applicable common law remedies, such as contract or breach of confidence.[5]

Practical Examples of the Application of Principle 3

The application of principle 3 may be illustrated by the following examples.

A bank collects data from an individual who is advised that the data purpose is the processing of the application and the servicing of accounts opened as a result. The bank:

- Transfers the data to a credit reference agency for advice on the applicant's creditworthiness. This use (ie transfer) will accord with the prescribed purpose provided that the credit agency is aware of the basis on which the data were initially obtained from the data subject. It will be covered by a standing arrangement rather than specifically applied to each case.

- The credit agency proposes transferring the data to a direct marketing company. As this is not a specified purpose nor a directly related purpose the data subject is contacted and his prescribed consent is obtained. The transfer therefore accords with the modified prescribed purpose provided that the direct marketing company is made aware of this new purpose.
- The direct marketing company transfers the data to a private investigator without seeking the data subject's consent to this change of data purpose. In these circumstances the direct marketing company would contravene principle 3, unless a relevant exemption in Part VIII applied.

Only data relevant to the prescribed purpose may be disclosed or transferred. Data will often be collected for a variety of purposes and their subsequent use, disclosure or transfer requires the continued segregation of these multiple purposes. Where data are collected for prescribed purposes A and B, a transfer or disclosure for purpose A cannot justify a transfer of all the other data previously collected. Thus in the bank example just given, a good deal of the data that the data subject provided the bank may not be relevant to the assessment of credit. A transfer will therefore accord with the prescribed purpose only to the extent that the data transferred are necessary for the fulfilment of that purpose.

Similarly, suppose a medical practitioner refers an overdue bill to a debt collector. Billing is certainly one of the purposes for which certain data may be collected from the patient data subject, but it is plainly not one for which data relating to his medical diagnosis may be legitimately collected. The doctor would plainly breach the principle if he were to disclose medical data to the debt collector.

Special Uses of Data: Data Matching and Transfers Out of Hong Kong

Regulating Matching Procedures

'Data matching' is a special form of data processing, and one that poses particular dangers to the data subject. Hence, the Ordinance has provided additional controls on this form of data processing, which are expected to come into force in the second half of 1997. Section 30 restricts data matching involving a 'matching procedure' which under the Ordinance:

> means any procedure whereby personal data collected for one or more purposes in respect of ten or more data subjects are compared (except by manual means) with personal data collected for any other purpose in respect of those data subjects where the comparison –
> (a) is (whether in whole or in part) for the purpose of producing or verifying data that; or
> (b) produces or verifies data in respect of which it is reasonable to believe that it is practicable that the data
>
> may be used (whether immediately or at any subsequent time) for the purpose of taking adverse action against any of those data subjects [s 2].

'Adverse action' in relation to an individual is defined in s 2 as 'any action that may adversely affect the individual's rights, benefits, privileges, obligations or interests (including legitimate expectations)'.

The definition of matching procedure is derived from the *New Zealand Privacy Act*, although the test in the Ordinance is cast in more objective terms. The provision is unique under the Ordinance in the following respects:

- Its application is restricted to automated processing. The comparison process must be carried out by automated and not manual means. Even then, only automated programmes involving at least ten data subjects are regulated. All the other provisions of the Ordinance apply to both automated and manual processing applied to a single individual.
- Only programmes which may result in 'adverse action' against data subjects are regulated. Elsewhere the Ordinance does not restrict its attention to processing attended by specific consequences. In this regard, (b) is carefully worded to extend the scope of (a), to cover not only programmes with the avowed aim of investigative matching but also those that, objectively speaking, produce data that can be so utilised. The concluding reference to 'immediately or at any subsequent time' further reduces the ability of data users to engage in these programmes surreptitiously. These refinements are a result of a Committee stage amendment, as the original Bill's provision omitted both (b) and the subsequent words in brackets.

The justification for these restrictions on the ambit of 'matching procedure' lies in the mischief being addressed. Matching procedures are mainly employed, usually by government, in large-scale programmes usually aimed at detecting fraud. Such programmes were pioneered by jurisdictions with large-scale social assistance programmes, such as the United States, Canada, Australia and New Zealand. Matching procedures were developed to combat the abuse of these programmes through, for example, the claiming of double benefits. The central element of the matching procedure is the comparison of data collected for one purpose with data collected for another. This will generally involve data collected by different organisations from or with reference to the same data subject. The data are then compared in order to identify discrepancies. For example, the data subject may have claimed a benefit with a residency requirement and immigration records show that he was out of the jurisdiction for the period claimed. Another example would be where a benefit is claimed on the basis of a stated income but a different income is indicated by data on the individual's spending.

The process culminates in the taking of adverse action against the individual ('the hit') identified as the subject of the apparently conflicting data. However, using data (such as notice of change of addresses by clients) which are used only to update existing records does not constitute data matching because no comparison is involved nor will adverse action result.

Matching programmes are the subject of special regulation under the Ordinance for several reasons. They pose particular privacy risks because they involve the transfer of data to the data user conducting the match for a purpose which will usually depart from that for which the data were originally collected. Accordingly a contravention of principle 3 will usually result (see above). As a matching procedure involves at least ten individuals, such transfers are on a large scale. As the Australian Privacy Commissioner points out, most of the individuals who are the subject of such data transfers will be of no interest to the data user conducting the matching, who instead will be focusing on any 'hits' identified.

Other concerns relate to the complex nature of the matching procedure, the resulting potential for error, and the impact on data subjects identified (either correctly or incorrectly) as 'hits'. A matching procedure is essentially an investigative tool dependent on inference. Ostensibly similar items are compared and any discrepancies identified may result in the data user taking action to the detriment of the data subject. The validity of this process, however, is dependent on the following kinds of requirements:

- A valid identifier, ie an identifier that uniquely identifies an individual. For example, a name will often be shared by different individuals. In Hong Kong, the most commonly used unique identifier is the identity card number;
- The accurate reference to that identifier. Evidence indicates that in Hong Kong, five to ten percent of ID card numbers are misstated.[6]
- The matching of identical items. Seemingly similar items may in reality be dissimilar. In one well known example, the matching of 'income' was flawed because of the disparate definitions of income.[7]

Restrictions on Matching Procedures

Section 30 of the Ordinance prohibits data users from engaging in matching procedures subject to conditions. Together with s 33 (discussed below), s 30 was one of the two sections of the Ordinance that was not brought into force on 20 December 1996. On 28 February 1997, the Privacy Commissioner announced that s 30 is planned to be brought into force 'by the middle of this year'.[8]

Section 30 provides that a matching procedure shall not be engaged in unless one of the following conditions are fulfilled:

- Consent of the data subject.
- Consent of the Commissioner.
- The procedure is covered by a class approval of the Commissioner.

These requirements are now examined.

Consent of the data subject

A matching procedure may be commenced where all the individuals subject to the proposed matching procedure have given their prescribed consent. In the case of large-scale programmes this is unlikely to occur. It will be recalled that 'prescribed consent' means expressed and informed consent. Simply advising a data subject that data previously supplied would now be deployed for matching purposes unless an objection was received would not suffice.

To constitute 'express consent', an agreement cannot merely be inferred. Similarly, a standard form or contract which requires the data subject's signature would nonetheless have to ensure that the individual was given an adequate indication of the types of data to be matched and what adverse consequences could ensue from being identified as a hit. Otherwise the consent, though expressed, would not be informed. Subject to a sufficient indication being given of these matters, consent could be sought for recurrent matching procedures.

Consent of the Commissioner

A matching procedure may be also undertaken where the data user has made an application under s 31 and the Commissioner has consented pursuant to s 32. Such an application must be made on the specified form, which became available in March 1997. Where two or more data users are involved, one data user may apply on behalf of all [(s 31(2)]. One application may also be made in respect of more than one matching procedure [s 31(3)].

In determining such an application, the Commissioner shall determine the matter within 45 days in accordance with the 'prescribed matters' specified in schedule 5, namely:

- Whether the carrying out of the matching procedure is in the public interest;
- The kind of personal data to be the subject of the matching procedure;
- The likely consequences to a data subject if the matching procedure were to result in any adverse action taken against the data subject;
- The practice and procedures, if any, that will be followed to enable a data subject to make a data correction request –
  - (a) in respect (of) any of the personal data produced or verified by the matching procedure; and
  - (b) before any adverse action is taken against the data subject.
- The practices and procedures, if any, that will be followed to ensure, so far as is practicable, the accuracy of any personal data produced or verified by the matching procedure;
- Whether any such data subject is to be informed of the procedure before it is first carried out;
- Whether there is any practicable alternative to the matching procedure; and

- The benefits to be derived from carrying out the matching procedure.

It is clear from these prescribed matters that the onus is on the data user to justify his use of a matching procedure. Upon determining the matter, where the Commissioner 'is satisfied as to those matters', he shall serve a notice stating his consent subject to any specified conditions. Where he is not so satisfied, he shall serve a notice stating his refusal, giving his reasons [s 32(1)(ii)]. An appeal lies to the Administrative Appeals Board against both refusal and any conditions imposed on the giving of consent [s 32 (3)].

Although the prohibition against engaging in a matching procedure is not expected to come into force until the second half of 1997, to allow the Commissioner adequate time for processing, applications for approval should be made a reasonable period before then. Data users currently engaged in data matching who fail to apply in time will have to cease using their matching procedures pending their receiving approval from the Commissioner.

Class approvals by the Commissioner

The third situation in which a matching procedure may be lawfully undertaken is when it belongs to a class of matching procedures specified in a notice under s 30(2). Such a notice must be gazetted and specify any applicable conditions. Before specifying such conditions, the Commissioner is required to consult with bodies representative of data users to which the conditions will apply and such other interested persons as he thinks fit. A notice under s 30(2) is deemed subsidiary legislation and accordingly is subject to the scrutiny of the Legislative Council.

The purpose of this mechanism is that by enabling the Commissioner to issue a general clearance to certain classes of matching procedures, he does not have to devote his time to approving individual instances falling within that class. Such a procedure also enhances openness in data processing. It assists data users to plan their activities more securely. At the same time, the consultation requirement should ensure that data subject concerns are taken into account and the oversight of the Legislative Council should also assist in this regard.

Personal Identifiers

These are defined in the Ordinance as follows:

> 'Personal identifier' means an identifier-
> - that is assigned to an individual by a data user for the purpose of the operations of the user; and
> - that uniquely identifies that individual in relation to the data user,
>
> but does not include an individual's name used to identify that individual (s 2).

Personal identifiers play a key role in data processing generally and in matching procedures and profiling specifically. As explained above, a matching procedure entails the collation of data compiled for different purposes with a view to their comparison. Profiling involves the collation of data from different sources. Both processes are dependent on the adequacy of an identifier to support a valid inference that the individual referred to in one data set is identical to the individual referred to in the other data set(s). In Hong Kong, the identity card number constitutes a unique identifier that is used in a variety of contexts.

The Commissioner is required to issue a code of practice addressing personal identifiers [s 12(8)]. The report of the Law Reform Commission observes that the collection of ID card numbers has become entrenched and indiscriminate in Hong Kong; individuals are routinely called upon to furnish their ID numbers when the justification for the practice is weak.[9]

Rights to Contest Results

In view of the data quality concerns about matching results, the Ordinance prescribes a procedure whereby the data subject is provided a seven-day grace period during which he may challenge matching results before adverse action is taken [s 30(5)]. A data user is required to give written notification of the proposed action with reasons and advising that the data subject has seven days to show why the proposed adverse action should not be taken.

Matching versus Profiling

'Profiling' is not a term of art but generally refers to that form of processing (usually automated) whereby personal data are collated and analysed. Profiling differs from a matching procedure in the following respects:

- The profiling process is classificatory rather than investigative, being based on the combination rather than the comparison of data;
- The data combined may have been collected for the *same* original purpose, whereas a matching procedure necessarily entails the bringing together of data originally collected for *different* purposes; and
- Adverse follow-up action is not an essential element of profiling.

Profiling and Principle 3

Does profiling constitute the use of personal data for a different data purpose, and hence require the consent of the data subject? Can a data processing process itself constitute a 'purpose'? The better view is in the negative: data processing should be generally viewed as a purely instrumental activity. But the use for a purpose does arise when the results of the processing are deployed for, say, direct marketing.

Data Matching and Principle 3

'Matching procedure' is defined as involving the comparison of data collected for *one* purpose with data collected for *another* purpose for the *further* purpose of taking adverse action against the data subject. This further purpose will usually depart from the purposes for which the data to be compared were originally collected. If so, there will be a contravention of principle 3. One could go further and argue that a matching procedure is a type of data processing which is *inherently* purposive – namely to identify 'hits'. Thus engaging in a matching procedure itself constitutes using the data for a new purpose, quite apart from the subsequent deployment of the matching results. According to this argument, a matching procedure *necessarily* involves using the data for a different purpose contrary to principle 3.

A matching procedure resulting in a contravention of principle 3 will not contravene the Ordinance provided that the matching procedure has been consented to either by all the data subjects involved, or by the Commissioner, whether on an individual or class basis as described above. This follows from the application of s 4 which provides that 'A data user shall not do an act, or engage in a practice, that contravenes a data protection principle, unless the act or practice, as the case may be, is required or permitted under this Ordinance'.

As consent under Part VI constitutes permission under the Ordinance, this provision absolves a contravention of principle 3 so that the data user does not have to take the additional steps of obtaining prescribed consent or invoking an exemption to that principle.

Transfer of Data Out of Hong Kong

Prohibition of Transfers Outside Hong Kong

As with s 30, s 33 was not brought into force with the rest of the Ordinance on 20 December 1996. Section 30 provides that 'a data user shall not transfer personal data to a place outside Hong Kong' except in specified circumstances. This includes two situations, namely transfers *from* Hong Kong, or transfers *between* two jurisdictions out of Hong Kong at the behest of a Hong Kong data user. The exceptions to this prohibition are discussed below.

Scope of Section 33

The section applies where the collection, holding, processing or use of the personal data either -

- Takes place in Hong Kong; or
- Is controlled by a data user whose principal place of business is in Hong Kong. A data user which is incorporated in Hong Kong is deemed to have its principal place of business in Hong Kong [s 34(5)(a)].

It will be recalled that the definition of 'use' in s 2 distinguishes 'transfer' from 'disclosure'. 'Transfer' conveys an active process of transmission and arguably does not extend to making the data available to those deciding they wish to retrieve it. Moreover, the requirement that the transfer be 'to a place outside Hong Kong' suggests that the destination is determined by the transferor.

Section 33 accords with a recommendation of the Law Reform Commission.[10] It reflects the increasing international concern over 'data havens' that lack legal protection for personal data. The concern is twofold. First, and most directly, data should not be transferred to a jurisdiction lacking adequate protections. Secondly, however, the data should not be further transferred via a jurisdiction that has protections to one that does not. The operation of s 33 ensures that Hong Kong does not become a staging post or conduit to data havens. The most influential expression of this concern is art 25(1) of the European Directive on Data Protection. This provides that member states shall, subject to exceptions, provide for transfers to other jurisdictions 'only if the third country in question ensures an adequate level of protection'.

Principle 3 is also relevant in this context and requires that all uses, transfers and disclosures of personal data accord with the purpose for which the data were collected. The principle applies both to transfers within Hong Kong and transfers to a jurisdiction outside of Hong Kong. The latter are *also* subject to s 33. Accordingly, transfers outside Hong Kong must comply with both principle 3 and fall within one of the exceptions to s 33. As a transfer in contravention of s 33 is subject to s 64(10), the data user is subject to prosecution in addition to a possible complaint by the data subject.

Following their transfer out of Hong Kong, the data user may retain control over the data, in which case the Ordinance will continue to apply to the data in the other jurisdiction. Alternatively, control may be relinquished and the Ordinance will cease to apply to regulate the data out of Hong Kong. In either case, the data will end up in another jurisdiction, which may or may not have adequate controls on its subsequent use or dissemination. And even if control is retained from Hong Kong, it may be difficult for the data user or the Commissioner to ascertain the situation. Clearly, the most prudent course is to regulate the data at the point of their transfer out of Hong Kong and this is what s 33 seeks to achieve.

Exceptions to Section 33

The transfer of personal data out of Hong Kong must satisfy at least one of the following requirements:

- The place outside Hong Kong has in force 'any law which is substantially similar to, or serves the same purposes as, this Ordinance'. The reference to 'law' imposes a significant restriction: a sectoral code lacking a statutory basis would be insufficient under this limb (but see also below), regardless of the extent of compliance. The place may be specified in a notice to be gazetted by the Commissioner pursuant to s 33(3), where he has reasonable grounds for believing that there is such a law. Failing the gazetting of such a notice, the data user's reasonable belief suffices.
- The data subject has consented in writing to the transfer. Elsewhere in the Ordinance, the data subject's consent is specified as 'prescribed consent', ie express consent given voluntarily, but not necessarily in writing.[11]
- The data user has reasonable grounds for believing that the transfer 'is for the avoidance or mitigation of adverse action against the data subject', and it is not practicable to obtain the written consent of the data subject or, if it was practicable, the consent would have been given. 'Practicable' is defined in s 2 as 'reasonably practicable'. 'Adverse action' is defined in s 2 as 'any action that may adversely affect the individual's rights, benefits, privileges, obligations, or interests (including legitimate expectations)'.
- The data are exempt from data protection principle 3 by virtue of an exemption under Part VIII of the Ordinance.
- The user has taken 'all reasonable precautions and exercised all due diligence to ensure' that the data will not be dealt with in a manner that would constitute a contravention of the Ordinance. Accordingly, the reasonable care test relates to the specific data in question and envisages an individualised solution.

Transborder Transfer Contracts

One method for discharging the due diligence test just mentioned is for the parties to the transfer to enter into a contract or other acceptable arrangement providing for the application of the data protection principles to the data upon their collection in the place outside Hong Kong. A contract is an agreement between the data user transferring the personal data and the recipient and supported by 'consideration'. A difficulty with this approach, however, is that under a common law principle known as 'privity of contract', only the parties to a contract may enforce it.[12]

Accordingly, the data subject is dependent on the data user seeking remedies if the transferor does not comply with his contractual obligations. This contrasts with continental legal systems which recognise the right of third parties to sue. The American Contract Law also permits third parties to sue when they are 'intended beneficiaries'. The difference in approach is important because the parties to a contract are free to choose the law applicable to their agreement. A choice of law provision is often incorporated which makes the applicable law explicit.

Following a joint study by the Council of Europe, the Commission of the European Communities and the International Chamber of Commerce, a model contract providing for the transfer of personal data was issued in 1992 by the Council of Europe.[13]

The virtue of a standard model agreement is that it creates a level playing field between multinational corporations with legal resources at their disposal, as well as smaller organisations that wish to comply with s 33. The model terms may be adapted and some of the clauses require adjustment to better accord with the requirements of the Ordinance. Items include:

- Modifying the obligations of the transferor to correspond with the Ordinance's formulation of the data protection principles. The obligations of the transferee should include a specific description of the purposes for which the data are to be used by the transferor, accompanied by a prohibition on the transfer of the data to other data users. This would require adopting a more restrictive definition of 'use' in this context than under the Ordinance (which defines 'use' as including transfer). The prohibition on further transfers is required because further transferees will not normally be a party to the contract.
- A clause needs to be added addressing data security in terms corresponding with principle 4 of the Ordinance.
- Similarly, there should be provision for the data exporting party to check the implementation of the contract. For example, in one notable recent case where the German railway company exported data to Citibank in the US, there was provision for the Berlin Data Protection Commissioner to conduct audits through local consultants.[14]

The Privacy Commissioner released in May 1997 a fact sheet on the transfer of data out of Hong Kong. It includes a model contract along the lines described above.

Non-contractual Agreements

Where the data users involved in the bilateral exchange of data are at arm's length, an agreement is unlikely to provide sufficient protection to discharge the due diligence requirement unless it is a legally binding contract. However, non-legally binding agreements may arguably discharge the due diligence requirement where there are organisational or institutional reasons disposing the parties to honour the agreement despite its not being legally enforceable. For instance, an agreement might be made between a company and an overseas affiliate where identical internal procedures are enforced.

Another example is an agreement between data users who are both subject to the same international code of practice applying to the processing of personal data in the relevant sector. An increasing number of international data users have a vital concern in the unhindered flow of personal data and have therefore adopted international codes. Accordingly, an agreement might be entered into between members of the sector subject to the code to abide by the terms of the model contract. Whether such an agreement discharged the due diligence test would depend on such factors as the extent to which the code provided for the protection of personal data and the extent to which the code was enforced.

Limitations of Agreements on Transfers Out of Hong Kong

While agreements between parties may be adequate for simple bilateral transfers, they may not be viable as regards more sophisticated transfers. International data transfers may pass through various intermediaries who may sub-transfer the data. The mechanics of arranging a vertical chain of agreements may become onerous and cumbersome.[15]

Application to the Internet

Internet electronic mail or file transfers are delivered in a store-and-forward manner. Providers and hence subscribers have no capability to limit the delivery of mail or files initiated by their clients via any jurisdiction reachable by the Internet. Section 2 (12) was accordingly inserted. This provides that a person is not a data user in relation to data which he is dealing with solely on behalf of another.

Direct Marketing Opt-out

Section 34 provides that where personal data are used to contact the data subject for direct marketing purposes, that individual must be provided the opportunity to opt out. The provision requires that where the data user has obtained personal data and uses them for direct marketing purposes, then 'the first time he so uses *those data*' (our emphasis) after 20 December 1996, he shall inform the data subject of his opt-out rights. The italicised words have the effect that the duty to so inform the data subject arises every time the data user uses new data for the purpose. As pointed out in chapter four, 'use' includes the simple search and retrieval of data. For example, a data user must provide the opt-out when first he first uses name and address data and if he subsequently also acquires telephone data, a further opt-out must be provided whether or not it deploys the new data to make contact with the data subject. This is because 'those data' do not extend to supplemental data. The opt-out must be expressed so as to inform the data subject that the data user is required, without charge to the data subject, to cease to so use those data if the data subject so requests.

'Direct marketing' is broadly defined to mean:

- The offering of goods or services;
- The advertising of the availability of goods, facilities or services; or
- The solicitation of donations or contributions for charitable, cultural, philanthropic, recreational, political or other purposes.

Section 34 applies to contact by means of sending goods or communicating information which is addressed to specific persons by name or by a telephone call made to specific persons.

Notes

* As a result of what we were informed was a misunderstanding, several passages from material contained in this chapter were substantially reproduced in a paper entitled 'Data Sharing and Interdisciplinary Collaboration' delivered at a conference 'The Implementation of the Personal Data (Privacy) Ordinance in Social Welfare Services: Interdisciplinary Collaboration' held on 15 April 1997 at the Hong Kong Trade and Exhibition Centre.

1 Australian Privacy Commissioner (1996) *Plain English Guidelines to Information Privacy Principles* 8-11, p 11, Human Rights Australia, Sydney.

2 See note 1 above, p 23.

3 See note 1 above, p 22.

4 See Chapter 3.

5 See Chapter 3.

6 See Law Reform Commission of Hong Kong (1994) *Reform of the Law Relating to the Protection of Personal Data* (Topic 27), p 131. (Hereafter referred to as 'LRC Report').

7 J Bing, (1991) Working Paper prepared for the 'Conference on Information Law: Towards the 21st Century', Amsterdam.

8 Office of the Privacy Commissioner for Personal Data, Press Release 28 February 1997. A pamphlet entitled *Matching Procedure: Some Common Questions* was released in conjunction with the Commissioner's announcement.

9 LRC Report p 125.

10 LRC Report p 215.

11 The requirement of written consent was the subject of discussion when representatives of American Express Inc met the Bills Committee. It argued that while consent could be requested in application forms that new or renewing members were required to complete, written responses from *existing* members (such as a consent form enclosed with the monthly statement) might not be forthcoming. This expectation was based on the highest response rate American Express had ever received in respect of a mailing soliciting a written reply: 55 percent for an offer of free cinema tickets. The statutory requirement was not, however, relaxed as a result of these concerns. In particular, inferring 'implied' consent from a failure to respond with written consent was rejected as incompatible with the reality of consent.

12 See Chapter 3.

13 *Model Contract to Ensure Equivalent Data Protection in the Context of Transborder Data Flows with Explanatory Memorandum,* Council of Europe, Strasbourg, 2 November 1992.

14 A Dix, *Privacy Laws & Business* December 1996, p 6.

15 See generally J Riedenberg 'The Privacy Obstacle Course: Hurdling Barriers to Transnational Financial Services' (1992) 60 *Fordham Law Review* 137.

8 Data Security

Introduction

Principle 4 addresses security of personal data and requires that all reasonably practicable steps be taken to ensure that personal data held by a data user are protected against unauthorised or accidental:

- Access;
- Processing, including 'amending, augmenting, deleting or rearranging the data, whether by automated means or otherwise' (s 2);
- Erasure; and
- Other use including to 'disclose or transfer the data' (s 2).

The OECD has characterised the security of information systems as the protection of availability, confidentiality, and integrity of data.[1] While principle 4 addresses confidentiality concerns with its reference to access, by also including reference to processing and erasure, it extends to the protection of the availability and integrity of data. The principle therefore adopts a comprehensive approach to data security. This mirrors the requirements of principle 2 in respect of data accuracy. It will be recalled that 'inaccurate' includes not only personal data that are incorrect or obsolete but also data that are misleading or incomplete. The unauthorised or accidental erasure or processing of data may result in incomplete and hence, misleading data.

In addition, just as the interests of the data subject and the data user in data quality coincide, the same overlap occurs in the case of data security. Losses that a data user may incur from security failures regarding personal data include:

- The loss of valuable information and loss of competitive advantage;
- The loss of orders or business;

- The loss of customer or supplier goodwill; and
- Public embarrassment and loss of credibility.

Scope of the Principle

Uniquely in the Ordinance, the security principle extends to 'data in a form in which access to or processing of the data is not practicable'. All the other provisions of the Ordinance regulate only data that are not only identifiable and attributable, but also processable, namely computerised manual data and structured manual files. Principle 4 dispenses with this restriction and thus acknowledges the fact that data that may not be in a reasonably retrievable or otherwise processable form may readily become so. For example, disorganised paper files can easily be fed through optical scanners onto a database. The principle accordingly regulates not only the secure retention of data, but also its disposal.

The five factors identified by principle 4 as particularly relevant in determining security measures are:

(a) *The kind of data and the harm that could result if any of those things should occur.*

'The kind of data' and the 'harm that could result' are distinct, if overlapping, tests. Reference to 'kind' of data acknowledges that personal data vary in their sensitivity. Some classes of data are considered inherently sensitive, regardless of their context. Cultures vary to some extent in respect of what data are considered sensitive. In a 1993 survey conducted in Hong Kong,[2] a majority of respondents said they would object to the public dissemination of data regarding their financial status, HIV status, income and medical history.

Inadequate security for other classes of data not considered intrinsically 'private', may also result in significant harm to the data subject. This was recognised by the respondents to the Hong Kong survey mentioned above. A higher proportion objected to the release of their address or telephone number than the more 'intimate' data mentioned above. This is presumably because such details provide the potential for continuing and unwelcome contact or intrusion.

(b) *The physical location where the data are stored.*
Adverse physical conditions may undermine secure data storage by:

- Corrupting data. Threats to maintaining computerised data integrity include power failures or surges, air conditioning malfunctions, water leaks, static electricity and dust. Most of these hazards are relevant also to the storage of manual data.
- Inadequately restricting physical access. In the case of manual files, restricting access will often be decisive in securing the data. In the case of computers, this is no longer the case. Whereas several decades ago it was practicable physically to segregate mainframe computers, the proliferation of microcomputers reduces the extent to which physical access by staff might be limited. Nonetheless, it remains a relevant factor and where the data processing takes place in public areas, the monitor should be positioned so as to prevent its contents being read casually by passers-by (this is a frequent source of complaints in other jurisdictions).

Proper procedures should extend beyond the filing cabinet or computer terminal or screen to address data disposal. Improper handling of storage media (eg paper, floppy discs, and computer printouts) may not only effectively release data but may also provide clues regarding system access.

(c) *Any security measures incorporated (whether by automated means or otherwise) into any equipment in which the data are stored.*
Earlier physical restrictions to computer access have been supplemented or replaced by logic or software controls. The obvious example is the use of passwords. Effective password systems require such factors as avoiding obvious passwords (such as one's date of birth), regularly changing them and avoiding the display of passwords. Also fundamental is a system for checking whether the data are valid and initiating the production of back-up copies.

Determining appropriate security measures also increasingly requires an appreciation of the sophisticated methods now available to breach data security. These include:

- Unauthorised access to a computer programme from another computer via a modem ('hacking'). Hacking is addressed by s 27A of the *Telecommunication Ordinance* but to date there have been few prosecutions.[3]
- Intentional attacks on the computer system such as the introduction of viruses through infected software, parasites, trap doors, Trojan horses, worms, and logic bombs.[4]
- Reading from a remote location the electromagnetic radiation emitted by computers.[5]

(d) *Any measures taken for ensuring the integrity, prudence and competence of persons having access to the data.*
This limb focuses on access by personnel, whether by remote means or on-site or, if the data are computerised, by remote means. It recognises that data security is largely a staff management issue, rather than a purely technical one. Ensuring the 'integrity' of staff means that access to data should be limited on a 'need to know' basis to trusted employees. A password system should be graduated accordingly; this is preferable to the use of a common password providing access to all levels of the system. Such measures should not be undermined by leaving active terminals unattended or passwords displayed on screens. A number of studies suggest that accidental harm to computers and their data account for more incidents than deliberate actions taken against them.[6] Ensuring the 'prudence and competence' of staff obviously requires adequate training programmes covering such rudiments as password systems and the need for back-up files. The UK Data Protection Registrar mentions as a relevant consideration whether disciplinary procedures are in force.[7]

(e) *Any measures taken for ensuring the secure transmission of the data.*
The most significant measure aimed at securing transmission is that of encryption, ie the scrambling of communications to prevent their being deciphered. Both hardware and software encryption solutions are now readily available to virtually guarantee protection against interception by third parties.[8]

In view of s 2(12), no duties are imposed on the telecommunications carrier in respect of the security of transmission, provided it does not step outside a pure agency role. But should it collect the data, or hold, process or use the data for any of its own purposes, it becomes a data user in relation to that data and is accordingly required to comply with the principles. It will be recalled that the unsolicited receipt of data does not suffice to constitute the collection of data (see Chapter 5).

All Practicable Steps

Principle 4 does not require that a data user *guarantee* the security of personal data. Absolute security is unattainable. What is required is that all reasonably practicable steps are taken to protect personal data, in the light of the above factors. This will require a comprehensive review of security in order to select those techniques that give the best value.

Future Directions

Data security concerns not only individual data users within their organisations. It is also important that mutual trust is established between data users. This can be achieved at two levels:

- Agreements may be entered into between data users. For example, American Express requires all vendors and consultants with whom it contracts to sign a data security confidentiality agreement. Contracts with merchants engaged in cooperative marketing efforts include clear privacy guidelines.[9]
- More generally, security should be accorded to entire networks. One possible obstacle is the availability of security measures such as access-control software that is compatible with an entire network in a multiple-vendor environment. At a still more general level, basic parameters for information security will need to be developed, perhaps accompanied by an accreditation mechanism. An example of a widely accepted code of practice is that developed by the UK Department of Trade and Industry.[10] Such solutions are subject to the OECD's caveat that:

  > [T]here can be no one security solution. Security needs vary considerably from sector to sector, company to company, department to department, and, as to given information systems, over time. Lack of an informed and balanced

> understanding of users' needs may create a significant risk of 'off-target' technology standardisation. A productive first step is recognition of the inherent diversity and heterogeneity of users' needs for information system safeguards.[11]

A Data Security Strategy

Data security must be approached systematically. A comprehensive strategy requires:

- Reviewing data holdings and classifying them according to their sensitivity;
- Identifying individuals with information responsibilities; and
- Assessing potential security threats and corresponding protective measures. Controls that can be employed to restrict access to systems and data include identification and authentication controls.

Relationship with Principle 3

Principle 3 regulates the disclosure and transfer of data. There are some situations in which the boundaries between that principle and the security principle overlap. An example is posting a letter with a window that enables the casual inspection of details such as the ID number of the addressee. This would certainly contravene the security principle and, arguably, principle 3.

Notes

1 Organisation For Economic Cooperation and Development 1992, *Guidelines for the Security of Information Systems*, OECD, Paris.

2 See *Report on Reform of the Law Relating to the Protection of Personal Data (Topic 27)* (1994) Law Reform Commission of Hong Kong, Appendix 2.

3 *Report on Privacy: Regulating the Interception of Communications* (1996) Law Reform Commission of Hong Kong, Chapter 4.

4 See P Mungo and B Clough, (1993), *Approaching Zero: The Extraordinary World of Hackers, Phreakers, Virus Writers and Keyboard Criminals*, Random House, London.

5 See M Wasik, (1991) *Crime and the Computer*, Clarendon Press, Oxford, pp 52-3.

6 See note 2 above, p 143.

7 *The Data Protection Act 1984, Guideline 4: The Data Protection Principles*, UK Data Protection Registrar (1989), Wilmslow, p 27.

8 See R Wacks, (1997) 'Privacy in Cyberspace: Personal Information, Free Speech, and the Internet' in Peter Birks (ed), *Privacy and Loyalty,* Clarendon Press, Oxford.

9 Lisa Skoog de Lamas, *Balancing Privacy Rights and Consumer Rights,* Asia Law and Practice Seminar, 6 November 1995.

10 A code of practice for information security management 1993, British Standards Institution, London.

11 *Guidelines for the Security of Information Systems* (1992), OECD, Paris.

9 Access to and Correction of Data

Introduction

Data protection principle 6 provides:

> Access to personal data
> A data subject shall be entitled to:
> (a) Ascertain whether a data user holds personal data of which he is the data subject;
> (b) Request access to personal data –
>   (i) within a reasonable time;
>   (ii) at a fee, if any, that is not excessive;
>   (iii) in a reasonable manner; and
>   (iv) in a form that is intelligible;
> (c) Be given reasons if a request referred to in paragraph (b) is refused;
> (d) Object to a refusal referred to in paragraph (c);
> (e) Request the correction of personal data;
> (f) Be given reasons if a request referred to in paragraph (e) is refused; and
> (g) Object to a refusal referred to in paragraph (f).

By providing for access, this principle enables the data subject to monitor the extent to which a data user is complying with the other five principles. And by conferring access rights, it provides data users with a crucial mechanism for enhancing data quality, for the data subject will frequently be best equipped to provide accurate and up-to-date data regarding himself. In these ways, principle 6 enables the data subject to participate in the proper management of data relating to him or her. Furthermore, such rights tend to discipline sweeping and unduly judgmental statements.

The mechanics of the access and correction process are elaborate and are spelt out in Part V of the Ordinance. Unlike the other data protection principles, the access principle is wholly subsumed by the specific provisions of the Ordinance and in the case of a conflict between them and the broad terms of principle 6, the former prevail. This follows from s 4 which prohibits an act or practice that contravenes a data protection principle unless that act or practice is required or permitted elsewhere under the Ordinance. Nevertheless, the specific provisions should themselves be interpreted in a manner that accords with the purpose of the Ordinance. This is stated in the long title of the Ordinance to be to protect the privacy of individuals in relation to personal data.

The access provisions of the Ordinance do not provide the only manner in which an individual may seek data relating to himself. In a number of organisations and relationships, informal channels also exist. An employer may, for example, have a practice of allowing an employee to inspect records compiled about him. Or the employer may periodically provide printouts of such data. The Ordinance does not displace such practices. It does, however, provide the individual with a legally enforceable right to a copy of all data relating to himself. Where informal channels of access are presently lacking, this right will necessitate data users establishing new systems to facilitate such access.

The access process under the Ordinance is instituted by an individual making a request under s 18(1) to:

- Ascertain whether the data user holds data on that individual; and/or
- Supply a copy of any data so held.

It is accordingly possible that a request may merely enquire whether data are held, unaccompanied by a request for a copy. In these circumstances the data user is entitled to treat such an enquiry as also requesting a copy of any data held 'in the absence of any evidence to the contrary' [s 18(3)]. To respond in this manner to an inquiry as to whether data are held by supplying a copy of any such data will usually be convenient for both the data subject and the data user; the data subject is spared the effort of making a follow-up request and the data user has to locate the data only once.

An access request may be in any form, but a data user may refuse to comply with a request that is not in writing in the Chinese or English language [s 20(3)(a)]. The Commissioner may specify forms for data access requests [s 67(1)] and non-compliance provides the data user with grounds for refusing the request [s 20(3)(e)]. The Bills Committee suggested that the Commissioner provide standard forms for different categories of data uses, or provide clear directives on what information should be included in the form.[1]

Pending any specification of forms by the Privacy Commissioner, individual data users may use their own forms. It would have to be made clear that the processing of the request is not dependent on completion of such a form, particularly as form-filling may deter some requesters from exercising their right of access. Standardised forms have the advantage of assisting requesters by indicating what details should be provided to fulfil the statutory requirement of sufficiently indicating the location of the data.[2]

The data user may wish to include other items that assist management. However, as this exercise involves the collection of personal data, the requirements of principle 1 must be complied with. It will be recalled from Chapter 5 that this requires that data only be collected when they are really necessary, and the data subject must be expressly notified of data purposes and classes of transferees. Accordingly, the forms should not attempt to solicit unnecessary data and should specifically provide notification of the matters referred to in principle 1(3).

Processing an Access Request

In very general terms, an access request requires that the data sought be considered in the following sequence:

- Are there 'personal data' of which the requester is the data subject?
- Are the data controlled by the data user?
- Is the requester entitled to a copy of the data?
- Is there a prohibition on the release of the data under s 20(1)(b) as involving the release of data relating to an individual other than the data subject without the former's consent?
- Are there applicable exemptions and if so, should they be invoked?

These requirements are now considered.

Personal Data

The first task of the data user will be to locate the personal data to which the request relates. The request should provide 'such information as the data user may reasonably require' to locate the data. Failure to supply this is a ground for not processing the request [s 20(3)(b)].

Assuming that data are located, the first issue is whether the data are 'personal data' as defined in the Ordinance. We examined this issue in detail in Chapter 4. We concluded that such data must be attributable, reasonably identifiable and reasonably processable or retrievable. Accordingly, upon receiving an access request the data referring to the individual making the request should be examined in accordance with the following criteria:

- Do the data 'relate to' the requester? This concerns the degree of relation and the opinions expressed by A about B 'relate' to B but not A. Similarly, the mere conjunction of those data with, or its application to, the requester is insufficient. Some nexus is required between the data and the requester. This excludes, for example, general criteria such as minimum income requirements.
- The second attribute of personal data are that they are identifiable. Accordingly, the next question is whether it is reasonably practicable to ascertain the identity of the requester from the data. For example, the data user may hold data indirectly linked to the requester's membership of a club. The data may criticise the attitude or goals of club members generally, without singling out specific individuals. If, however, other data held by the data user receiving the request list the requester as a member, then the critical data would be identifiable.
- The third attribute for the data to constitute 'personal data' and hence be subject to an access request is that the data are reasonably processable and retrievable. Experience elsewhere indicates, however, that refusing access on the basis that the data, if they exist, are not readily retrievable will create more problems than it apparently solves. A complaint may well result and it will then be incumbent on the data user to demonstrate to the Commissioner that it has made reasonable efforts to retrieve the data. This approach has been adopted by the Privacy Commissioner of New Zealand in an instructive ruling. It arose from the New Zealand Department of Social Welfare advising the complainant that it was unable to locate the requested data.

Section 29(2)(b) of the New Zealand *Privacy Act* provides that a data user may refuse an access request if 'the information requested is not readily retrievable or . . . does not exist or cannot be found'. In applying this provision, the New Zealand Commissioner ruled that:

> In order to ascertain whether all reasonable steps had been taken to find the information, I asked the department to provide me with a report outlining the steps taken to locate the information requested. The department reported the details of an extensive search it had conducted. Inquiries revealed the file had been transferred to another office and later transferred again. A complete search of all current and past files of the office where the file was last transferred was carried out. This included searching files held in storage and archives. A further check was also made at the originating office, and the previous director of that office had been approached. Contact was also made with a former staff member who had been involved with the file but she was unable to provide any material help in locating it. In the circumstances of this case, it appeared that the department had taken all reasonable steps to locate the information sought. I was not aware of any further steps available to locate the information.[3]

No Requirement to Identify Basis of Decision

The requirement that a data user supply a copy of the data is not accompanied by an express duty to identify *which* items of the data formed the specific basis of a decision relating to a data subject. For example, an employer may decline to promote an individual on account of his inexperience, whereas it could instead have based its decision on other data such as level of education. Upon requesting access, the data subject must be provided the data relating to both his experience and education. However, the employer is not subject to any express statutory duty to identify which of these sets of data formed the basis of its decision. Of course, should the employer become aware that the factual basis of its decision had been flawed, it may wish to reconsider the decision in any event, but that would be a matter for the employer to decide: the data subject would not be entitled to demand that information.[4]

It is, however, arguable that certain classes of decision have a sufficient impact on the individual to warrant his being alerted to the nature of the data being relied on, such as an adverse credit report. Although the Ordinance does not specifically attend to the notion of 'adverse action' in its treatment of access rights, it does so in the context of matching procedures under s 30. This is a fairness issue that may accordingly require addressing in codes of conduct. Also relevant is principle 2 dealing with accuracy – alerting a data subject to vital data obviously facilitates their prompt access and correction.

If, but only if, the data are attributable, and reasonably identifiable and reasonably processable or retrievable, then it is necessary to confirm that the data are controlled by the data user.

Control of the Data

It will be recalled that a 'data user' is defined as the person, alone or jointly, who controls the collection, holding, processing or use of the data (s 2). While a data user will generally both hold the data and control their use, the data may be held by another person but remain under the control of the data user. In this situation, the data user is nonetheless deemed to hold the data and is accordingly required to comply with the request. The degree of control required to bring the provision into play is whether the data user 'controls the use of the data in such a way as to prohibit the data user who does hold the data from complying (whether in whole or part) with a data access request which relates to the data' [s 18(4)].

For example, a bank may contract out part of its data processing operations to a data bureau. Under such an arrangement, the bank may cease holding the data which it has transferred to the bureau. Nonetheless, it retains effective control over such data. In this situation where the data user controls the data which is held by another person, the access request may be received not by the data user, but by the person holding the data. The data user subject to the prohibition may refuse the request insofar as he is prohibited from complying with it [s 20(3)(d) and s 20(4)]. Upon receiving the request, however, that person must advise the requester of the name and address of the data user retaining control [s 21(1)(c)]. Failure to do so will result in the controlling data user not complying with the request. As the controlling data user is deemed to hold the data and hence is responsible for complying with the request, this will result in his being in breach of the requirements of the Ordinance notwithstanding the fact that he never actually received the request.

To ensure compliance, a data user should clearly instruct those holding data on their behalf [5] to respond to the request in a manner that facilitates the data user complying with it. The agent could advise the data subject to approach the data user directly, or could itself refer on the request. A more comprehensive arrangement might be preferred whereby the data user authorises its agent to comply with the request without recourse to the data user. In assessing whether such an arrangement is desirable, it should be borne in mind that the exemptions from access are many and complex[6] and the agent would have to be conversant with their application. It may be that the data user would prefer to make such assessments itself, particularly as policy issues arise in determining whether to invoke exemptions even when they are applicable (see Chapter 12).

Verifying the Identity of the Requester

Access and correction rights under the Ordinance are vested solely in the *data subject* or his representative ('relevant person'). Furthermore, it would clearly be a serious violation of the data subject's privacy for data relating to him to be transferred to a third party who has no legitimate interest in receiving it. Accordingly, the Ordinance provides that the data user *shall* refuse to comply with a data access request if the data user is not provided with 'such information as [it] may reasonably require' to satisfy it as to the identity of the requester [s 20(1)(i)].

In establishing procedures in respect of proof of identity, the requirements of principle 4 addressing data security are relevant. It will be recalled that this requires that all reasonably practicable steps shall be taken to ensure that personal data are protected against unauthorised or accidental access.[7] Of the five factors there identified, the most relevant is 'the kind of data and the harm that could result' from providing the data to the wrong person [principle 4(a)]. Accordingly, the stringency of proof of identity should correspond to the likely impact on the data subject arising from the unauthorised release of the class of data in question.

The UK Data Protection Registrar's guidance on this is that for non-sensitive data a signature would suffice, but for sensitive data further proof may be appropriate, such as ID number, date of birth, or the witnessing of a signature which can be compared with that on file.[8]

Where the data subject is out of Hong Kong, special procedures may be necessary. The use of an agent or 'relevant person' may be invoked.[9] A rigorous form of verification is provided for under the *Registration of Persons Ordinance*. An applicant from out of Hong Kong must supply fingerprints when applying for an ID card.

A breach of the security principle exposes the data user to compensation for damage (s 66). On the other hand, procedures to establish identity which are excessively strict are likely to be the subject of complaints to the Commissioner. As with other areas where the Commissioner concludes that practices are defective, he may issue an enforcement notice (s 50).

Relevant Persons

Where the request is received from a 'relevant person', the data user's duty is twofold:

- To satisfy himself as to the identity of the individual on whose behalf the requester is purporting to act; and
- That the requester has the necessary relationship to the individual whose data is sought [s 20(1)(ii)]. The relationship in question must be one of the following (s 2):
  - (i) A person who has parental responsibility for a minor. 'Minor' is a person under 18 years' of age;[10]
  - (ii) A person appointed by a court to manage the affairs of an individual incapable of managing his own affairs; and
  - (iii) A person authorised in writing by an individual to make the data access and/or correction request. Even if the requisite relationship exists, the data user must ensure that the individual has been authorised to make the specific request received, ie for data access and/or data correction [s 2(2)] as an individual acting outside his remit will not fall within the definition of 'relevant person'.

Although a relevant person may make an access request on behalf of a member of these classes of persons, there is nothing in the Ordinance to exclude requests from such persons themselves. Indeed, minors and protected persons may be vitally concerned not only with access to their data generally but specifically with what their parents and protectors are recording about them.

It follows that the access rights of relevant persons co-exist with the rights of the individuals on whose behalf they act. But a situation may arise in which it may be apparent to the data user that the relevant person is seeking access despite the objections of the minor or protected person. In such a case it may be asked whether the relevant person is indeed seeking access 'on behalf of' the individual concerned under s 18(1) and whether access should not be declined.

This issue is of relevance to access requests by parents rather than those representing protected persons. The latter have been deemed to be incapable of managing their own affairs and a data user would be acting reasonably in treating an access request by the appointed person as being sufficient.

The position regarding parents and children, however, is more difficult. The Ordinance arguably treats the relevant person's access request as being 'on behalf of' the individual simply by virtue of his being in the requisite relationship. This is reinforced by the fact that s 20 omits any reference to the individual's consent or otherwise. There will often be good reasons why a parent should be entitled to access to the personal data relating to his child despite the latter's objections. Generally speaking, we do not believe that the data user should be required to adjudicate in such disputes, particularly as the Ordinance makes no reference to this role nor to the criteria to be applied. In responding to requests from a relevant person the data user will be required only to consider the matters specifically set out, namely verification of identity and relationship.

There will be cases, however, where the data user is particularly reluctant to grant access to a parent because to do so would breach an undertaking to the child that the data be treated confidentially. Social welfare, medical and educational data may be compiled on this basis. In these circumstances, the data user may wish to resist the application for access by the parent to data that the child objects to the release of. As mentioned earlier, a purposive interpretation of the provisions of the Ordinance must be adopted so as to best achieve its objective of protecting the privacy of the data subject. This approach is required by the long title to the Ordinance and should be read together with s 19 of the *Interpretation of General Clauses Ordinance*. In addition, this approach could invoke the provisions of the Convention on the Rights of the Child[11] as an interpretative aid to these difficult provisions of the Ordinance.

We believe that the collective weight of these provisions would justify, if not actually require, a data user to refuse access to a parent where the data has been collected from the child on the basis of confidentiality.

Data Relating to Another Individual

There is a prohibition on complying with an access request to the extent that the request entails the release of data relating to an individual other than the data subject without the former's consent [s 20(1)(b)]. In one sense, an individual's expressed opinions about a data subject may be said to be a manifestation of that individual. However, as mentioned above, when analysing personal data, 'relate to' is, by definition, a relative term and under the Ordinance, it does not extend to the expression of an individual's opinion about the data subject. Recorded opinions by A about B constitute personal data relating only to the latter. To hold otherwise would seriously undermine the access provisions by precluding access to opinion data whenever the source was identifiable.

Nonetheless, there are two situations contemplated by the Ordinance where data may 'relate to' an individual other than the data subject. These are, first, reference to another individual, and, secondly, comparative data.

References to another individual

References to any other individual should be edited out where this is feasible. It is readily achievable with plain text, but may be more difficult with other media. For example, the New Zealand Privacy Commissioner considered the application of a similar provision to photographs depicting the complainant and another person of an 'extremely explicit nature'.[12] He upheld the refusal of access on this basis. The ruling does not discuss the possibility of providing access only to those parts of the photographs depicting the complainant, presumably because of the artificiality of such a solution.[13]

Comparative data

Data refer also to another individual when comparisons are drawn with the data subject, eg Charles is more intelligent than Henry. Simply removing reference to Henry strips the remainder of the judgement of any meaning. In such situations, the data user may release the data only where it is satisfied that the other individual has indicated his consent to the disclosure to the requester. The provision does not go so far as to require the data user specifically to seek such consent.

Identification of sources

Data relating to another individual may comprise information identifying an individual as the source of the data being requested. However, the prohibition against the release of data relating to another individual only extends to such information which 'names or otherwise explicitly identifies that individual' [s 20(2)(a)]. For example, the official title of a supervisor would explicitly identify a source. However, other data may suffice to identify the source to the data subject, such as the nature of the comments or even its date. Such data must be disclosed, subject only to the omission of names or other identifying particulars [s 20(2)(b)].

But a number of exemptions sanction the refusal of access to data from which the identity of the source may be inferred by the data notwithstanding the absence or removal of identifying details. These are addressed in Chapter 12 and recognise that in areas such as law enforcement, there are public interest grounds for protecting sources such as informers.

Editing Data Before Release

The effect of the above provisions is that an access request will often necessitate an editing exercise. Two case notes of the New Zealand Privacy Commissioner provide practical examples of how the broadly similar provisions of the New Zealand legislation have been applied in practice:

> A complainant sought review of access to the notes made by a social worker regarding his step-daughter. The Social Welfare Department considered such information to be confidential to the step-daughter. Under the Privacy Act, however, this did not provide a blanket exemption from access. The issue remained whether any data related to the complainant. The notes did contain such data. It was in the form of the step-daughter's allegations. The Commissioner recommended that these be extracted from the notes and supplied to the complainant. However, the Commissioner considered that comments made by the step-daughter about her feelings or reactions to the complainant's actions constituted data relating to her and should be withheld.[14]

> A complainant sought access to two letters which had alleged that she had sold drugs at school. The Commissioner accepted that information should not be disclosed that could result in the identification of informants. Nonetheless, the complainant was entitled to be informed of the substance of the letters and to request correction of them if necessary. The Commissioner therefore recommended that the allegations be extracted from the letters.[15]

Supply of the Data

The Ordinance requires only that a copy of the data be supplied. The original need not be supplied and this will in any event not normally be practicable. Nor is any formal procedure prescribed such as that of 'certified copies'. As mentioned above, the access provisions of the Ordinance are not intended to displace existing informal channels for access and these will often involve showing the individual the original document for his inspection.

A copy of personal data supplied to the requester must so far as reasonably practicable be:

- Intelligible, unless it is a true copy of document unintelligible on its face (eg a computer print out with no alterations) [s 19(3)(c)(i)];
- Readily comprehensible, with any codes adequately explained [s19(3)(c)(ii)]; and
- In the language (Chinese or English) specified in the request, unless the data are held in a different language. If no language is specified, they should be in the language (Chinese or English) used in the request, unless the data are held in a different language and a corresponding copy is provided [s19(3)(c)(iii)].[16] The Ordinance does not specifically provide for translations. Translating the data would arguably constitute a change of purpose and the data subject's prescribed consent should be obtained.
- In the form specified in the request; if this is not reasonably practicable, then:
  (i) if there is only one form which is practicable, to supply this accompanied by an explanation; and

(ii) If there is more than one form which is practicable, to ask the requester in writing to specify his preference within 14 days and to comply accordingly. If the requester fails to respond within the required time the data user should supply the data in the form he prefers [s 19(4)].

- Supplied by reference to the data at the time the request is received, except that the copy may incorporate any subsequent processing which would have been made irrespective of the receipt of the request [s 19(3)(a)]. This proviso takes into account the periodic data processing cycles often adopted. While these are often automated, the proviso would extend to the incorporation of manually effected amendments which would ordinarily take place within the 40-day period. For instance, an examination script being re-marked following an appeal by the candidate. Such routine updates aside, should the data user become aware of inaccuracies, the data user must nonetheless provide the data in their uncorrected form. However, it would be acceptable for the requester to be informed that inaccuracies have been detected and that the data user proposes effecting corrections following the processing of the request.
- Furthermore, a transition period is provided whereby for the first year that the Ordinance is in force (ie until 19 December 1997), the data user is allowed to correct the data and provide the data subject only with the residue, together with a notice advising that the data have been corrected [s 19(3)(a)(ii)] and s 19(5)]. Precise details of the corrections effected need not be provided. As 'correction' means rectification, erasure or completion (s 2), this provides data users with a major opportunity in the first year that the Ordinance is in force to clean up their personal data.

The Mechanics of Access

The Bills Committee explored the possibility of access being provided which would not entail supplying a copy of all the data to the requester. The concern was that a data subject may well not know how much data are held and that they may be extensive and hence costly to supply. It was accordingly suggested that a room be set aside where the requester could peruse the data and determine which parts he wanted copied and supplied. These data would, however, have to be vetted beforehand by the data user to exclude data which are related to other individuals or which may be the subject of an exemption. In any event, the proposal was not adopted and under the Ordinance the data subject is entitled only to a copy of the relevant data. It should be emphasised, however, that this does not preclude the data user from handling the matter in the manner proposed, if so requested. So, for example, a patient may informally ask his doctor if he may inspect a document during a consultation. But even when a request is lodged under the Ordinance the patient cannot insist on examining the original records.

Repetitive Requests

A data user may refuse to comply with a request that follows at least two similar requests 'and it is unreasonable in all the circumstances for the data user to comply with the request' [s 20(3)(c)]. This reasonableness test would take into account the fundamental nature of access rights in enabling the individual to monitor compliance with the principles generally. Refusal on this basis would therefore be likely to require evidence that the access right was being exercised vexatiously or abused in some way.

Time Limit for Compliance

Section 19(1) provides that the data user must comply with an access request 'not later' than 40 days. This should not be treated as a standard response period and with most requests a more reasonable response time will be several days. In particular, where the data are of critical importance to the data subject, delaying until just before the expiration of the 40 days may be quite unreasonable. Where, however, a data user is unable to comply within 40 days, he must notify the data subject prior to the expiration of 40 days providing reasons and comply to the extent that he can [s 19(2)].

Notification of Refusal of Access

Upon determining that it will refuse the access request, the data user must so notify the requester in writing within 40 days, identifying [subject to s 21(2)] which of the following grounds is applicable, namely:

- No verification of the identity of the requester or the relationship of the relevant person;

- The request entails disclosure of data about another individual;
- The request is not in writing in Chinese or English;
- There is insufficient information to locate the data;
- There have been repeated requests;
- The data are controlled by another data user;
- There has been non-compliance with the specified form for requests; and
- An exemption is applicable.[17]

Whereas a data user 'shall refuse' under the first ground, the Ordinance uses the permissive 'may' regarding refusal under the remaining grounds.

Non-disclosure of Grounds

Where the data which are subject to a request are:

(a) Exempt from access under ss 57 or 58 (addressing security, law enforcement etc); and
(b) The interest protected by that exemption would be likely to be prejudiced by disclosing the existence or non-existence of those data;

then the data user may, instead of specifying the grounds for refusal, merely advise that it has no personal data the existence of which he is required to disclose to the requester [s 21(2) and s 63]. For example, prematurely alerting a suspect to the fact that he has come to the notice of the authorities could abort investigative efforts. The difficulty confronting the data user in this situation, however, is that merely resorting to this formula may tip off a savvy individual that this is a coded admission that he is under suspicion. The only way to avoid this would be for the investigative agency not to restrict its use of this notification to the situation which it specifically addresses. Specifically, it could also be used in *complying with* (as opposed to refusing) requests where there are no data. Whether a request is framed under (a) or both (a) *and* (b) of s 18(1), if there are no relevant data on record, then so informing the data subject constitutes compliance. This is because (a) specifically asks whether there are data and (b) includes this question.

Forced access

Access rights are conferred on data *subjects*. There may be occasions, however, when a data *user* may be tempted to avail itself of this mechanism to collect data via the data subject. A prospective employer could, for example, ask the data subject to exercise his access rights regarding specified data users (eg former employers) and furnish the prospective employer with the results. This may be referred to as 'forced access'.

Forced access is incompatible with the requirement that personal data shall be collected by means which are 'lawful; and fair in the circumstances of the case' [principle 1(3)]. As the right of access is a right of the data subject, the Commissioner may well take the view that for a data user essentially to subvert the mechanism for its own purposes would constitute unfair means of collection.[18]

Moreover, the notion of prevailing upon an individual to hand over the entire records of designated data users is likely to offend the requirement that only such data may be collected as are necessary for or are directly related to a lawful purpose directly related to a function or activity of the data user [principle 1(1)].

Finally, a central purpose of obtaining access is to enable the data subject to correct data relating to him. It would therefore be essential that he check the data and obtain corrections to incorrect data. This could take several months. The alternative of the data subject passing on inaccurate data would result in a mechanism aimed at enhancing data quality resulting instead in the propagation of inaccuracies. For these reasons there are objections both in principle and practice to a data user asking an individual to exercise his rights of access as a data collection tool.

Forced access is a concern not only for data subjects. It is an issue for certain data users holding data that may be the target of such requests. Prime targets will be those data users holding sensitive data that would not be ordinarily transferred directly to other data users, such as criminal records or medical data. The temptation will then arise for data users to attempt to use the data subject instrumentally to obtain data that would otherwise be unavailable. Hence the concern of data users holding crucial but confidential data is that they will be subjected to a flood of access requests originally emanating from other data users.

Data users particularly concerned about being recipients of forced access should consider adopting a strategy to combat such attempts. A useful mechanism is provided by the Ordinance which permits a data user to inform the data subject orally that it holds no personal data on that individual. Forced access involves the data user exerting pressure on the data subject to produce data which it cannot obtain directly. However, it can be generally assumed that the data subject will be reluctant to allow his access rights to be exploited in this way. He may feel obliged, however, at least to convey compliance with the request. Accordingly, the data subject may be expected to welcome any assistance in foiling such requests. By adopting a general practice of informing data subjects orally whenever no data are held, data users provide this assistance.

The data subject can therefore quite legitimately claim that his access request has not provided any data – not even a letter saying there are no data. Nor can the data user seeking forced access be sure whether the data subject has obtained data or not (the other data user is constrained by principle 3 not to confirm that a request was received or its outcome). When data users seeking to impose forced access are confronted with a situation where they cannot expect even a piece of paper from an obliging data subject, they are likely to desist – they have lost their leverage over the data subject, who may ignore such efforts to subvert their access rights.

Data Correction

Where the individual receiving personal data under the access provisions considers that the data are inaccurate, he may apply for data correction, ie the rectification, erasure or completion of the data [s 22(1) and s 2].

Transfers Pending Consideration of the Correction Request

Following receipt of the correction request, but before responding to it, the data user may have occasion to disclose the data in question to a third party. Such disclosures are permissible, but the data user must take all reasonably practicable steps to advise the third party that a correction request is under consideration [s 22(3)].

Where the data user is satisfied as to the inaccuracy, he should:

- Make the necessary correction of the data [s 23(1)(a)]; and
- Supply the requester with a copy of the corrected data [s 23(1)(b)].

It follows that it is essential that the correction is effected with reference to the original record (database or manual file, etc) with this being reflected in the copy supplied to the requester. The correction need not involve the alteration of the original, where such correction is not practicable. It is not, for instance, practicable to edit microfilm records. In these circumstances it will suffice if the correction is tagged or otherwise recorded in a manner that will ensure that it is read together with the original.

Transfer of Corrections

The transfer of corrections requires data users to have in place a system for effecting corrections. The Ordinance does not stipulate specific methods and this accords with the approach suggested by the Law Reform Commission:

> One method would be to maintain audit trails on all disseminate data. We consider this an unduly onerous duty to impose in all cases. Nor would such tagging of data be the only possible method of checking where data had been transferred to. For example, if the transferor only discloses data on a regular basis to a limited list of transferees, then he could simply propagate all updates to those listed, on the basis of an agreement that they apply the updates. Another possibility for credit checks would be to notify a central agency for distribution of corrections as required.[19]

Time Limits for Corrections

Ordinarily, a data user must comply with a data correction request within 40 days [s 23(1)]. He should comply to the extent possible, but if additional time is required, he should within the specified period so advise the requester, giving reasons [s 23(2)(a)]. He should comply thereafter as soon as reasonably practicable.

This procedure precludes a data user from merely discontinuing its processing of a particular request which presents processing problems and seeking a new request (and fee!) enabling it to recommence afresh.

Notification of Refusal

Upon determining that it intends to refuse the correction request, the data user must so notify the requester in writing within 40 days, giving reasons [s 25(1)(a)] applicable, namely:

(a) No verification of identity of requester or relationship of relevant person [s 24(1)(a) and (b)];
(b) The data user is not satisfied that the data are inaccurate [s 24(3)(b)];
(c) The data user is not satisfied that the correction requested is accurate [s 24(3)(d)];
(d) The request is not in writing in Chinese or English [s 24(3)(a)];
(e) Insufficient information is provided to locate the data [s 24(3)(c)](see above); and
(f) The data are controlled by another data user [s 23(3)(e) and s 23(4)]. Section 25(1)(b) requires that the requester be provided with the name and address of the data user controlling the data (see above).

As pointed out above, whereas a data user 'shall' refuse under (a), he 'may' refuse under the remaining grounds. Accordingly, whereas a data user must refuse under (a), he has discretion whether or not to refuse under the other paragraphs, depending on the circumstances.

Correction of Opinion

Personal data are not restricted to factual details but include 'an expression of opinion'. This is defined as including 'an assertion of fact which is unverifiable; or in all the circumstances of the case, is not practicable to verify' [s 25(3)]. As the Law Reform Commission comments:

> The distinction [between factual and evaluative statements] is often a matter of form and difficult to draw. Data protection laws are concerned with material upon which decisions are made affecting the individual. Evaluative data will often be more influential in this regard than factual data. There is the additional argument that people will be less prone to make sweeping assessments if aware that they may be scrutinised.[20]

Opinions possess a subjective element. Unlike the case of purely factual data, it is not simply a question of substituting the 'accurate' opinion for the inaccurate. Accordingly, a procedure is prescribed which recognises that more than one opinion may be legitimate and relevant. Where the 'correction' relates to opinion data which the data user is not satisfied is inaccurate, he must nonetheless note the matters in respect of which the opinion is considered by the requester to be inaccurate. This must be annexed to the challenged opinion data in a manner that ensures it is not overlooked [s 25(2)]. A copy must be attached to the notification to the requester of the refusal to correct.

Log Book

Experience elsewhere indicates that a significant proportion of the complaints received by the Commissioner will relate to refusals to provide access. Thus the New Zealand Privacy Commissioner reports that 47 per cent of complaints received involved an access review.[21]

To facilitate the Commissioner's investigation of access complaints, the Ordinance requires all data users to keep a running record in the form of a log book recording in Chinese or English:

- Particulars of the reasons for refusal of all access requests [s 27(2)(a)]. The simplest procedure will be to record the reasons given to the requester when notifying him of the refusal of access. Where specifying the grounds for refusal is likely to prejudice the interest protected by an exemption, the data user may merely advise that he has no personal data the existence of which he is required to disclose to the requester [s 21(2) and s 63]. He must nevertheless log particulars of the prejudice that would be caused if the existence or non-existence of the data are disclosed [s 27(2)(b)];
- Particulars of the reasons for refusing to correct data [s 27(2)(c)]; and
- Any other particulars specified by regulation [s 27(2)(d)]. No such regulations have been promulgated to date.

The required details must be recorded in the log book on or before the relevant notice is served on the requester advising of the refusal to provide access or correction respectively [s 27(3)]. This ensures that should the Commissioner subsequently have to respond to a complaint, the investigation will not be hampered by the data user being unable to recall why the request was refused and/or that the existence of data were not conceded. The log book entries may also reveal patterns in handling requests which may assist in identifying any systemic problem areas. Not only should this provide assistance to the Commissioner in resolving difficulties regarding specific data users, but it will provide also a statistical basis for sectoral solutions. To this end, a log book entry must be retained for four years, subject to any regulations to the contrary [(s 27(1)(c)].

A data user must permit the Commissioner to inspect and copy the log book at any reasonable time. All reasonable assistance should be provided to the Commissioner without charge [s 27(4)(b)]. It is an offence to resist, obstruct, or hinder the Commissioner [s 64(9)].

Fees

A fee, which shall not be excessive, may be charged for complying with a data access request [s 28(2) and (3)]. No other fee may be levied [s 28(1)]. The request may be:

(a) To be informed whether the data user holds data relating to the requester [s 18(1)(a)]. Informing the data subject either 'yes' or 'no' is to comply with the request and accordingly a fee is payable; and

(b) To be supplied with a copy of such data [s 18(1)(b)]. To supply such data is to comply with the request and a fee is payable.

A request under both (a) and (b) is to be treated as a single request [s 18(2)]. This avoids duplication of fees under both (a) and (b). Furthermore, a request under (a) may also be treated as a request under (b).

Modern record-keeping methods allow some choice of format, and the selection made will determine the expense incurred in providing a copy of the data. For example, providing the hard copy of a lengthy document may be far more expensive than giving a disk containing the data. The Ordinance accordingly provides that where the data user may comply with the request by supplying the data in several forms, he must charge according to the fee he imposes for the least expensive option. This is regardless of whether a more expensive option is actually adopted [s 28(4)].

That the Ordinance does not envisage that fees be set at commercial levels is underscored by the alternative formula specified for copies of data previously supplied [s 28(6)]. The fee for a further copy is to be 'not more than the administrative and other costs incurred'. Fees set at high levels are likely to be the subject of complaint to the Commissioner. While there is no specific provision under the Ordinance requiring that data users provide a schedule of fees, principle 5 requires all practicable steps be taken to ensure that a person can 'ascertain a data user's policies and practices in relation to personal data'.

Notes

1 Bills Committee to study the Personal Data (Privacy) Bill, note of 8th meeting, p 11.

2 See s 20(3)(b) discussed below.

3 New Zealand Privacy Commissioner Case note 0575.

4 Questions of compensation are less straightforward. See Chapter 13.

5 We use the term 'agent' here, although, as a matter of law, no relationship of agency may actually exist.

6 See Chapter 12.

7 See Chapter 8.

8 *The Data Protection Act 1984, Guideline 5*: Office of the UK Data Protection Registrar (1989), Wilmslow, pp 10-11.

9 See below.

10 Age of Majority (Related Provisions) Ordinance s 2(1).

11 1989. Doc A/RES/44/25. Reprint 28ILM 1448.

12 Section 29(1)(a) of the New Zealand Act provides that an agency may refuse to disclose any information requested if 'the disclosure would involve the unwarranted disclosure of the affairs of another individual'.

13 New Zealand Privacy Commissioner Case note 008W.

14 New Zealand Privacy Commissioner Case note 0567.

15 New Zealand Privacy Commissioner Case note 1666.

16 We confess some uncertainty as to the precise meaning of s 19(3)(c)(B).

17 Exemptions are discussed in Chapter 12.

18 This is the position adopted by the German Deputy Federal Data Protection Commissioner. See U Danman, 'Major Changes Ahead for Data Protection in Germany' *Privacy Laws and Business* September 1995 at 14.

19 Law Reform Commission Report, on Reform of the Law Relating to the Protection of Personal Data, 140.

20 Law Reform Commission Report, on Reform of the Law Relating to the Protection of Personal Data, 182.

21 New Zealand Privacy Commissioner (1995), Annual Report, p 12.

10 Office of the Privacy Commissioner

Establishment of the Office of the Privacy Commissioner

The office of the Commissioner is a corporation sole with perpetual succession and as such is capable of suing and being sued [s 5(2)]. This is a comparatively unusual approach in Hong Kong; another example is the office of the Financial Secretary.

Section 5 provides also for the appointment of a person to be the Commissioner. Appointment is by the Governor (Chief Executive) and shall be for a period of five years with the option of not more than one renewal for the same period. No professional or other restrictions are specified.

As with the Commissioner for Administrative Complaints, the Commissioner's independence is secured by the requirement that he or she may be removed only by the Chief Executive with the approval of a resolution of the Legislative Council on the ground of inability to perform the functions of office or misbehaviour (s 5). The Legislative Council can merely approve the Chief Executive's decision to remove the Commissioner and cannot itself initiate such a step. The Commissioner shall not be regarded as a servant or agent of the Government nor as enjoying any status, immunity or privilege of the Government [s 5(8)]. He is, however, deemed to be a public servant for the purposes of the *Prevention of Bribery Ordinance*. He shall not engage in any outside work without the Chief Executive's approval (s 6). The filling of a temporary vacancy is addressed by s 7.

Functions of the Commissioner

These are specified in s 8 and may be classified as follows:

Supervision and Education

The Commissioner's principal function is to monitor and supervise compliance with the provisions of the Ordinance [s 8(1)(a)]. To this end, he has an educational role in promoting awareness of the law. Relevant to the Commissioner's educational role are the following functions and activities:

- Promoting awareness and understanding of the Ordinance, and in particular the data protection principles [s 8(1)(c)]. The Commissioner has acted expeditiously to this end and released guidance notes on access and correction rights under principle 6 and guidelines on the remaining principles. The publication of the Commissioner's annual report will also assist in this regard. As in other jurisdictions, the annual report will provide accounts of how the data protection principles should be applied to cases eliciting complaints;
- Publish in the *Government Gazette* 'guidelines not inconsistent with this Ordinance, indicating the manner in which he proposes to perform any of his functions, or exercise any of his powers, under this Ordinance' [s 8(5)]; and
- Promote codes of practice [s 8(1)(b)]. The role of codes of practice is not solely educational, however, and is fully addressed below.

Monitoring Developments Impinging on Privacy

Both legal and technical developments may impinge on privacy. Accordingly, the Commissioner shall:

- Examine any proposed legislation that may impinge on privacy and report the results to the person proposing it [s 8(1)(d)]. A legislative proposal may emanate not only from the Government, but also from a legislator or a special interest group; and
- Undertake research and monitor developments in the processing of data and computer technology impinging on privacy [s 8(1)(f)].

These additional functions require that the Commissioner endeavour to anticipate legal, technical, and administrative developments that may impinge on data privacy. They acknowledge the experience acquired in other jurisdictions establishing the need for early consultation on relevant developments.[1] Developments being mooted in Hong Kong that warrant examination would include the use of smart cards and electronic road pricing. The effective examination of such issues obviously requires that the Commissioner has adequate resources at his disposal. The current office structure makes no provision for full-time research staff, although some research has been contracted out.

International Contacts

The protection of data privacy benefits from sharing the experiences of other jurisdictions with similar laws. Accordingly it is expressly provided that the Commissioner shall liaise and co-operate with his counterparts in other jurisdictions [s 8(1)(g)]. There is an established international network of privacy commissioners and they hold an annual conference. The Commissioner shall accordingly participate in these arrangements.

Delegations

The Commissioner may delegate in writing any of his functions or powers under the Ordinance with the exception of:

- The power of delegation provided by s 10;
- Regulations which specify that they are not delegable [s 10(2)(b)]; and
- Any provisions of Schedule 2 (dealing with the Commissioner's finances) which are specified as not delegable [s 10(2)(c)].[2]

Personal Data (Privacy) Advisory Committee

A Personal Data (Privacy) Advisory Committee has been established 'for the purpose of advising the Commissioner upon any matter relevant to the privacy of individuals in relation to personal data or otherwise relevant to the operation of this Ordinance' (s 11). Chaired by the Commissioner, the committee comprises eight members appointed by the Secretary for Home Affairs for such duration and on such terms as he determines. The only statutory restrictions on membership are that at least one member shall have five years' data processing experience and not more than one member shall be a public officer. The committee members are all part-time.

The Bills Committee raised the issue of whether members of the Advisory Committee would have access to personal data. In response, it was pointed out that the secrecy provision [s 46] would preclude the Commissioner from disclosing personal data pertaining to individual cases to the Advisory Committee. Instead, it was envisaged that the committee would only advise on general functions and practice.

The remainder of Part II addresses housekeeping matters that are unlikely to concern those not involved with the operation of the office of the Commissioner. Reference is made in s 8(2) to the acquisition and holding of property, contracts, trusts, gifts and donations, and membership or affiliation with international bodies. Section 8(3) addresses the Commissioner's powers to execute documents and s 8(4) deals with the evidential effect of the Commissioner's use of a seal. Section 9 provides the Commissioner with comprehensive powers regarding the employment of staff, the engagement of consultants and the remuneration or payment and providing benefits thereto.

Codes of Practice

The Role of Codes

While s 8 identifies as a function of the Commissioner his promotion of and assistance in the preparation of codes, Part III comprehensively addresses the role of codes of practice. The principal function of such codes is to provide 'practical guidance' [s 12(1)] in complying with the necessarily general provisions of the Ordinance. As with similar legislation in other jurisdictions, the core requirements are contained in the data protection principles. These are powerful and flexible enough to regulate personal data regardless of the sphere of activity concerned. But while the promulgation of codes of practice are not essential to the operation of a data privacy law, they provide a valuable aid to its successful implementation.

This importance derives from the rather general nature of the data privacy principles and the desirability of elaborating on their application to the different sectors. Codes of practice are accorded an important role in data privacy regulation in a number of jurisdictions.

Nature of Codes of Practice

Codes of practice perform a similar role under the Ordinance as they do under the UK *Data Protection Act*. The UK Registrar has issued helpful guidance notes on the role of codes and the following discussion draws heavily on his discussion.[3] The Registrar regards a code as:

> A document which provides guidance to organisations in a particular industry or sector on how they should comply with the Data Protection Act and, in particular, with the data protection principles. Codes of practice should be aimed at senior management and those responsible for data protection within organisations, although they should be intelligible to the lay reader, and should be made available publicly.
>
> To command respect codes of practice must not simply paraphrase the Act or be exhortative – they must state clear practical actions which are to be followed. They must support the Act's objectives and requirements and not try to diminish or bypass them.

The UK Registrar usefully distinguishes codes of practice from two other forms of guidance on the protection of personal data:

- Cross-sectoral guidelines in the form of technical or professional advice on such general issues as computer security; and
- Internal operational procedures. These address specific aspects of data protection as they apply to particular groups of employees or functions. Matters which need addressing include the allocation of responsibilities amongst staff for compliance with the Ordinance, training and discipline. While the development of operational procedures will be a matter for individual data users, they should be reviewed to take account of a code of practice once it has been issued.

The UK Registrar sees these three different forms of guidance 'as complementary rather than necessarily hierarchical or sequential'.[4]

A code of practice might address:

- The types of data subjects about whom data are held;
- The status of rights of those individuals flowing from the data protection principles;

- The data users affected by the code: the types of organisations and their main activities ;
- How the data protection principles apply to the data users affected and their relationship with the particular practices embodied in the code. For example, a firm recommendation may be made that data held for a certain purpose should be deleted a specified period after the last transaction. Or a more flexible 'guideline' may be preferred which stipulates that the issue of deletion should be conducted at specified intervals, taking into account specified factors;
- Reference to other statutory provisions or guidance from other regulatory bodies affecting the processing of personal data;
- Which data users are committed to the code of practice. Where the representative body is a membership organisation conferring commercial or other benefits, compliance with the code could be made a condition of the membership;
- The sanctions that may follow from a breach of the code by a data user; and
- Arrangements for periodical review, monitoring its effectiveness, publicising its requirements, administration, and advisory services for both individuals and data users.

The New Zealand Privacy Commissioner has also issued a guidance note on codes of practice.[5] He makes two supplementary points:

- The paraphrasing of the data protection principles should be avoided. Rather the emphasis should be on how compliance with each principle is to be secured; and
- To be most useful, codes should include practical examples.

Section 12(8) of the Ordinance stipulates that a code addressing the use of personal identifiers must be approved within one year. The most pervasive personal identifier used in Hong Kong is the identity card number.

Part III comprises enabling provisions regarding the issue of codes of practice. Pursuant to s 12, the Commissioner may approve and issue a code of practice whether or not he has prepared the code. Alternatively, he may approve a code issued or proposed to be issued by the sector concerned.

Where the code is not being prepared by the Commissioner, he may approve it in parts [s 12(7)]. Commenting on the similar provisions of the UK Act, the Data Protection Registrar noted that the phased introduction of codes allows 'useful guidance to be issued without waiting for the resolution of particularly complex or controversial issues'.[6]

The approval of a code requires its gazettal [s 12(2)], as does the code's revision (in whole or in part) [s 12 (3)] or withdrawal of approval [s 12(5)]. It is not provided that a notice of gazettal shall be in the form of subsidiary legislation. Accordingly, the approval of the Legislative Council is not required pursuant to s 34 of the *Interpretation and General Clauses Ordinance.*

No criteria are specified regarding the selection of areas to be addressed by codes, but relevant factors include the nature of the data and their capacity adversely to affect the interests of the data subject. Sensitive data such as medical data and data having an impact on financial prospects such as banking and employment should be priority areas for the issue of codes.

Before approving or revising a code, the Commissioner is required under s 12(9) to consult with:

- such bodies representative of data users to which the code or the code as so revised, as the case may be, will apply (whether in whole or in part); and
- such other interested persons,

as he thinks fit.

In April 1997 the Commissioner issued its first code for public consultation. The draft Code on Consumer Credit Reference Services made a number of proposals relating to the processing of personal data by credit reference agencies. The consultant engaged to prepare the initial draft of the code was former Australian Privacy Commissioner, Kevin O'Connor. The proposals include restricting the personal data which a credit reference agency may hold to what is commonly called 'negative' or 'black' data regarding defaults and requiring a credit provider to inform an individual when it has taken into account a credit report from a credit reference agency in making a decision to refuse credit.

The Legal Effect of Codes

Given the role of codes in providing 'practical guidance' in respect of the requirements of the Ordinance', it follows that their provisions may elaborate on but not abridge or amend the substantive statutory requirements, any more than a regulation may. To provide worthwhile guidance, a code should not restrict itself to an arid repetition of the data protection principles but should elaborate on their implications in specific contexts. Accordingly, a purposive approach should be adopted in the development of codes, so that the spirit of the principles are given practical effect.

The legal effect of the code differs from that of regulation and failure on the part of any data user to observe any provision of an approved code of practice does not of itself render the data user liable to any civil or criminal proceedings [s 13(1)]. But where in any proceedings under the Ordinance a data user is alleged to have contravened a requirement thereunder, then a failure to observe a relevant provision of the code is admissible [s 13(2)]. Such a contravention will constitute proof of contravention of the Ordinance in the absence of evidence that such requirement was complied with other than by way of observance of the code.

Data User Guidelines

The development of a code of practice is a major undertaking. Following his appointment, the Commissioner indicated in his meetings with data user groups that as an initial step they should take the initiative in drawing up guidelines. The Commissioner provides his comments on drafts submitted and the resultant guidelines then provide a sound basis for the development of a code.

Data User Returns

Part III addresses codes of practice and also comprises enabling provisions equipping the Commissioner with tools to deploy as he sees fit. The notification provisions of Part IV empower the Commissioner to specify a class of data users required to submit returns giving details of their personal data systems.

Notification requirements are widespread amongst the data protection laws of other jurisdictions. A notification requirement can provide a list of those data users which the Privacy Commissioner should monitor. Similarly, it can provide a register which may assist in directing individuals to where information relating to them is held.

The precise mechanism varies, but can be classified as follows:

- Pure notification systems: the data user is required only to notify the supervising authority of its data processing systems (eg the Netherlands);
- Registrations systems: the data user is required to obtain the approval of the supervising authority to its processing of personal data. However, it may commence such processing pending the authority's consideration of the application (eg the United Kingdom); and
- Licensing systems: the prior approval of the supervising authority is required to process personal data (eg Sweden).

Part IV adopts the least onerous variant, namely the data user is required only to notify the supervisory authority that it is processing personal data. Uniquely among legislation adopting this pure notification option, however, the Ordinance does not itself require notification as a legal requirement. Instead, it empowers the Commissioner to do so by specifying by notice in the Gazette the class of data users required to furnish him with returns [s 14(1)]. As with codes of practice, no statutory criteria are stipulated to guide him in identifying the appropriate classes. The Commissioner has a wide discretion on the matter. However, because the gazetted notice is deemed to be subsidiary legislation [s 14(9)(a)] his subjecting a class of data users to this notification requirement falls to be scrutinised by the Legislative Council.

Theoretically, an option open to the Commissioner would be to require all data users to notify him under the Ordinance. It is significant that the Ordinance chose not to implement a recommendation of the Law Reform Commission that the law impose a requirement to this effect. Since the Ordinance refrains from adopting this approach, the implication is that the Commissioner should proceed selectively. Reinforcing this conclusion are the reasons why the government declined to impose a legal notification requirement at the outset. It accepted criticism from the commercial sector that this would impose a bureaucratic burden on the 400,000 active businesses in Hong Kong. It also heeded overseas experience indicating that a mandatory, across-the-board notification requirement constituted a substantial diversion of a Privacy Commissioner's resources without deriving any commensurate benefit to data privacy.

Processing notification requires resources, as does pursuing those who fail to notify. For example, the UK *Data Protection Act* requires all data users to notify by registering. Enforcing this provision has proved a major undertaking, with 61 prosecutions being brought in the year ending 31 March 1995 alone.[7]

The Mechanics of Data User Returns

Upon identifying a prospective class of data users to be subject to the notification requirement, the Commissioner must consult with bodies representative of data users belonging to the proposed class and such other interested parties as he thinks fit [s 14(2)].

Upon gazettal, members of the prescribed class are required to submit to the Commissioner a data user return. The return must contain the six categories of information prescribed in Schedule 3 of the Ordinance, namely:

- The name and address of the data user;
- A description of the kind of personal data used;
- A description of the purpose(s) of the data;
- A description of any class of transferees of the data;
- The details of transfers or proposed transfers of personal data outside Hong Kong; and
- Contact details of the individual to whom data access requests should be directed.

The return must be submitted not later than the anniversary of either the date of the notice gazetted by the Commissioner or the date that the data user joined the class there specified, whichever is the sooner, in the specified form and be accompanied by the prescribed fee [s 14(4)]. The Commissioner must make arrangements to have available the necessary forms [s 14(5-7)]. The Commissioner must be advised of any material changes within one month [s 14(8)].

The matters to be addressed in returns are to some extent covered elsewhere in the Ordinance. A description of data purposes and classes of transferees must be provided to comply with principle 1(3) upon collecting personal data from the data subject. Also, prior to the use of data collected in these circumstances, the data subject must be provided with the contact details of the individual handling access requests. Similarly, a description of the kind of data held must be available under principle 5. However, there is no provision requiring that the data subject be advised of transfers out of Hong Kong.

In requiring information on all these matters, data user returns provide a potentially useful source of information on data processing patterns – not only to the Commissioner but also to data subjects. This is recognised by the provision that establish a public register in the form of a database (s 15). To this end, the Commissioner may require further and better particulars supplementing the data user return [s 15(3)]. The Commissioner is required to provide facilities making the contents of the register available for inspection free of charge [s 16(1)]. On payment of a fee, the Commissioner shall furnish a copy of the requested particulars contained in the register [s 16(2)]. These provisions further the objectives of data protection principle 5 addressing openness in data processing.

The Ordinance does not specify factors relevant to the Commissioner's decision to require a class of data users to submit returns. We submit that they might include:

- Whether the class of data users is one processing sensitive data that could seriously impact on the data subject, such as those in the medical sector or the banking sector;
- The extent to which the Commissioner's investigations of complaints and/or conduct of inspections identifies problem areas; and
- Whether the sector comprises data users who do not have direct contractual links with data subjects and accordingly operate in effect 'behind a screen'. Some classes of data users act as reference agencies to other data users who require data on potential customers. For example, data bureaux may provide assessments of the creditworthiness of applicants for services. Such reference agencies may operate on an industry-wide basis, such as in connection with employment, insurance or tenancies. Even where their operation is more fragmented, they may occupy a strategic role in the provision of vital services. Their operation is moreover such that data subjects tend to be unaware of their mode of operation and even their existence.

  Data users providing reference services pool pre-collected data rather than collect direct from the data subject. This denies the data subject the opportunity afforded by principle 1(3) to be informed of data purposes and classes of transferees. This lack of visibility could create disparate results. On the one hand, it will tend to elicit fewer complaints. On the other, it will reduce the number of access and consequent correction requests. This effective exclusion of the data subject from the data processing cycle may adversely affect the quality of potent data. A notification requirement in these circumstances could redress the problem by increasing transparency.

Notes

1 Flaherty demonstrates how the post-implementation scrutiny of new systems is inefficient and may be ineffective. D Flaherty (1989), *Protecting Privacy in Surveillance Societies*, Chapel Hill: University of North Carolina Press, p 30.

2 The Commissioner delegated a number of his functions relating to investigations and inspections with effect from 30 January 1997. See GN 665 *Government Gazette* 7/1997.

3 *Guidance Note 6: Code of Practice – Second Explanatory Statement*, Office of the UK Data Protection Registrar (1989), Wilmslow. The New Zealand Privacy Commissioner's Guidelines of 5 December 1994 are to similar effect. Unlike codes under the Ordinance and the UK Act, however, codes under the *New Zealand Privacy Act* may amend the principal legislation. In 1994 New Zealand issued a comprehensive Health Information Privacy Code.

4 *Guidance Note 6: Code of Practice – Second Explanatory Statement*, Office of the UK Data Protection Registrar (1989), Wilmslow.

5 New Zealand Privacy Commissioner, 5 December 1994.

6 See note 4 above.

7 1995 (145) NLJ 1505.

11 Powers and Procedures of the Commissioner

Introduction

As with other regulatory schemes imposing statutory requirements, the Ordinance provides for the investigation of possible contraventions. Part VIII makes it clear that the focus of investigations is the data user, ie the organisation controlling the use of the personal data concerned (s 2). Data users can, of course, act only through their employees and under the Ordinance the data user is generally liable for the acts of employees done in the course of their employment (s 65; see Chapter 13). Investigations will therefore necessarily involve the Commissioner obtaining information from employees in determining whether the data user has contravened the Ordinance.

But such individuals will not be the formal subject of the investigation. The subject will be 'the relevant data user', ie the data user specified in the complaint (s 2). And the various procedures and powers detailed in Part VII all relate to the relevant data user. Should the Commissioner decide that a particular individual be the specific subject of an investigation, the individual would have to be identified as the relevant data user.

This focus on organisations processing personal data accords with the regulatory aims of the Ordinance, namely securing *systemic* compliance. A contravention may result from the actions of a relatively junior employee. However, the employee will, as part of a larger organisation, reflect the norms, instructions, and level of training provided by that organisation. It would be neither productive nor fair to treat the employee as an isolated culprit. He is part of a larger system, and the contravention should be addressed on an organisation-wide basis to achieve systemic compliance.[1]

The Commissioner may investigate a data user:

- In response to a complaint; or
- On his own initiative. The Commissioner will often be alerted to possible contraventions which the data subject will be oblivious

of. Other complaints may reveal a contravention, as may press reports and anonymous tip-offs. For example, the Australian Commissioner has exercised his power to initiate investigations upon receiving telephone calls or following up on press reports on the dumping of personal files on roadsides.[2]

Complaints

An individual may complain to the Privacy Commissioner provided that all the following requirements of s 37 are fulfilled:

- He is the data subject or a 'relevant person'[3] acting on his behalf, and may be representing other complainants as well [s 37(2)];
- The complaint is written in Chinese or English, or such other form acceptable to the Commissioner [s 37(3)]; and
- The complaint specifies an act or practice that has been done or engaged in, or is being done or engaged in by the data user specified in the complaint ('the relevant data user') and which may be a contravention of a requirement of Ordinance [and s 37(1)].

The Commissioner is under a duty to assist complainants seeking assistance in formulating the complaint [s 37(4)].

Discretion to Decline Investigation

Where the Commissioner receives a complaint or has reasonable grounds for believing that there has been a contravention of the Ordinance then subject to s 39 he must carry out an investigation (s 38). The Commissioner *may* decline to investigate a complaint on various grounds specified in s 39. Most of these matters stipulated as relevant to his discretion whether to investigate will be apparent to the Commissioner at the outset, namely:

- The complainant or relevant person had actual knowledge of the matter complained of for more than two years [s 39(1)(a)];
- The complainant is anonymous or cannot be identified or traced [s 39(1)(b) and (c)];
- There is no link with Hong Kong because none of the following applies:

(i) The complainant was a resident of Hong Kong or the data user was able to control the data in or from Hong Kong [s 39(1)(d)(i)]; or
(ii) The complainant was in Hong Kong when the complaint arose [s 39(1)(d)(ii)]; or
(iii) The act or practice complained of may prejudice the enforcement of any right or the exercise of any privilege acquired in Hong Kong [s 39(1)(d)(iii)];

- The relevant data user ceased being a data user for at least two years [s 39(1)(e)];
- The Commissioner has previously dismissed a substantially similar complaint [s 39(2)(a)]; and
- The complaint is frivolous or vexatious or its subject matter is trivial [s 39(2)(b) and (c)].

The grounds for declining to investigate that are more likely to be known to the recipient of the complaint than the Commissioner are that the complaint was not made in good faith [(s 39(2)(c)] or that the subject of the complaint had ceased being a data user for at least two years [s 39(1)(e)]. Though a data user may inform the Commissioner that either these or any of the other above factors exist, it cannot necessarily be expected to deter him from proceeding. Given the Commissioner's ancillary power to investigate at his own initiative, his decision whether or not to proceed will primarily depend on the view he takes of the contravention complained of. This is because complaints may reveal systemic problems and the earlier they are addressed, the sooner problems with other data subjects are avoided.

That the role of the complainant is only one consideration determining whether a complaint should be pursued is underscored by s 40 which declares that the Commissioner may continue his investigation of a complaint following its withdrawal.

In addition to these specific grounds for declining to investigate, the Commissioner may so refuse where 'any investigation or further investigation is for any reason unnecessary'. As discussed below, this ground will apply if the parties are able informally to resolve the matter satisfactorily.

Informal Attempts to Resolve Complaints

Upon receiving a complaint, the Commissioner may immediately proceed formally to investigate, thereby availing himself of all his evidence-gathering powers under the Ordinance. However, experience in other jurisdictions indicates that prior to instituting an investigation it will often be worth endeavouring to resolve the matter informally.

Thus, the Australian Privacy Commissioner frequently uses his discretion not to investigate a complaint until the complainant has first complained to the respondent in writing and has given the respondent an adequate opportunity to respond. An assessment of the complaint is made and preliminary inquiries may be undertaken. The complainant is then given assistance formulating his submission to the respondent. The complainant is also invited to revert to the Commissioner if he or she is not satisfied with the respondent's reply. Alternatively, the Commissioner will forward the complaint to the respondent with the consent of the complainant.[4]

A similar approach is adopted in New Zealand regarding complaints that are likely to be resolvable. The Privacy Commissioner indicates to the complainant how the allegations may be viewed under the Privacy Act should the complaint be pursued because the data user proves unresponsive. Such indications will generally avoid making specific rulings.

The Ordinance accommodates a similar strategy to that adopted in Australia and New Zealand so that the Commissioner may postpone investigating for up to 45 days following his receipt of a written complaint pending initial efforts to resolve the matter informally. The success of such efforts will depend on the co-operation of the parties, because until an investigation is commenced, the Commissioner is not entitled to resort to his formal evidence-gathering powers described below. It is in the interests of all concerned, however, that complaints are resolved informally wherever possible without the need for the Commissioner to investigate formally. Not later than the expiration of the 45 days after receiving the complaint the Commissioner must either proceed with a formal investigation or notify the complainant in writing of his refusal to investigate, giving reasons [s 39(3)]. The notification of refusal must be accompanied by a copy of s 39(4), which provides the complainant with a right of appeal to the Administrative Appeal Board [s 39(3)].

The complainant's right of appeal is against the Commissioner's refusal 'to carry out or continue' an investigation and therefore extends to the situation in which the Commissioner has commenced an investigation within the 45 days but has discontinued it. Where the parties have succeeded in negotiating an informal settlement by this time this will be a reason for the Commissioner refusing to commence or continue a formal investigation on the basis that it would be 'unnecessary' [s 39(2)(d)].

The Commissioner's decision to pursue a complaint is not subject to appeal by the data user. Furthermore, the complainant's right to appeal under s 39 lapses should the Commissioner discontinue an investigation more than 45 days after receiving the complaint. This follows from the requirement that the Commissioner's notice of refusal to investigate must be issued not later than 45 days after receiving the complaint [s 39(3)]. However, the statutory scheme envisages that investigations will not be discontinued after 45 days but instead will be completed and hence subject to the appeal provisions under s 47.

Procedures for Investigation of Alleged or Suspected Breaches

A possible contravention may be of such a nature that informal attempts to resolve the matter may be inappropriate. Alternatively, such efforts may have been unsuccessful. In these circumstances where the Commissioner determines that an investigation is warranted, either in response to a complaint or at his own initiative, he must first advise the relevant data user in writing of his intention to investigate [(s 41(1)].

'Relevant data user' is defined as the data user specified in the complaint or, in any other case, the subject of the investigation (s 2). This notice requirement is waived where the Commissioner believes on reasonable grounds that such notice may prejudice the investigation [s 41(2)]. For example, he may anticipate the destruction of evidence.

The manner in which the Commissioner investigates possible contraventions is a matter for him to determine. A graduated approach is provided for under the Ordinance. Section 43(1) provides that:

> the Commissioner may, for the purpose of any investigation:
> - be furnished with any information, document or thing, from such persons, and make such inquiries as he thinks fit; and
> - regulate his procedure in such manner as he thinks fit.

This very broad provision confers on the Commissioner the flexibility required to respond appropriately to the alleged or suspected contravention. Accordingly, the Commissioner will often commence his investigation with a simple request for certain information. When directed to the data user, the request will often be included in the letter the Commissioner is required to send him under s 41 advising of his intention to investigate.

More formal powers are also provided which the Commissioner can call upon should informal approaches be insufficient. A request for information under s 43 may be ignored or matters may emerge that necessitate a more formal approach. Indeed, it may be apparent at the outset that a request under s 43 may not be productive and that the Commissioner should immediately adopt more searching methods. These are provided for under s 44 under which he may summon the complainant or any other person possessing relevant information and require that person to answer the Commissioner's questions. Such questions may be administered under oath [s 44(4)]. A failure to comply with these requirements would constitute an offence under s 64(9).

Experience under the New Zealand *Privacy Act* suggests that these formal evidence-gathering powers seldom need to be invoked, perhaps precisely because data users realise that they are available if required. One situation where subpoena powers may be necessary is where an employee is concerned that his appearing to give evidence willingly would be perceived as constituting disloyalty to his employer.

The Ordinance provides also that the Commissioner may require the production of any document or thing under his possession or control [s 44(1)]. It is important to note that with its references to 'furnish' and 'produce', the Ordinance carefully defines the Commissioner's powers so as to exclude his unilateral seizure of evidence. This reflects the concern voiced during the legislative process that this newly established investigative body not be vested with full powers of search and seizure.

Overriding of Secrecy Provisions and Public Interest Immunity

These powers might be thwarted by a range of legal constraints with regard to the providing of information. Section 45 addresses this issue. It provides that during investigations persons 'shall have the same privileges in relation to the giving of information, the answering of questions, and the production of documents and things, for the purposes of an investigation, as witnesses have in civil proceedings in the Supreme Court'. The section proceeds, however, to override certain legal constraints upon providing information which could otherwise seriously undermine the Commissioner's investigative powers, namely statutory secrecy provisions and a common law principle rendering inadmissible disclosures that may prejudice the public interest:

- A large number of Ordinances make it a criminal offence for agencies and their staff to provide information or furnish documents for purposes which are not strictly related to the functions of the agency. The wording of these secrecy provisions vary. The *Inland Revenue Ordinance* represents the strict end of the spectrum and identifies the only bodies to which information may be passed on. Other provisions are formulated to provide some leeway. Hence the *Insurance Companies Ordinance* imposes a secrecy requirement 'except in the exercise of any functions under the Ordinance'. But s 44(8)(a) of the Ordinance provides that legal obligations to maintain secrecy shall not apply to disclosures for the purpose of investigations. This operates to override even the strictest secrecy provisions.
- Under the common law doctrine known as 'public interest immunity', evidence which is relevant and admissible under the ordinary rules of evidence will be excluded if its disclosure is contrary to the public interest. Either party may apply to the court for a ruling to this effect. For example, evidence of the identity of informants in welfare cases has been ruled as inadmissible. The House of Lords has held that if their identities were liable to disclosure, the sources of information would dry up, hindering prosecution efforts.[5] Section 45(1) abrogates the operation of this general principle in investigations.

Privilege Against Self-incrimination

Section 45(1) does, however, provide that every person shall have the same privileges in relation to the giving of information and documents as witnesses in the Supreme Court. Accordingly, the privilege against self-incrimination is available to persons in the course of investigations. The privilege entitles a person to refuse to answer the question or produce the document if to do so would tend to expose that person to proceedings for a criminal offence.[6] The test is whether, from the circumstances of the case and the nature of the evidence sought there is a reasonable ground to apprehend real danger to the witness by responding.[7]

The principle arises because contraventions of the requirements of the Ordinance (save for the data protection principles) are offences under s 64 (see Chapter 13). Section 45(2) protects witnesses as regards evidence given in the course of any investigation by rendering such evidence inadmissible in other proceedings. But this protection does not extend to the trial of a person for perjury 'or for an offence under this Ordinance'.

Hence, where a witness provides information or documents to the Commissioner in respect of an investigation for a contravention of a requirement under the Ordinance (other than a data protection principle), the privilege against self-incrimination may be applicable. Its relevance will depend on whether the witness will be exposing himself to prosecution.[8] Generally, however, it will not be the witness who is exposed but the data user who employs him. As mentioned earlier, the focus of Part VII is on data users, ie organisations controlling the use of personal data. Similarly an employee of a data user will be liable under the criminal law only where the provisions of the *Criminal Procedure Ordinance* apply in relation to aiding and abetting (s 89) or a member of the management has consented to or connived at the commission of the offence (s 101E; see Chapter 13).

Commissioner Subject to Secrecy

In view of the statutory abrogation of statutory secrecy provisions and common law constraints on disclosing information that may prejudice the public interest, alternative controls are clearly necessary. Section 46 accordingly requires the Commissioner and his staff to maintain secrecy regarding matters coming to their attention in the performance of their duties. Criminal sanctions are prescribed for a breach of secrecy [s 64(6)]. This secrecy requirement is qualified by the Commissioner's reporting functions which are addressed below.

Hearings

The Commissioner's broad discretion regarding procedures permit him to proceed inquisitorially. Section 43(2) mentions the possibility of convening a hearing. A 'hearing' is a proceeding of relative formality with definite issues of fact or law to be tried.[9] They are likely to be rarely held under the Ordinance. Where the parties are contesting the facts or matters of principle, however, the Commissioner may consider it necessary to convene a hearing. It is entirely at his discretion and neither party is entitled to the adoption of such a procedure [s 43(4)]. Experience in other jurisdictions suggests that witnesses are generally more forthcoming when interviewed alone, rather than when others, such as their superiors, are present.

Where a hearing is conducted, counsel and solicitors do not have a 'right of audience', ie the right to make submissions and question witnesses [s 43(3)]. Legal representation is solely at the discretion of the Commissioner, such as where skilled cross-examination is warranted or legal issues emerge.

Hearings in Public

It follows from the above that 'hearings' are likely to be rare. Where they are required, the Ordinance recognises the general principle that hearings shall be held in public in order that justice should be seen to be done [s 43(2)]. This is necessarily qualified where privacy issues arise. A hearing must be heard in private if the complainant so requests in writing [s 43(2)(b)]. To provide otherwise and subject the complainant to the prospect of publicity could act as a serious disincentive to his taking action.

Even where the complainant does not require a private hearing, the Commissioner has a discretion to order one [s 43(2)(a)]. This enables him to consider the interests of the data user as well as the wider public interest. In considering whether the public interest would be served by a private hearing, the Commissioner would have to take into account his broad investigative powers discussed above. The statutory abrogation of other secrecy requirements will increase the potential for public disclosure of matter of some delicacy. Whilst the Commissioner and his staff are themselves subject to secrecy requirements, these would not of course operate against those attending public hearings repeating evidence.

Powers of Entry

In carrying out an investigation, the Commissioner may enter premises occupied by the data user or on which is situated his personal data system, or part of it [s 42(2)]. 'Personal data system' is defined (s 2) as encompassing both manual and automated systems and includes both documents and equipment forming part of the system. Before effecting entry, the Commissioner must either:

- Have served written notice at least 14 days earlier advising of the proposed entry and specifying the premises [s 42(3)(a)]; or
- Have obtained a warrant [s 42(5)]. The warrant must be produced for inspection by an occupant who challenges the power of entry [s 42(10)].

As obtaining a warrant enables the Commissioner to enter without prior warning, the issuing magistrate must be satisfied upon oath that providing the usual notice may substantially prejudice the investigation [s 42(6)]. For example, there may be a significant risk that the data user may destroy evidence.

Additional requirements are imposed for entry to domestic premises, which are defined as premises which are constructed or intended to be used for habitation [s 42(11)]. Whereas the general 14 day notice requirement becomes effective upon its expiration as regards non-domestic premises, in the case of domestic premises, a resident adult's consent is necessary within the 14 days [s 42(4)]. Should such consent not be forthcoming, the Commissioner must obtain a warrant upon satisfying a magistrate that the investigation may otherwise be substantially prejudiced [s 42(7)].

The Commissioner must exercise his powers in a manner that does not unduly disrupt the operations carried out there by the data user or any other person [s 42(8)]. However, the data user must, without charge, afford the Commissioner all reasonable facilities and assistance required to carry out the investigation [s 42(9)].

Notice of Result

Upon completing an investigation (whether initiated by complaint or instituted by the Commissioner), s 47(2) provides that the Commissioner must inform the data user of:

- The result of the investigation;
- Any recommendations;
- Any report that he proposes to publish under s 48;
- Whether he proposes serving an enforcement notice on the data user; and
- Any other comments he thinks fit.

Where the investigation has resulted from a complaint, the complainant must also be advised of all these matters, as well as any comments from the data user regarding the Commissioner's recommendations and proposed report [s 47(3)]. If the Commissioner does not propose serving an enforcement notice the complainant must also be informed of his right to appeal to the Administrative Appeals Board under s 47(4).

Negotiated Settlements

As mentioned above, the Ordinance provides the Commissioner with the opportunity to effect an informal resolution of a complaint before he has to institute an investigation. Experience elsewhere suggests that most investigations can themselves be resolved through a disputes resolution process. The Australian Commissioner has reported a high success rate in negotiating settlement of complaints between the Commissioner's office and the data user:

> The majority of privacy complaints can be resolved on the basis that the respondent to the complaint has adequately dealt with the complaint. Normally, once a complaint has been received, the allegations are verified and the objectives of the complainant are canvassed. The allegations are then put to the respondent for a response. Once the views of the respondent are known, negotiations commence to clarify the issues, to ensure that in the future, the respondent's conduct complies with the provisions of the Act and to obtain a satisfactory result for the injured party.[10]

The crucial role played by privacy commissioners in resolving complaints is indicated by figures showing that approximately of 50 per cent of complaints received by the Australian Commissioner are substantiated and would not have been resolved without an investigation by his office.[11] Remedial action generally consists of an apology to the complainant together with revised procedures (including staff training) to minimise the risk of a future breach of the Act, including improving security. Data may also require amending.[12]

Enforcement Notices

Where during an investigation the Commissioner has been unsuccessful in negotiating a settlement or where such negotiations were inappropriate, he may conclude that formal enforcement action is necessary. By serving an enforcement notice, the Commissioner puts the data user on formal notice that he must comply with the Ordinance. Failure to comply with an enforcement notice constitutes a criminal offence punishable by two years imprisonment and a daily fine of $1000 [s 64(7)].

The Commissioner may serve an enforcement notice under s 50 (1) when in his opinion the data user:

- Is contravening a requirement under the Ordinance; or
- Has contravened such a requirement in circumstances that make it likely that the contravention will continue or be repeated.

In determining whether a notice should issue, the Commissioner must consider whether the contravention has caused the data subject damage or distress, or is likely to do so [s 50(2)].

The notice must state that he is of the opinion that there is a contravention of a specified requirement under the Ordinance, giving reasons, and direct the data user to take specified remedial steps within a specified period, but not less than the 14-day period within which the data user may appeal against the notice to the Administrative Appeals Board [s 50(1)]. Where the Commissioner considers the taking of remedial steps as urgent, he may direct that they be taken not less than seven days following notice being served [s 50(5)]. A copy of s 50 must also be provided. The notice may be framed with reference to an applicable code of practice and may afford the data user a choice between different ways of remedying the contravention [s 50(3)].

The Commissioner may also serve an enforcement notice before completing an investigation, where he considers the matter urgent [s 50(8)]. In addition to the matters stipulated above, he must give reasons for the urgent service.

The Commissioner may cancel an enforcement notice by serving the data user notice in writing [s 50(6)].

The provisions regarding enforcement notices are derived from the UK *Data Protection Act*. Although not a statutory requirement, the UK Registrar has adopted an early warning system prior to the issue of enforcement notices. The Registrar first serves a 'preliminary notice' which states that the Registrar is intending to issue a statutory enforcement notice for specified reasons. The notice is sent by registered mail informing the data user that it has 28 days to respond either orally or in writing. The advantage of such a procedure is that it provides the parties with a final opportunity to resolve the matter less formally. A similar approach may be adopted under the Ordinance.

Reports on Investigations

Upon completing an investigation or inspection, the Commissioner may publish a report setting out any recommendations relating to the promotion of compliance with the Ordinance by the class of data users to which the complained party belongs [s 48(2)]. He may also make 'such other comments arising from the investigation as he thinks fit to make'. The report shall be so framed as to prevent the identity of individuals, other than the data user and the Commissioner [s 48(3)]. The Australian Commissioner has found that there is sometimes little choice but to name the data user. The description of the conduct may clearly identify the data user in any event. Alternatively, naming the data user may be necessary in order adequately to describe the conduct.[13]

The Commissioner's power to publish reports represents a significant potential sanction against errant data users. A critical report may have a serious impact on a company's public relations.

The provisions of s 47 on notification of parties and s 48 on reports do not apply where:

- The result of the investigation is that there is no contravention because of the application of an exemption under Part VIII; and
- The interest protected by that exemption would be likely to be prejudiced by the application of ss 47 and 48.

Instead, the Commissioner is required only to inform the data user of the result of the investigation together with any comments. If the investigation was initiated by a complaint, the complainant shall be informed only that 'the result of the investigation is that (the Commissioner) is satisfied that the act or practice the subject of the investigation is not a contravention of the Ordinance' [s 49(ii)(B)].

Inspections

One of the functions of the Commissioner is 'to carry out inspections, including inspections of any personal data systems used by data users which are departments of the government or statutory corporations' [s 8(1)(e)]. Inspections, like investigations at his initiative, provide the Commissioner with the opportunity to exercise a proactive role. However, inspections play a fundamentally different role under the Ordinance.

Whereas investigations are conducted in relation to suspected breaches of the Ordinance, inspections represent systematic audits of selected personal data systems. Accordingly, their purpose is not to uncover breaches but rather to provide a comprehensive vetting of the personal data system's general compliance with the Ordinance. Not all other jurisdictions confer on the Commissioner this audit role, but those that do report that it is a crucial component of an effective regulatory scheme.[14]

The Commissioner is not required to give prior notice before entry to non-domestic premises to inspect a personal data system situated there, but entry must be at a reasonable time [s 42(1)]. Entry to domestic premises to conduct an inspection requires the consent of an adult residing there.

The Commissioner must exercise his powers in a manner that does not unduly disrupt the operations carried out there by the data user or any other person [s 42(8)]. However, the data user must, without charge, afford the Commissioner all reasonable facilities and assistance required to carry out the inspection [s 42(9)].

Published Reports of Inspections

Upon completing an inspection, the Commissioner may publish a report setting out any recommendations relating to the promotion of compliance with the Ordinance by the class of data users to which the complained party belongs [s 48(1)]. The report shall be framed so as to protect the identity of individuals, other than the data user and the Commissioner [s 48(3)].

The Australian Commissioner's approach on the issue provides useful guidance on how this power should be used:

> The Privacy Commissioner has taken the view that routine publication of audit reports might adversely affect private sector organisations, because they may be exposed to disadvantage in the market if publicity were to be given to minor infractions or relevant standards, especially where there is a preparedness to remedy the difficulties identified. But the PC reserves the possibility of 'naming' organizations

in cases of major or flagrant breach of standards. No situations of that kind have arisen in the current reporting year.[15]

Restricted Powers of the Commissioner Regarding the Media

The Commissioner's proactive powers of investigation and inspection have been carefully curtailed under the Ordinance regarding the media. Section 61 provides that news organisations are exempt from the Commissioner's power to institute an investigation for an alleged contravention until the data are published or broadcast or any suspected breach under s 38(b). They are also exempt from the Commissioner's power to conduct an inspection under s 36. These restrictions on the Commissioner's powers apply to personal data held by a data user:

- Whose business or part of whose business, consists of a news activity; and
- Solely for the purposes of that activity (or any directly related activity.

'News activity' is defined as meaning any journalistic activity and includes news gathering and the preparation, compiling or dissemination to the public news articles or programmes or observations on news or current affairs [s 61(3)].[16] These restrictions on the powers of the Commissioner were proposed by the Law Reform Commission to preserve the institutional integrity of the media.

Notes

1 The data user has a defence if it took reasonably practicable steps to prevent the contravention [s 65(3)].

2 Australian Privacy Commissioner, 5th Annual Report, p 24.

3 Section 2.

4 Australian Privacy Commissioner, 5th Annual Report, p 83.

5 *D v National Society for the Prevention of Cruelty to Children* [1978] AC 171. See Chapter 3.

6 *Evidence Ordinance,* s 65.

7 *Cross & Tapper on Evidence* 8 ed (1995) Butterworths, London, pp 453-9.

8 The privilege is restricted to the person who claims it. So, for example, it does not extend to questions the answers to which would tend to incriminate a spouse: see *Rio Tinto Zinc Corporation v Westinghouse Electric Corporation* [1978] AC 547, per Lord Diplock at 637.

9 (1983) *Black's Law Dictionary* 5 ed, West Publishing Co, St. Paul, Minn.

10 Australian Privacy Commissioner, 4th Annual Report, p 59.

11 Australian Privacy Commissioner, 5th Annual Report, p 87.

12 Australian Privacy Commissioner, 7th Annual Report, p 65.

13 Australian Privacy Commissioner, 6th Annual Report, p 59.

14 See D Flaherty (1989), *Protecting Privacy in Surveillance Societies*, Chapel Hill: University of North Carolina Press.

15 Australian Privacy Commissioner, 4th Annual Report, p 13.

16 The argument in support of this limitation on the powers of the Commissioner to inspect or investigate news organisations may be found in the Report of Law Reform Commission, pp 234-241.

12 Exemptions

Introduction

The requirements imposed on data users by the Ordinance are qualified by the exemptions set out in Part VIII. Save in respect of data used by individuals for domestic purposes, exemptions are provided only to:

- *Principle 3 – regulating the use of data.* As explained in Chapter 2, this provides that personal data shall not, without the data subject's prescribed consent, be used (including transferred or disclosed) for any purpose other than the purpose for which the data were to be used at the time of the collection of the data, or a directly related purpose.
- *The right of access.* Access rights are conferred by principle 6 but are also addressed in detail in Part V, including s 18(1)(b). Accordingly, an exemption from access is expressed as being an exemption 'from the provisions of data protection principle 6 and s 18(1)(b)', ('the access provisions').
- *Notification.* Principle 1(3) requires that the data subject be notified of such matters as the purpose of data upon their collection. The principle provides, however, that the data user collecting the data is exempted from these notification requirements if their fulfilment is likely to prejudice the purpose of collection and that purpose is exempt from the access provisions.

The Subject Matter for Exemptions

The exemptions addressed in Part VIII vary in content but they all identify circumstances where providing access and/or the strict application of principle 3 may be undesirable or impractical. The exemptions may broadly be grouped according to whether they relate to specified public interests, to employment or whether they are held for domestic purposes.

Public Interest

The exemptions address the following public interests: security, defence, and international relations in respect of Hong Kong (s 57), law enforcement and regulation (s 58), and health (s 59).

These exemptions impose a harm test and provide that where prejudice to the stated interest is likely to result from:

- Providing access to data held for those purposes; and/or
- Complying with principle 3 regarding data used for those purposes (whether or not the data are held for those purposes);

then the data user is exempt from providing access and/or principle 3 in respect of such data.

Another interest which is similarly accorded an exemption from both access and principle 3 relates to freedom of expression (s 61). But this exemption does not explicitly articulate a harm test; it refers instead to a 'news activity'.

A further public interest which is couched in terms of an activity but has been accorded an exemption only from principle 3 (but not from the right of access) is that of the carrying out of research (s 62).

Employment

A further cluster of exemptions relate less to the protection of a competing public interest than to qualifying access rights as they relate to two specific relationships, namely that of employment (s 53, s 54 and s 56) and legal professional privilege (s 61). This shift from the principled to the pragmatic is further reflected by the qualifying of access rights during a decision-making process (s 55). These exemptions do not impose a harm test and relate only to access.

Domestic Sphere

The recognition that legal regulation should not extend to the domestic sphere has resulted in a broad exemption for data held by individuals in a personal capacity (s 52).

Before proceeding to examine these exemptions in more detail, certain general points need to be made:

Effect of an exemption
Section 51 provides that in so far as personal data are exempt from a provision of the Ordinance, that provision neither confers any right nor imposes any requirement on any person.

Exemptions may overlap
The interests identified by the various exemptions are not mutually exclusive and often more than one exemption may be applicable. For example, the prosecution of tax offenders would relate both to the detection of crime [s 58(1)(a)] and to the collection of tax [s 58(1)(c)].

Exemptions apply to data rather than records
As with other applications of the Ordinance, exemptions relate to data, not records as such. An exemption may relate to an entire record, but it will often pertain only to a part or parts of a record, whether computerised and/or manually held. Applying an access exemption will therefore often require that an editing process be undertaken.

Permissive nature of exemptions
Exemptions *allow* the data user to alter the use of data and/or bar access – they do not *require* it do so. This is indicated by the Ordinance's use of the permissive 'may' instead of the mandatory 'shall' – which is used, for instance, in the case of s 20(1)(b), prohibiting the release of data disclosing personal data of which any other individual is the data subject. The data user must accordingly weigh the factors for and against departing from principle 3. The issue is whether the public interest in question is likely to be prejudiced, unless the data are used for a purpose other than that for which they were collected.

If an access exemption is being considered, another relevant factor is the data quality implications for the data user's own records. Access and correction rights enhance data quality, as the data subject will normally be best informed about himself. Conversely, to deny access is to miss an opportunity to remove inaccuracies and bias. We have shown that maintaining accurate data is a requirement under principle 2 and that a breach of this principle may render the data user liable for compensation. Providing access and correction rights accordingly best ensures compliance with the other provisions of the Ordinance.

As the use of exemptions is discretionary, it is important that data users develop policies which ensure that they are applied in a consistent manner.

Application of Access Exemptions to Data 'Held' for Specified Purposes

Most of the access exemptions dealt with below are expressly limited to data 'held' for specified purposes. This expression is found also in various contexts in the *UK Data Protection Act*. The UK Data Protection Registrar has observed that:

> [T]here is a difficulty in the practical application of the Act in determining for what purposes data are actually held ... I take the view that the best guide to this is the purpose for which the information was originally obtained by the data user.[1]

This limitation that data are held for the purpose applicable to access exemptions does not apply to the exemptions from principle 3 as these are stated to apply whether or not the data are held for an exempted purpose.

Exemptions may be Invoked only on Reasonable Grounds

The exemptions in s 58 (security) and s 59 (law enforcement and regulation) impose a harm test whereby the exemption may be invoked if prejudice to the stated interests is 'likely'. The UK Data Protection Registrar has interpreted this requirement in the following way:

> The Act does not explain the meaning of the phrase 'likely to prejudice'. The Registrar takes the view that, for the exemption to apply, there would have to be a substantial chance, rather than a mere risk, that, in a particular case, the purposes would be noticeably damaged. A data user needs to make a judgment as to whether or not prejudice is likely in relation to the circumstances of each individual case. The exemption cannot justify the disclosure of personal data relating to a number of individuals, when in fact those purposes would only be likely to be prejudiced by a failure to make the disclosure in the case of some of them.[2]

The 'likelihood' test is easier to state than apply. Determining the likelihood of prejudice will tend to be more difficult in the case of change of use than with access. The problem is most acute when data held by data user A are requested by data user B for a purpose other than that for which A originally collected them. In the absence of the data subject's prescribed consent, A may transfer or disclose the data only if its failure to do so is likely to prejudice the interest asserted by B. But A will frequently be less able to assess this likelihood of prejudice than B. Nonetheless, it is A who must determine whether to invoke the exemption and who is vulnerable to challenge from the data subject. For example, data held by the Social Welfare Department may be requested by the Police. Or client data held by a stockbroker may be sought by the Securities and Futures Commission. In neither case is the data user who holds the data well placed to make an independent assessment of a claim that unless the specified data are released an investigation will be prejudiced.

It does not follow, however, that a data user holding data may simply acquiesce in any such assertion. This is made clear by s 58(2) which provides a defence to a contravention of principle 3 for the data user 'to show that he had reasonable grounds for believing' that failure to use the data for the altered purpose 'would have been likely to prejudice' any of the matters stated in that section. As explained below, s 58 addresses a variety of regulatory interests. Although the other exemption provisions omit explicit reference to this reasonableness test, we believe that they should be approached in a similar manner.

What constitutes reasonable grounds for invoking an exemption will obviously depend on the circumstances, but relevant considerations include the nature of the data requested and the explanation provided. If the data relate to specific items of one or more data subjects, such as presence on certain premises at a specified time or involvement in particular transactions, then the test will be more readily satisfied than if general data are sought. Broadly speaking, the more general the data sought, the more detailed B's explanation will need to be in order to satisfy A that reasonable grounds exist. The mere assertion by B that the data are needed is most unlikely to satisfy the test, as it would countenance data fishing expeditions contrary to the spirit of the Ordinance.

Access Exemptions may Apply only on an Interim Basis

A related point arises when considering whether the interest in question is likely to be prejudiced by granting access. Whether such prejudice is likely will depend on the timing of access. This is illustrated by a ruling of the New Zealand Privacy Commissioner under similar provisions. It related to his reviewing the application of an exemption, similar to that contained in s 58, where access would be likely 'to prejudice the maintenance of the law, including the prevention, investigation and detection of offences, and the right to a fair trial':

> The complainant had been refused access to personal information held by the Commerce Commission, which is a financial regulator. The commission proposed interviewing the complainant in relation to a price fixing investigation it was conducting. The commission had interviewed other persons and obtained documents pursuant to warrant and the complainant sought access to such data insofar as it related to himself prior to any further interview with the commission. The commissioner upheld the refusal of access. He noted that the responses by the complainant to questions posed on the basis of this material would determine the direction of its investigation:
>
> In such circumstances if the complainant were to have access to the information before the commission has had the opportunity to pose its questions and gauge the response, then the efficacy of the whole investigative process would be diminished and the commission would be prejudiced in its investigation of whether or not an agreement that substantially lessened competition had occurred.
>
> I noted, however, that this finding was based on the stage which the investigation had reached. Once the interview had been concluded and the commission had formed a decision then this concern would no longer be relevant.[3]

It will be recalled that a data user has 40 days to respond to an access request [s 19(1)]. If an exemption is applicable upon receipt of the access request but is likely to cease to apply in 40 days, the simplest course is for the data user to delay providing a copy of the data accordingly.

Access Exemptions must be Logged

It was pointed out in Chapter 9 that s 27 requires that where a data user refuses to comply with an access request the particulars must be entered in a log book maintained for the purpose. Where the data user declines to disclose even the existence of the data to the data subject on the basis that this would prejudice the interest protected by the exemption, reasons must be logged.

Exemptions Relating to both Access and Principle 3

We identify below those purposes which are expressed as being subject to exemptions from both the application of the access provisions and principle 3. In both cases there must be a reasonable likelihood that providing access or the application of principle 3 is likely to prejudice the interest protected by the exemption. It does not follow, however, that their application to the same data will necessarily result in the exemption applying equally; it may be permissible to bar access but not to depart from principle 3 or vice versa. This point is well illustrated by so-called 'black lists'. Such a list may, for instance, be distributed to loan providers identifying individuals with a history of fraudulently obtaining and defaulting on loans. The exemptions relating to the prevention or remedying of unlawful or seriously improper conduct may justify using data derived from business records to compile a list for this altered purpose. It would, however, be more difficult for a data user holding the list to argue that providing access to an individual named on it would prejudice these purposes. But providing access to a 'stop list' of wanted persons held at immigration check-points could arguably prejudice the apprehension of offenders by tipping-off those wanted by the authorities.

Domestic Purposes

Personal data held by an individual and concerned only with the management of his personal, family or household affairs, or for recreational purposes are exempt from all the data protection principles, the data user return provisions (under Part IV), the access and correction provisions (under Part V), as well as the Commissioner's powers of inspection and investigation (under ss 36 and 38).

Whereas the other exemptions are expressed to apply to 'data users' (encompassing both legal persons and individuals), this exemption is restricted in its application to individuals. The exemption is intended to cover personal records such as Christmas card mailing lists or personal correspondence. Provided such data are used solely for the stipulated purposes they have little potential to harm the interests of data subjects. To impose, for example, the access requirements of the Ordinance on such data would not only be cumbersome but would also unduly intrude on the individual's personal and family life. Should, however, the individual transfer or disclose such data to a data user in administrative or commercial spheres contrary to the limitations of the exemption then the exemption would terminate.

Security, Defence, and International Relations in Respect of Hong Kong

Data held for the purposes of safeguarding security, defence or international relations in respect of Hong Kong are exempt from the access provisions and principle 3 where their application would be likely to prejudice those purposes [s 57(1)].

This exemption has the following procedural features that are not applicable to other exempted purposes:

- The Chief Executive or Chief Secretary may determine and accordingly sign a certificate to the effect that the exemption 'is or at any time was required' in respect of the personal data [s 57(3)]; and
- The certificate may also direct the Commissioner not to carry out an investigation or inspection in respect of the data to which the certificate relates 'and for the reasons specified in that certificate'. The Commissioner must comply with such a direction [s 57(5)].

The certificate procedure is not a prerequisite of the application of this exemption. That is determined by the harm test. The certificate procedure provides, however, evidence that the harm test has been satisfied [s 57(4)]. When accompanied by a direction not to investigate, that evidence is, as regards the Commissioner, effectively conclusive. As such, the application of this exemption is less transparent than the other exemptions. Abuse of the provision is nevertheless likely to be constrained by three factors:

- Unlike other exemptions (save for those relating to news) the scope of the exemption from access, but not use, is limited not only by the purposes for which the data are held but by the identity of the data user holding such data. Specifically, the data must 'be held by or on behalf of the Government' for the specified purposes;[4]
- The certifying party must be either the Chief Executive or the Chief Secretary. This power is not delegable. However, a document purporting to be a certificate under this provision is, in the absence of evidence to the contrary, deemed to be properly issued [s 57(6)]; and
- Unless the certificate provides to the contrary, the Commissioner is entitled to examine the data which are the subject of the certificate to confirm that the exemption applies. A certificate to the contrary stating that the Commissioner should not so investigate or inspect must be accompanied by reasons. A court would be entitled to look behind the certificate, and the requirement to give reasons would broaden its powers of judicial review.

Though the phrase 'security, defence or international relations' in respect of Hong Kong is not defined, 'security' 'includes the prevention or preclusion of persons (including persons detained in accordance with the provisions of the *Immigration Ordinance,* entering and remaining in Hong Kong who do not have the right to enter and remain in Hong Kong' [s 57(7)].

Law Enforcement and Regulation

Section 58 provides an exemption from the access provisions and from principle 3 in relation to the following purposes sharing a broad regulatory aim:

- The prevention or detection of crime and the apprehension, prosecution or detention of offenders [s 58(1)(a)&(b)];
- The assessment or collection of any tax or duty [s 58(1)(c)]. This language is likely to cover only charges levied by such agencies as the Inland Revenue Department or the Department of Customs and Excise, and would not extend to such items as the recovery of debts, whether or not they are imposed by statute; and
- Unlawful or seriously improper conduct, or dishonesty or malpractice [s 58(1)(d)].

Section 58(1)(d) exempts data relating to the prevention, preclusion or remedying (including punishment) of unlawful or seriously improper conduct, or dishonesty or malpractice, by persons. Several of these expressions warrant elaboration.

'Unlawful conduct' encompasses breaches of both statute and the common law as it relates to both civil and criminal wrongs.

'Seriously improper conduct' is defined under the Ordinance to include:

(i) Conduct whereby a person would cease to be a fit and proper person where such fitness is a requirement of that person's office, profession or occupation [s 2(9)]; and

(ii) Any conduct by which a person has or could become a suspended disqualified person under the Hong Kong Jockey Club Rules of Racing and Instructions by the Stewards [s 2(13)].

The reference to 'seriously improper conduct' is not limited by this inclusive definition and embraces a broad range of regulatory activity focusing on behaviour which is not unlawful as such. Examples would include the enforcement of regulatory codes of conduct, disciplinary proceedings, and the regulation of other behaviour that may have escaped formal inclusion in codes or disciplinary rules but is nevertheless such that it is not tolerated by the community generally or the professional sector concerned.

The words 'prevention, preclusion or remedying' indicate, however, that data transfers for these purposes must be to persons performing roles relevant to these activities, such as regulatory agencies or disciplinary bodies.

- Prevention of financial loss:
  The prevention or preclusion of significant financial loss arising from –
  (i) any imprudent business practices or activities of persons; or
  (ii) unlawful or seriously improper conduct, or dishonesty or malpractice, by persons.

Not only financial regulators but also banks hold information for the protection of their depositors. Such information relates to such matters as 'black lists' of known fraudsters and those with a history of failed business ventures. Subject to the harm test being satisfied, such data are exempt from access. Releasing data to data users playing a preventive role will be exempt from principle 3.

- Ascertaining whether the character or activities of the data subject are likely to have a significantly adverse impact on any thing
  - (i) to which the discharge of statutory functions by the data user relates; or
  - (ii) which relates to the discharge of functions which are subject to s 58(3).

The application of this limb is limited to the public sector. Whereas those other s 58 exemptions addressed above relating to 'seriously improper conduct' and 'malpractice', etc focus on blameworthy conduct, this limb goes further. The term 'character and activities' may characterise matters relating to the data subject which are of legitimate concern to the data user even though they do not involve blameworthy conduct. For example, an individual may apply for or hold an important position for which, through no fault of his own, he is unsuited by temperament or for which he is insufficiently qualified. Or an individual may be engaging in share transactions on a scale which may distort the market and hence impinge on the Stock Exchange of Hong Kong's statutory function of ensuring the operation of an orderly and fair market.

Section 58(3) applies to any functions of a financial regulator:

(i) For protecting members of the public against financial loss arising from various forms of misconduct by persons undertaking specified financial services;
(ii) For maintaining or promoting the general stability or effective working of the specified financial services; and
(iii) A function specified by the Governor [s 58(4)]. Such a notice is subsidiary legislation [s 58(5)(b)].

These provisions are without prejudice to the application of the other exemptions [s 58(5)(a)]. As mentioned above, exemptions are not mutually exclusive and will often overlap.

Protection of Sources

Data held for the above purposes specified in s 58 are exempted also from access where this would be likely to directly or indirectly identify the person who is the source of the data [s 58(1)(g)(ii)]. It will be recalled that there is a general prohibition against providing access to data relating to another individual but that only identifying particulars may be removed. The data must be provided even if the identity of the source can be inferred. The access exemption under s 58 is, however, broader and allows a data user to deny access to all those data which are likely to lead to the identification of the source, whether explicitly or inferentially. Allegations may be such as to allow the source to be readily identified. For example, a relative may record allegations about specific events which the data subject knows were witnessed only by a particular person. In such circumstances the data may be withheld.[5]

News and the Media

Access exemption for journalistic data

An access exemption is accorded to data held by a data user whose business, or part of whose business, consists of a news activity and are held solely for the purpose of that news activity. 'News activity' is defined as any journalistic activity and includes the gathering of news, preparation or compiling of articles or programmes concerning news; or observations on news or current affairs for the purpose of dissemination to the public. Similarly exempted is the dissemination to the public of any article or programme of or concerning news, or observations on news or current affairs.

Unlike the exemptions discussed above, the competing public interest is in this case a well recognised individual right. Freedom of expression is, like the right to privacy, protected by the International Covenant on Civil and Political Rights. That protection is replicated by the *Bill of Rights Ordinance*. The fundamental constitutional significance of free speech was recognised by the Hong Kong Law Reform Commission. The Commission accepted that the right of free speech is enjoyed both by speaker and audience. Accordingly, measures that undermine the activities of the news media may adversely affect the audience's right to receive information. The access exemption accorded to news is therefore broader than the other access exemptions as the data held solely for news purposes are exempt 'unless and until the data are published or broadcast'. Hence the access exemption extends to all unpublished data, including journalists' notebooks. The provision reflects concerns that affording data subject access rights to unpublished data could thwart investigative journalism. Thus if an individual were able to obtain access to data relating to a current investigation it may alert him to the possibility of sources being approached; he may therefore attempt to silence them by warning them not to speak.

Exemption from principle 3 for journalistic sources

It was pointed out above that s 58 contains a whistle-blower provision whereby a data user collecting personal data may alter the purpose to avoid prejudicing certain interests. Similarly, s 61(2) provides that personal data are exempt from principle 3 where the use of the data consists of disclosing them to a news organisation by a person who reasonably believes that their publication or broadcasting would be 'in the public interest'. This is the only reference made by the exemptions to a general public interest test. As mentioned above, the regime of exemptions has endeavoured to crystallise the relevant forms of public interest that may justify public disclosure of personal data. Including a general public interest test in this exemption reflects the vital role of the news media in keeping the community aware of matters of general concern. The requirement that the publication be in the public interest would, however, exclude matters that may be merely interesting to the public. This is now a fairly well established rule in the context of disclosures in breach of confidence, though the concept of 'public interest' would seem to be narrower than its more generous meaning in s 61 (2) (see Chapter 3).

The courts have repeatedly adopted Lord Wood V-C's statement that:

> [T]here is no confidence as to the disclosure of an iniquity. You cannot make me the confidant of a crime or a fraud, and be entitled to close up my lips upon any secret which you have the audacity to disclose to me relating to any fraudulent intention on your part: such a confidence cannot exist.[6]

And it has been held that there 'may be cases where the misdeed is of such a character that the public interest may demand, or at least excuse, publication on a broader field, even to the press'.[7]

In *British Steel Corporation v Granada Television Ltd*,[8] Granada Television broadcast a programme seeking to show that the huge losses being incurred by British Steel at the time were due to mismanagement and poor quality control. This information, which Granada knew to be confidential, had been passed to them by an unknown person. The only contended issue was an order granted to British Steel that Granada disclose its source. In spite of this, the House of Lords took it upon themselves to consider the public interest test. In the words of Lord Wilberforce:

> There is an important exception to the limitations which may exist upon the right of the media to reveal information otherwise restricted. That is based on what is commonly known as the 'iniquity rule'. It extends in fact beyond 'iniquity' to misconduct generally . . . It must be emphasised that we are not in this field in the present case. The most that it is said the papers reveal is mis-management and government intervention.[9]

Similarly, in *Lion Laboratories Ltd v Evans*,[10] the decision involved intoximeters manufactured by the plaintiff to be used to breath-test drivers suspected of exceeding the prescribed alcohol limit. Two ex-employees of the plaintiff had disclosed internal memoranda to a newspaper relating to their concern about the accuracy of the device in calibration tests. At first instance, the court granted the plaintiff an interlocutory injunction. The Court of Appeal, without hesitation, discharged the injunction on the ground that the information contained in the memoranda concerned matters in the public interest. In the course of his judgment, Stephenson LJ stressed four issues:

- That the courts were concerned only with what was *in* the public interest, not what was *of* interest to the public;
- That the media have their own private interest in increasing circulation;
- That the public interest is not always best served by disclosure to the press; and
- That the public interest test was not confined to cases of iniquity. Stephenson LJ expressed the view that iniquity was 'merely an instance of just cause or excuse for breaking confidence'[11] and accordingly there was no need to show misconduct on the part of

> the plaintiff. He believed that the just cause or excuse in the instant case was 'the public interest [in admittedly confidential information]'.[12]

In *X v Y*[13] an employee of a health authority leaked the names of two practising doctors who had contracted AIDS. The information was given to a newspaper reporter in return for the payment of a sum of money. The plaintiffs, the health authority, obtained an order restraining the newspaper from publishing or using the information. The newspaper nevertheless published an article implying that there were doctors in the health service who were continuing to practise despite having contracted AIDS and suggesting that the Department of Health and Social Security wished to suppress this information. The newspaper intended to publish a further article identifying the doctors. The plaintiffs sought, *inter alia*, an injunction restraining the newspaper from disclosing the identity of the doctors.

The court granted a permanent injunction; it held that the public interest in preserving the confidentiality of hospital records identifying actual or potential AIDS sufferers outweighed the public interest in the freedom of the press to publish such information because victims should not be deterred by fear of discovery from coming forward for treatment. Protecting the confidentiality of the names of sufferers would not stifle free and informed public debate about the disease. Moreover, as Rose J put it,

> The risk of identification is only one factor in assessing whether to permit the use of confidential information. In my judgment to allow publication . . . would be to enable both defendants to procure breaches of confidence and then to make their own selection for publication. This would make a mockery of the law's protection of confidentiality when no justifying public interest has been shown.[14]

The kinds of arguments that have been adopted by the courts in drawing the contours of legitimate breaches of confidence may provide useful pointers when it comes to determining the extent to which and manner in which the Ordinance's public interest test in s 61 might be interpreted.[15] The scope of principle 3 is, however, less rigid than the common law since it is not primarily concerned to protect the confidentiality of relationships.

Exemptions from Access Only

Legal Professional Privilege

Section 60 provides that personal data are exempted from access 'if the data consist of information in respect of which a claim to legal professional privilege could be maintained in law'. This exemption covers both aspects of legal professional privilege, namely confidential data held by a solicitor and privilege relating to data where litigation was contemplated or pending when they were created. The former category is broader and the test is whether the communication or other document is made confidentially for the purposes of giving legal advice. This would attach not only to actual legal advice, but also to data exchanged between solicitor and client for the purposes of keeping each informed, and may extend to advice about what should be sensibly done in the relevant legal context.[16] As the privilege is enjoyed by the client – not the lawyer – this exemption cannot be invoked against the lawyer's own client.

Relevant Process

This access exemption is interim in nature and only defers access rights during certain decision-making processes. Having to respond to an access request prior to the completion or conclusion of a particular process (say, of appointment or promotion) may cause considerable disruption and inconvenience to the data user. On the other hand, permanently denying access and correction rights thereafter may prejudice not only the interests of the data subject but the integrity of the decision-making process itself.

Section 55 addresses these considerations by exempting from access personal data which are being considered for the purpose of determining the suitability, eligibility or qualifications of the data subject for:

- Employment or appointment for office;
- Promotion in employment or office or continuance in employment or office;
- Removal from employment or office;
- The granting of contracts, awards (including academic and professional qualifications), scholarships, honours or other benefits, or their continuance, modification or cancellation; and

- Whether any disciplinary action should be taken against the data subject for a breach of the terms of his employment or appointment to office.

'Employment' is defined as employment under a contract of service or of apprenticeship or a contract personally to execute any work or labour (s 2).

This exemption does not apply where no appeal 'whether under an Ordinance or otherwise', may be made against any such determination [s 55(2)(b)]. An example of a non-statutory right of appeal is that provided by the Civil Service Regulations regarding staffing decisions.

The scope of the exemption appears to have generated some misunderstanding, particularly regarding its application to employment data. It has, for instance, been suggested that it could be used to deny access during the continuance of lengthy contracts of employment on the basis that consideration of the data subject's performance throughout the contract will be relevant to the issue of renewal. This ignores the mischief which the exemption seeks to address. The Law Reform Commission recommendation on this point explains that there is a need for 'an exemption from interim access to data relating to an evaluative process which will be seriously disrupted by affording access before a decision has been made and where appeal rights exist'.[17] Moreover, the concept of a 'process' connotes a focused activity of short duration. A relevant process will often be short. As a data user has 40 days to respond to an access request, if a relevant process is under way upon receipt of the access request but is likely to cease to apply within 40 days, the data user need merely delay providing a copy of the data.

Employment Data

Prior to the Ordinance, organisations were entitled to establish their own policies governing employee access to their data. The Law Reform Commission's consultation process elicited a variety of responses on the matter, but generally speaking, organisations were fairly cautious about the prospect of making such personal data available to employees. This caution is reflected in the extensive exemptions from providing access to staff data.

Some employers adopt open reporting systems for staff data, and the Ordinance's exemption does not require that this be reversed.

As with the other exemptions, those discussed below are discretionary and afford employers considerable flexibility in responding to access requests. In addition to the cost and data quality implications of refusing access generally, in respect of employment data the impact on both morale and staff relations must be taken into account. While the nature of the data may be such that their release may be expected to damage the employee's morale, denying access may generate suspicion and mistrust. In respect of staff relations, much depends on the nature of the data in question. They may, for example, actually confirm what the subject has been told thereby enhancing trust or confidence. Or the data may, on the other hand, contradict what the assessor has directly informed the employee or may indicate obvious prejudice or partiality. Whatever the effect, the general objective of the Ordinance is plain: access should be denied only on legitimate policy grounds – not merely to avoid embarrassment for the data user or discomfort for the data subject. This is reflected by the limited scope of the exemptions relating to staff data, examined below.

We suggest that the most effective solution to problems generated by biased or needlessly tactless personal assessments is for the data user to take the initiative and amend the data before an access request is received. As pointed out in Chapter 9, until 19 December 1997 the data user may correct the data upon receipt of an access request [s 19(3)(a)(ii) and s 19(5)]. After that date, however, the data user is required to provide whatever data it holds on the data subject. Employers would therefore be well advised to regularly review their personal files and destroy doubtful assessments.

It is plainly important that employers develop coherent policies regarding their attempt to bring their activities under the umbrella of the exemptions. Their inconsistent application will become readily apparent to a data user's workforce.

In addition to the exemption regarding relevant process addressed above, the following access exemptions are relevant to employment data.

Staff planning

As with other aspects of their operations, organisations need to plan their staffing needs. Such projections will necessarily be provisional. They may range from future promotion paths to expected redundancies. Organisations may be understandably reluctant to share these projections with those employees identified as being affected. Both hopes and fears may be prematurely generated among those potentially affected.

Accordingly, s 53 provides:

> Personal data which consist of information relevant to any staff planning proposal to –
> (a) fill any series of positions of employment which are presently, or may become unfilled; or
> (b) cease any group of individuals' employment,
> are exempt from the provisions of data protection principle 6 and s 18(1)(b).

The reference to 'series of positions' and 'group of individuals' indicate that the exemption is limited to plans referring to more than one individual. Thus, integrated projections, and not unrelated predictions, are the subject of this exemption. This is explicable on the basis that in the latter case, affording access to any one individual could result in all the affected staff being tipped off; this would engender obvious difficulties for the management.

Transitional provision

Employers may be concerned that data compiled before the Ordinance came into force on 20 December 1996 may contain comments that could adversely affect staff relations for a variety of reasons. Data compiled before the Ordinance came into force will frequently have been recorded without any expectation that it would ever be seen by the data subject. Such data may be candid to the point of bluntness or likely to cause offence. An individual making an assessment of an employee may thus have good reason to wish to resist access by the subject to his evaluation of him. He may, for example, want to prevent the subject's feelings being hurt. Or he may simply wish to shield the source from possible embarrassment.

Similar considerations will, of course, extend to other classes of data compiled before the appointed date, such as credit data. The general policy of the Ordinance is that access should nevertheless be granted to the data subject, for generally speaking he has more to lose from the use of inaccurate or biased data than does the evaluator by being made unexpectedly accountable for having compiled it. Section 54 departs from this general policy to some extent and provides:

> Personal data –
> (a) held by a data user –
>   (i) immediately before the appointed day;
>   (ii) who is the employer of the data subject; and
>   (iii) relating to the employment of the data subject; and
> (b) provided by an individual on the implicit or explicit condition that the subject would not have access to the data,
>
> are exempt from the provisions of data protection principle 6 and section 18(1)(b) until the expiration of 7 years following the enactment of the Ordinance.

According to the administration, this provision was 'made to avoid the possible disruption to the staff management relationship by opening up to subject access employment-related personal data provided in confidence, such as personal assessments'.[18] The transition period would allow the sensitivity of the data to decline.

There are two limitations to this exemption. First, the data must have been compiled on the condition, whether explicit or implicit, that the subject would not have access to them. Traditionally, of course, there has been something of an assumption by record keepers that staff would not see the contents of their files, no matter how innocuous they may be. Nonetheless, a good deal of data would have been provided regardless of whether the subject would see them or not. Such data are not exempted: the statutory requirement that the data were provided on the *condition* that they not be shown to the subject goes further than the simple belief that this would be the result. The data must be such that they would not have been provided if subject access was envisaged. Factual data are unlikely to be provided on such conditions of confidentiality. The exemption is primarily aimed at subjective evaluations provided on the basis of confidentiality.

Secondly, the provision applies only to employment data held prior to the Ordinance coming into force on 20 December 1996 and which relate to an individual who remains on the staff. It accordingly lapses upon the individual ceasing employment by resignation or retirement. Nor does it apply to deny access rights as against another data user to whom the data have been transferred. These limitations reflect the policy objectives of the provision, namely that the continuing employment relationship may be damaged by revealing confidential data. Upon the termination of that relationship, or outside it, the general requirements of transparency through access prevail.

Personal references
Section 56 recognises that personal references play a unique role in personnel management. It provides an access exemption for:

> Personal data held by a data user which consist of a personal reference –
> (a) given by an individual other than in the ordinary course of his occupation; and
> (b) relevant to another individual's suitability or otherwise to fill any position of employment or office which is presently, or may become, unfilled,
>
> are exempt from the provisions of data protection principle 6 and section 18(1)(b) –
> (i) in any case, unless the individual referred to in paragraph (a) has informed the data user in writing that he has no objection to the reference being seen by the individual referred to in paragraph (b) (or words to the like effect); or
> (ii) in the case of a reference given on or after the day on which this section comes into operation, until the individual referred to in paragraph (b) has been informed in writing that he has been accepted or rejected to fill that position or office (or words to the like effect),
>
> whichever occurs first.

The words 'other than in the ordinary course of his occupation' identify a defining characteristic of a *personal* reference, namely that it is provided in a personal capacity and not on behalf of an organisation. Internal assessments are accordingly excluded from the ambit of this exemption. Nonetheless, there will be borderline cases such as where an academic regularly receives requests which he responds to during working hours. In such circumstances a useful test is whether the referee could be required by his employer to respond to requests for references. If providing the reference is at the referee's discretion it may be characterised as a personal reference.

This provision and s 54(1) are the only exemptions whose operation is determined according to whether the data were compiled before or after 20 December 1996. If they were, the exemption applies unless or until the referee consents in writing to disclosure to the data subject. If the reference was provided after that date, access may be denied only until the position has been filled and the data subject has been informed in writing that he has been accepted or rejected for the position or office in question.

General references written for an individual leaving employment are normally couched in broad terms, reciting attributes possessed and experience acquired. As it is customary for the referee to furnish the subject with a copy directly, access will not in these circumstances be an issue. In practical terms, therefore, the exemption is aimed at references furnished directly to a prospective employer concerning a specific position.

The provision therefore assumes that the employer will abide by the courtesy of informing an unsuccessful applicant of the rejection in writing. It might be argued that by failing to do so, the employer may retain the reference for future use. This, however, neglects the more general provisions of principle 2(2) and s 26(2) requiring that personal data shall not be kept longer than is necessary for the fulfilment of the purpose (including any directly related purpose) for which the data are to be used. A reference will usually have fulfilled its purpose upon the filling of the position. It should then be returned to the referee or purged. Only if the prospective employer reasonably expects that a similar vacancy will arise in the foreseeable future should he retain the reference. To this extent (ii) is otiose. An additional reason for not holding references longer than strictly necessary is provided in Chapter 3 addressing possible liability for negligent misstatement.[19]

Health Data

Personal data relating to the physical or mental health of the data subject are exempt from access where it would be likely to cause serious harm to the physical or mental health of the data subject or any other individual. 'Health' conveys that the likely harm must have lasting impact and not merely occasion a fleeting disturbance.

Whereas the previous exemptions require that data be *held* for certain purposes, the application of this exemption is solely determined by the application of the harm test.

Exemption from Principle 3 Only

Research Data

Section 62 provides an exemption from principle 3 where the data are to be used solely for preparing statistics or 'carrying out research'. The latter expression extends to non-statistical research and accommodates transfers between data users of data relating to identifiable individuals required to complete the research exercise. For example, an organisation may collect personal data such as contact details in order to service its customers. It may subsequently wish to conduct a customer satisfaction survey with a sample of those customers. To this end, it may need to transfer the contact details to a market researcher to enable it to contact those individuals to collect additional data from them through the conducting of interviews. The transfer of the contact details would be for the purpose of carrying out research.

Commissioner's Role in Reviewing Application of Exemptions

Upon being refused access on the basis of an exemption, the data subject is entitled to complain to the Commissioner who will then review whether the exemption was properly invoked. The question arises whether in reviewing a refusal to provide access, the Commissioner should restrict his attention to the exemption invoked by the data user. The New Zealand Commissioner has interpreted his role as wider than this:

> I noted that in investigating a decision to withhold information I was not bound to consider only those particular withholding provisions relied on by the agency. The Privacy Act identifies interests which it seeks to protect by enabling an agency to withhold personal information [pursuant to an exemption] where its disclosure would have certain prejudicial results. Investigating an agency's decision to withhold information will, then involve me in an assessment of the likely results of release of the information at issue. I therefore considered the complainant's file in the light of all the [exemptions].

The Ordinance, like the New Zealand *Privacy Act*, does not specifically provide that the Commissioner may consider the application of exemptions that are not invoked. Nor are we convinced that such an approach is appropriate. As mentioned above, the exemptions are not mandatory – whether a data user invokes an exemption is a discretionary exercise. Furthermore, where a data user does invoke an exemption it must identify it in a log book and advise the data subject when refusing access. Moreover, the Ordinance's exemption provisions are considerably more elaborate than those in the New Zealand legislation.

Notes

1 UK Data Protection Registrar, (1989) 5th Report, HMSO, London, p 67.

2 UK Guidelines, Third Series, November 1994, p 99.

3 New Zealand Privacy Commissioner. Case note 084W.

4 This limitation resulted from an amendment at the committee stage of the bill, which reflected concern that data users outside government should not be entitled to invoke these interests to bar access to personal data.

5 This is reflected in the common law's concern to protect sources in cases where to allow disclosure might result in sources drying up and so undermine the operation of agencies that rely on such data in order to pursue their legitimate functions. See, for instance, *D v National Society for the Prevention of Cruelty to Children* [1977] 1 All ER 589.

6 *Gartside v Outram* (1856) 26 LJ Ch 113 at p 114. Cf *Weld-Blundell v Stephens* [1919] 1 KB 520. See also *Initial Services v Putterrill* [1968] 1 QB 396 at 405.

7 *Initial Services v Putterrill* [1968] 1 QB 396 at 405-6 per Lord Denning MR.

8 [1981] AC 1096.

9 At 1169.

10 [1985] 1 QB 526.

11 At 538.

12 At 537.

13 [1988] 1 QB 526.

14 At 661. In *R v Egdell* a mental health review tribunal was considering whether the detention in a mental hospital of a schizophrenic who had killed five persons should be continued. At the request of his solicitor, the patient was examined by an independent psychiatrist who discovered that he had an obsession with firearms and explosives which predated his development of schizophrenia. This aspect of his illness had not been evident to any of the psychiatrists who were responsible for his care or who had previously reported on his condition. Having been expressly refused permission by the patient's solicitor, the independent psychiatrist sent this information to the tribunal, to a doctor in the hospital, and to the Home Office.

The Court of Appeal held that this was a permissible breach of the patient's confidence. It acknowledged that the law recognised that there was a public interest in maintaining patients' confidence (for otherwise the health of patients would suffer because they would be less willing to reveal information required by their physicians). The patient's interest was, the court said, not merely a private one. The independent psychiatrist was, it concluded, entitled to breach confidence because suppression of the material contained in his report would have deprived both the hospital and the Secretary of State of vital information directly relevant to questions of public safety.

15 For an analysis of recent developments see R Wacks (1995), *Privacy and Press Freedom*, Blackstone Press, London.

16 *Supreme Court Practice* 1997 (1996), Sweet & Maxwell, London, Vol 1 Part 1, pp 431-2.

17 The Law Reform Commission of Hong Kong (1994) *Reform of the Law Relating to the Protection of Personal Data* (Topic 27), p184.

18 Bills Committee to study the Personal Data (Privacy) Bill, note of 1st meeting, p 7.

19 See *Spring v Guardian Assurance* [1995] 2 AC 296.

13 Offences and Compensation

Offences

While, under s 65, a company may be vicariously liable for the acts of its employees, sub-section (4) specifies that such liability applies only to civil – not criminal – liability. Accordingly, it is necessary to establish the scope of criminal liability under the Ordinance by reference to its other provisions and the relevant provisions of the *Criminal Procedure Ordinance*.

The *Personal Data (Privacy) Ordinance* distinguishes between 'persons' and 'data users', and expressly imposes direct liability on data users for most of the offences specified in s 64, namely:

- Supplying false information in relation to a data user return [sub-s (1)];
- Supplying false information in relation to a matching procedure [sub-s (4)];
- Contravening a matching requirement [sub-s (5)];
- Contravening an enforcement notice [sub-s (7)]; and
- Contravening any other provision of the Ordinance [sub-s (10)].

On the other hand, the other offence provisions in s 64 apply to a 'person', namely one who:

- Supplies false information in relation to a data access request [sub-s (2)];
- Supplies false information regarding deletion from the register where that person has ceased to be a data user [sub-s (3)]; and
- Obstructs, hinders or fails to comply with the Commissioner's requirements in relation to an inspection or investigation, or makes a false statement which he knows to be false [sub-s (9)].[1]

'Person' is defined by the *Interpretation and General Clauses Ordinance* as including 'any public body, any body of persons, corporate or unincorporate' including where 'person' occurs in a provision creating an offence. The Ordinance's reference to 'a person' rather than 'the data user' for these offences is explicable by their subject matter: they pertain more to situations where personal liability is contemplated and encompass data subjects sub-s (2) as well as employees of data users sub-s (9).

By way of contrast, the offences which specify the 'data user' are more likely to address the offences of 'strict liability' which are characteristic of regulatory legislation generally. Strict liability offences (unlike, for example, making a knowingly false statement) do not require proof of a mental element (*mens rea* or 'guilty mind'). The law recognises that requiring proof of such a mental element on the part of a company would in most cases render a successful prosecution impossible.

The above offences must also be considered in conjunction with the relevant provisions of the *Criminal Procedure Ordinance*:

- Section 101E provides that where a person by whom a statutory offence has been committed by a company (this would include both a 'person' or a 'data user' under the Ordinance) and it is proved that the offence was committed with the 'consent or connivance' of a director or other officer concerned in the management of the company, that director/officer is personally liable. This provision codifies the common law recognition that individuals may play a role such that they may be viewed as part of the directing mind of the company; and
- Section 89 provides that any person who aids, abets, counsels or procures the commission of an office is similarly liable.

The effect of these provisions is that individuals may be prosecuted not only for the offences which refer to 'persons' but also for those that refer to 'the data user'.

The offence provisions specify various levels of fines and these are currently as follows:

Levels	Fines
Level 1	\$1-\$2,000
Level 2	\$2,001-\$5,000
Level 3	\$5,001-\$10,000
Level 4	\$10,001-\$25,000
Level 5	\$25,001-\$50,000
Level 6	\$50,001-\$100,000

Compensation

Section 66 of the Ordinance provides that an individual who suffers damage by reason of a contravention of a requirement of the Ordinance by a data user which relates, wholly or partly, to personal data of which that individual is the subject, shall be entitled to compensation from the data user for that damage. Such damage may be or include injury to feelings.

Sub-section (3) provides two defences. First, that the data user has taken reasonable care to avoid the contravention concerned. Secondly, that where the contravention relates to inaccurate data, that the data accurately record data received or obtained by the data user concerned from the data subject or from a third party. In the case of inaccurate data, sub-s (4) declares that no compensation may be obtained in respect of that part of the damage that occurred within the first year of the operation of the section (ie until 20 December 1997).

It is to be noted therefore that the section provides relief only where the data subject has failed to exercise 'such care as in all the circumstances was reasonably required to avoid the contravention concerned'. It will thus be open to a data user to show that, in the context of the particular collection, use or transfer of the personal data, he acted reasonably. Similarly, a data user who has collected personal data either directly from the data subject or from a third party, will avoid liability if such data were received in this inaccurate form.

Injury to Feelings

A data subject who suffers damage as a result of a contravention of the Ordinance by a data user which relates to the data subject's personal data may be able to recover damages for his injured feelings. Where, for example, sensitive medical information is transferred without the data subject's consent, negligently or intentionally, to a third party, it is not unlikely that the feelings of the data subject may be injured. To this extent, the Ordinance represents a recognition of the individual's right to or interest in 'privacy' as a feature of one's '[t]houghts, emotions and sensations'[2] the violation of which may occasion 'mental pain and distress, far greater than could be inflicted by mere bodily injury'.[3]

The common law acknowledges that, both in contract[4] and tort[5], insult and injured feelings warrant compensation. And statutory declarations of this right, such as in s 66(2) of the Ordinance,[6] merely restate the common law position.

In determining the appropriate principles to be applied in order to arrive at suitable quantum, the court may look to decisions in which injured feelings have attracted damages at common law or under statutes such as the anti-discrimination legislation in Britain.

In the former category, the courts have long recognised that damages might include compensation for non-pecuniary loss. The tools of measurement are admittedly blunt, but a combination of experience and relativity seems to be the guiding principle.[7] So, in Hong Kong, damages for injured feelings have been awarded where the plaintiff has been defamed[8], suffered injury through negligence[9] or assault,[10] or where Vietnamese refugee seekers had been falsely imprisoned.[11]

In the latter case of statutory awards, the courts in Britain have been disposed to grant modest awards to victims of discrimination.[12]

It is unlikely that our courts will wish to display excessive generosity under this head of damages.

Liability of Employers and Principals

Section 65 of the Ordinance lays down the general rule of vicarious liability: that employers are generally liable for the acts of their employees, principals for the acts of their agents, committed in the course of their employment,[13] whether or not the employer or principal are themselves negligent or, in the words of s 65(1), in the case of an employer, 'whether or not it was done or engaged in with the employer's knowledge or approval'.

A wrongful act by an employee is deemed to be within the scope of his employment if it is either a wrongful act authorised by the employer, or a wrongful and unauthorised mode of doing an act authorised by his employer.[14] This will be a matter of fact to be determined in each case. The net of vicarious liability is cast fairly widely, and it is no defence at common law for an employer to show that he expressly prohibited the wrongful act in question, if the act was merely a mode of carrying out the employee's duties.[15]

Nevertheless, sub-s (3) provides a defence for an employer who can prove that he took such steps as were practicable to prevent the employee from doing the act or engaging in the practice in question, or from doing or engaging in, in the course of his employment, acts or practices of that description. This would appear to modify the common law distinction between prohibitions that limit the sphere of employment, on the one hand, and those which relate to specific conduct within that sphere. The common law rule is that only where an employee contravenes a prohibition of the latter kind, will his employer be liable for his negligent acts. A contravention of the former type places the employee outside the scope or sphere of his employment.[16] Sub-section (3) seems to place both kinds of prohibitions on the same footing, and to afford the employer a defence even in circumstances in which the employee acts in a prohibited manner within the course of his employment.

Much will presumably depend on the nature of the data user's work. In some cases an admonition by an employer to his employee, or a principal to his agent, to comply with the terms of the Ordinance, will necessarily be of a fairly general kind. It is difficult to imagine, for example, a bank employee being totally prohibited from dealing with personal data. Hence the scope of his employment is likely to be sufficiently wide to result in the employer being held liable for breaches of the Ordinance on a fairly large scale. Hence perhaps the need for a wider defence. Employers will nevertheless wish to ensure that sub-s (4) provides that s 65 does not apply in cases of any criminal proceedings under the Ordinance.

Notes

1 There is, in addition, the offence (not strictly relevant in the present context) of disclosing the identity of an informant or failing to maintain secrecy provisions (6). It relates primarily to the Office of the Privacy Commissioner.

2 Warren and Brandeis, "The Right to Privacy" (1890) 4 *Harvard Law Review* 193, 195.

3 *Ibid*, at 196.

4 See *Jackson v Horizon Holidays Ltd* [1975] 1 WLR 1468, *Jarvis v Swan Tours Ltd* [1973] QB 233, *Bliss v South East Thames Regional Health Authority* [1987] ICR 700, *Hardwick v Spence Robinson* [1975] HKLR 425. See S Nossal (1996) 'Recovery in Contract of Damages for Mental Distress' 26 HKLJ 162.

5 *Wilkinson v Downton* [1897] 2 QB 57. For a discussion of compensation for injured feelings in Hong Kong, see, for example, *Wong Melvin v Jockey Daily News Ltd* [1985] 2 HKC 528 (defamation), *Wong Kwai Fun v Li Fung* [1994] 1 HKC 549 (threats of violence), *Attorney General v Yiu Yun* [1990] 2 HKC 238 (negligence), *Kahn Mohammed Yaqub v Attorney General* [1983] 2 HKC 186 (corruption), and *Kan Chung Nin Tony v Li Kwong Ming* [1987] 1 HKC 487 (defamation).

6 The identical provision appears in Section 76(6) of the *Sex Discrimination Ordinance* and Section 72(5) of the *Disability Discrimination Ordinance*.

7 See for example, Lord Diplock's analysis in *Wright v British Railways Board* [1983] 2 AC 773, and Lord Halsbury's judgment in *The Mediana* [1900] AC 113, especially at 116.

8 See for example, *Cheung Ng Sheong Steven v Eastweek Publisher Ltd* [1995] 3 HKC 601; *Wong Melvin v Jockey Daily News Ltd* [1985] 2 HKC 528. See generally P Rhodes, 'Damages for Defamation in Hong Kong' (1981) 11 HKLJ 167.

9 See for example, *Attorney General v Yiu Yun* [1990] 2 HKC 239.

10 See for example, *Wong Kwai Fun v Li Fung* [1994] 1 HKC 549.

11 *Pham Van Ngo v Attorney General* [1993] HKLY 468; HCA No A4895 of 1990.

12 See for example, *Murray v Powertech (Scotland) Ltd* [1992] IRLR 257; *Ministry of Defence v Sullivan* [1994] ICR 193; *Ministry of Defence v Mutton* [1996] ICR 590.

13 Section 2 defines 'employment' as employment under (a) 'a contract of service or of apprenticeship, or (b) a contract personally to execute any work or labour'.

14 *Warren v Henlys Ltd* [1948] 2 All ER 935 at 937; *Ilkiw v Samuels* [1963] 1 WLR 991 at 997, 1002 and 1004.

15 *London County Council v Cattermoles (Garages) Ltd* [1953] 1 WLR 997 at 1005; *Limpus v London General Omnibus Co* [1862] 1 H&C 526; 1158 ER 993 *Fung Lo Sze v Fan Shuk Ching* (1986) unrep, Civ App No 119 of 1986.

16 *Plumb v Cobden Flour Mills Co Ltd* [1914] AC 62. Compare *Twine v Bean's Express Ltd* [1946] 1 All ER 202 and *Iqbal v London Transport Executive* (1974) 16 KIR 329 *R v Secretary of State for the Home Department ex parte Iqbal* [1979] 1 All ER 675, affirmed [1979] 1 All ER 685.

Appendix

Personal Data (Privacy) Ordinance

CHAPTER 486

PERSONAL DATA (PRIVACY)

An Ordinance to protect the privacy of individuals in relation to personal data, and to provide for matters incidental thereto or connected therewith.

[ ]

PART I

PRELIMINARY

1. Short title and commencement

(1) This Ordinance may be cited as the Personal Data (Privacy) Ordinance.

(2) This Ordinance shall come into operation on a day to be appointed by the Secretary for Home Affairs by notice in the Gazette.

2. Interpretation

(1) In this Ordinance, unless the context otherwise requires—

"act" (作為) includes a deliberate omission;

"adverse action" (不利行動), in relation to an individual, means any action that may adversely affect the individual's rights, benefits, privileges, obligations or interests (including legitimate expectations);

"appointed day" (指定日) means the day appointed under section 1(2);

"approved code of practice" (核准實務守則) means a code of practice approved under section 12;

"code of practice" (實務守則) includes—

(*a*) a standard;

(*b*) a specification; and

(*c*) any other documentary form of practical guidance;

"Commissioner" (專員) means the Privacy Commissioner for Personal Data established under section 5(1);

"Committee" (諮詢委員會) means the Personal Data (Privacy) Advisory Committee established under section 11(1);

"complainant" (投訴人) means the individual, or the relevant person on behalf of an individual, who has made a complaint;

"complaint" (投訴) means a complaint under section 37;

"correction" (改正), in relation to personal data, means rectification, erasure or completion;

"daily penalty" (每日罰款) means a penalty for each day on which the offence is continued after conviction therefor;

"data" (資料) means any representation of information (including an expression of opinion) in any document, and includes a personal identifier;

"data access request" (查閱資料要求) means a request under section 18;

"data correction request" (改正資料要求) means a request under section 22(1);

"data protection principle" (保障資料原則) means any of the data protection principles set out in Schedule 1;

"data subject" (資料當事人), in relation to personal data, means the individual who is the subject of the data;

"data user" (資料使用者), in relation to personal data, means a person who, either alone or jointly or in common with other persons, controls the collection, holding, processing or use of the data;

"data user return" (資料使用者申報表) means a data user return referred to in section 14(4);

"disclosing" (披露), in relation to personal data, includes disclosing information inferred from the data;

"document" (文件) includes, in addition to a document in writing—

(*a*) a disc, tape or other device in which data other than visual images are embodied so as to be capable, with or without the aid of some other equipment, of being reproduced from the disc, tape or other device; and

(*b*) a film, tape or other device in which visual images are embodied so as to be capable, with or without the aid of some other equipment, of being reproduced from the film, tape or other device;

"employment" (僱用) means employment under—

(*a*) a contract of service or of apprenticeship; or

(*b*) a contract personally to execute any work or labour,

and related expressions shall be construed accordingly;

"enforcement notice" (執行通知) means a notice under section 50(1);

"financial regulator" (財經規管者) means any of—

(*a*) the Monetary Authority appointed under section 5A of the Exchange Fund Ordinance (Cap. 66);

(*b*) the Securities and Futures Commission established by section 3 of the Securities and Futures Commission Ordinance (Cap. 24);

(*c*) a clearing house within the meaning of section 2(1) of the Commodities Trading Ordinance (Cap. 250) or a recognized clearing house within the meaning of the Securities and Futures (Clearing Houses) Ordinance (Cap. 420);

(*d*) the Exchange Company within the meaning of section 2(1) of the Commodities Trading Ordinance (Cap. 250);

(*e*) the Exchange Company within the meaning of section 2(1) of the Stock Exchanges Unification Ordinance (Cap. 361);

(*f*) the Insurance Authority appointed under section 4 of the Insurance Companies Ordinance (Cap. 41);

(*g*) the Registrar of Occupational Retirement Schemes appointed under section 5 of the Occupational Retirement Schemes Ordinance (Cap. 426);

(*h*) a person specified in a notice under subsection (7) to be a regulator for the purposes of this definition;

"inaccurate" (不準確), in relation to personal data, means the data is incorrect, misleading, incomplete or obsolete;

"inspection" (視察) means an inspection under section 36;

"investigation" (調查) means an investigation under section 38;

"log book" (紀錄簿), in relation to a data user, means the log book kept and maintained by the data user under section 27(1);

"matching procedure" (核對程序) means any procedure whereby personal data collected for 1 or more purposes in respect of 10 or more data subjects are compared (except by manual means) with personal data collected for any other purpose in respect of those data subjects where the comparison—

(*a*) is (whether in whole or in part) for the purpose of producing or verifying data that; or

(*b*) produces or verifies data in respect of which it is reasonable to believe that it is practicable that the data,

may be used (whether immediately or at any subsequent time) for the purpose of taking adverse action against any of those data subjects;

"matching procedure request" (核對程序要求) means a request under section 31(1);

"personal data" (個人資料) means any data—

(*a*) relating directly or indirectly to a living individual;

(*b*) from which it is practicable for the identity of the individual to be directly or indirectly ascertained; and (*c*) in a form in which access to or processing of the data is practicable;

"personal data system" (個人資料系統) means any system, whether or not automated, which is used, whether in whole or in part, by a data user for the collection, holding, processing or use of personal data, and includes any document and equipment forming part of the system;

"personal identifier" (個人身分標識符) means an identifier—

(*a*) that is assigned to an individual by a data user for the purpose of the operations of the user; and

(*b*) that uniquely identifies that individual in relation to the data user,

but does not include an individual's name used to identify that individual;

"practicable" (切實可行) means reasonably practicable;

"prescribed officer" (訂明人員) means a person employed or engaged under section 9(1);

"processing" (處理), in relation to personal data, includes amending, augmenting, deleting or rearranging the data, whether by automated means or otherwise;

"register" (登記冊) means the register of data users kept and maintained by the Commissioner under section 15(1);

"relevant data user" (有關資料使用者), in relation to—

(*a*) an inspection, means the data user who uses the personal data system which is the subject of the inspection;

(*b*) a complaint, means the data user specified in the complaint;

(*c*) an investigation—

(i) in the case of an investigation initiated by a complaint, means the data user specified in the complaint;

(ii) in any other case, means the data user the subject of the investigation;

(*d*) an enforcement notice, means the data user on whom the notice is served;

"relevant person" (有關人士), in relation to an individual (howsoever the individual is described), means—

(*a*) where the individual is a minor, a person who has parental responsibility for the minor;

(*b*) where the individual is incapable of managing his own affairs, a person who has been appointed by a court to manage those affairs;

(*c*) in any other case, a person authorized in writing by the individual to make a data access request, a data correction request, or both such requests, on behalf of the individual;

"requestor" (提出要求者), in relation to—

(*a*) a data access request or data correction request, means the individual, or the relevant person on behalf of an individual, who has made the request;
(*b*) a matching procedure request, means the data user who has made the request;

"specified" (指明), in relation to a form, means specified under section 67;
"third party" (第三者), in relation to personal data, means any person other than—
(*a*) the data subject;
(*b*) a relevant person in the case of the data subject;
(*c*) the data user; or
(*d*) a person authorized in writing by the data user to collect, hold, process or use the data—
(i) under the direct control of the data user; or
(ii) on behalf of the data user;

"use" (使用), in relation to personal data, includes disclose or transfer the data;
"would be likely to prejudice" (相當可能損害) includes would prejudice.

(2) For the avoidance of doubt, it is hereby declared that paragraph (*c*) of the definition of "relevant person" shall not be construed—
(*a*) to entitle a person who has only been authorized to make a data access request on behalf of an individual to make a data correction request on behalf of the individual;
(*b*) to entitle a person who has only been authorized to make a data correction request on behalf of an individual to make a data access request on behalf of the individual.

(3) Where under this Ordinance an act may be done with the prescribed consent of a person (and howsoever the person is described), such consent—
(*a*) means the express consent of the person given voluntarily;
(*b*) does not include any consent which has been withdrawn by notice in writing served on the person to whom the consent has been given (but without prejudice to so much of that act that has been done pursuant to the consent at any time before the notice is so served).

(4) Subject to section 64(10), it is hereby declared that any reference in this Ordinance to the effect that a data user (howsoever described)—
(*a*) has contravened a requirement under this Ordinance; or
(*b*) is contravening a requirement under this Ordinance,

includes—
(i) where paragraph (*a*) is applicable, any case where the data user has done an act, or engaged in a practice, in contravention of a data protection principle;
(ii) where paragraph (*b*) is applicable, any case where the data user is doing an act, or engaging in a practice, in contravention of a data protection principle.

(5) Notwithstanding any other provisions of this Ordinance, a complaint may be made (and an investigation, if any, initiated by the complaint may be carried out) in relation to a person who has ceased to be a data user except any such person who has not at any time been a data user during the period of 2 years immediately preceding the date on which the Commissioner receives the complaint and, accordingly, a person in relation to whom such a complaint is made shall for the purposes of such complaint (and an investigation, if any, initiated by such complaint) be deemed to be a data user, and the other provisions of this Ordinance shall be construed accordingly.

(6) Any reference in this Ordinance to a data protection principle followed by a number is a reference to the principle bearing that number set out in Schedule 1.

(7) The Governor may, by notice in the Gazette, specify a person to be a regulator for the purposes of the definition of "financial regulator".

(8) It is hereby declared that a notice under subsection (7) is subsidiary legislation.

(9) Where a person—

(*a*) holds any office, engages in any profession or carries on any occupation; and

(*b*) is required by any law, or by any rules made under or by virtue of any law, to be a fit and proper person (or words to the like effect) to hold that office, engage in that profession or carry on that occupation,

then, for the purposes of this Ordinance, any conduct by that person by virtue of which he ceases, or would cease, to be such a fit and proper person shall be deemed to be seriously improper conduct.

(10) Subsection (9) shall not operate to prevent seriously improper conduct including, for the purposes of this Ordinance, conduct by virtue of which a person ceases, or would cease, to be a fit and proper person notwithstanding that the conduct is not conduct to which that subsection applies.

(11) Words and expressions importing the neuter gender in relation to any data user shall include the masculine and feminine genders.

(12) A person is not a data user in relation to any personal data which the person holds, processes or uses solely on behalf of another person if, but only if, that first-mentioned person does not hold, process or use, as the case may be, those data for any of his own purposes.

(13) For the avoidance of doubt, it is hereby declared that, for the purposes of this Ordinance, any conduct by a person by virtue of which he has or could become a disqualified person or a suspended person under the Rules of Racing and Instructions by the Stewards of the Royal Hong Kong Jockey Club, as in force from time to time, is seriously improper conduct.

3. Application

(1) This Ordinance binds the Government.

(2) Where there is any conflict or inconsistency between the provisions of this Ordinance and the provisions of any other Ordinance, then the provisions of this Ordinance shall, to the extent of that conflict or inconsistency, as the case may be, prevail over the provisions of that Ordinance.

4. Data protection principles

A data user shall not do an act, or engage in a practice, that contravenes a data protection principle unless the act or practice, as the case may be, is required or permitted under this Ordinance.

PART II

ADMINISTRATION

5. Establishment, etc. of Privacy Commissioner for Personal Data

(1) For the purposes of this Ordinance, there is hereby established an office by the name of the Privacy Commissioner for Personal Data.

(2) The Commissioner shall be a corporation sole with perpetual succession and—

- (*a*) shall have and may use a seal; and
- (*b*) shall be capable of suing and being sued.

(3) The Governor shall, by notice in the Gazette, appoint a person to be the Commissioner.

(4) Subject to subsection (5), the person appointed to be the Commissioner shall hold office for a period of 5 years and shall be eligible for reappointment for not more than 1 further period of 5 years.

(5) The person appointed to be the Commissioner may—

- (*a*) at any time resign from his office by notice in writing to the Governor; or
- (*b*) be removed from office by the Governor with the approval by resolution of the Legislative Council on the ground of—
  - (i) inability to perform the functions of his office; or
  - (ii) misbehaviour.

(6) The Governor shall determine—

- (*a*) the emoluments; and
- (*b*) the terms and conditions of appointment,

of the person appointed to be the Commissioner.

(7) The provisions of Schedule 2 shall have effect with respect to the Commissioner.

(8) Subject to subsection (9), the Commissioner shall not be regarded as a servant or agent of the Government or as enjoying any status, immunity or privilege of the Government.

(9) The person appointed to be the Commissioner shall be deemed to be a public servant—

(*a*) within the meaning of section 2 of the Prevention of Bribery Ordinance (Cap. 201); and

(*b*) for the purposes of that Ordinance.

6. Commissioner to hold no other office

The person appointed to be the Commissioner shall not, without the specific approval of the Governor—

(*a*) hold any office of profit other than his office as Commissioner; or

(*b*) engage in any occupation for reward outside the functions of his office.

7. Filling of temporary vacancy

(1) Where the person appointed to be the Commissioner—

(*a*) dies;

(*b*) resigns;

(*c*) is removed from office;

(*d*) is absent from Hong Kong; or

(*e*) is for any other reason unable to perform the functions of his office,

then the Governor may, by notice in writing, appoint a person to act as the Commissioner until, as the case requires—

(i) a new Commissioner is appointed under section 5(3); or

(ii) the Commissioner resumes his office.

(2) A person appointed under subsection (1) to act as the Commissioner, whilst he is so appointed—

(*a*) shall perform the functions; and

(*b*) may exercise the powers,

of the Commissioner under this Ordinance.

(3) Section 6 shall apply to a person appointed under subsection (1) to act as the Commissioner as if that person were the Commissioner.

8. Functions and powers of Commissioner

(1) The Commissioner shall—

(*a*) monitor and supervise compliance with the provisions of this Ordinance;

(*b*) promote and assist bodies representing data users to prepare, for the purposes of section 12, codes of practice for guidance in complying with the provisions of this Ordinance, in particular the data protection principles;

(*c*) promote awareness and understanding of, and compliance with, the provisions of this Ordinance, in particular the data protection principles;

(*d*) examine any proposed legislation (including subsidiary legislation) that the Commissioner considers may affect the privacy of individuals in relation to personal data and report the results of the examination to the person proposing the legislation;

(*e*) carry out inspections, including inspections of any personal data systems used by data users which are departments of the Government or statutory corporations;

(*f*) for the better performance of his other functions, undertake research into, and monitor developments in, the processing of data and computer technology in order to take account of any likely adverse effects such developments may have on the privacy of individuals in relation to personal data;

(*g*) liaise and co-operate with any person in any place outside Hong Kong—

(i) performing in that place any functions which, in the opinion of the Commissioner, are similar (whether in whole or in part) to any of the Commissioner's functions under this Ordinance; and

(ii) in respect of matters of mutual interest concerning the privacy of individuals in relation to personal data; and

(*h*) perform such other functions as are imposed on him under this Ordinance or any other enactment.

(2) The Commissioner may do all such things as are necessary for, or incidental or conducive to, the better performance of his functions and in particular but without prejudice to the generality of the foregoing, may—

(*a*) acquire and hold property of any description if in the opinion of the Commissioner such property is necessary for—

(i) the accommodation of the Commissioner or of any prescribed officer; or

(ii) the performance of any function which the Commissioner may perform, and, subject to the terms and conditions upon which such property is held, dispose of it;

(*b*) enter into, carry out, assign or accept the assignment of, vary or rescind, any contract, agreement or other obligation;

(*c*) undertake and execute any lawful trust which has as an object the furtherance of any function which the Commissioner is required or is permitted by this Ordinance to perform or any other similar object;

(*d*) accept gifts and donations, whether subject to any trust or not;

(*e*) with the prior approval of the Governor, become a member of or affiliate to any international body concerned with (whether in whole or in part) the privacy of individuals in relation to personal data;

(*f*) exercise such other powers as are conferred on him under this Ordinance or any other enactment.

(3) The Commissioner may make and execute any document in the performance of his functions or the exercise of his powers or in connection with any matter reasonably incidental to or consequential upon the performance of his functions or the exercise of his powers.

(4) Any document purporting to be executed under the seal of the Commissioner shall be admitted in evidence and shall, in the absence of evidence to the contrary, be deemed to have been duly executed.

(5) The Commissioner may from time to time cause to be prepared and published by notice in the Gazette, for the guidance of data users, guidelines not inconsistent with this Ordinance, indicating the manner in which he proposes to perform any of his functions, or exercise any of his powers, under this Ordinance.

9. Staff of Commissioner, etc.

(1) The Commissioner may—

(*a*) employ such persons (including technical and professional persons); and

(*b*) engage, other than by way of employment, such technical and professional persons,

as he thinks fit to assist him in the performance of his functions, and the exercise of his powers, under this Ordinance.

(2) The Commissioner shall determine—

(*a*) the remuneration and terms and conditions of employment of any person, or any person belonging to a class of persons, who may be employed under subsection (1)(*a*);

(*b*) the remuneration and terms and conditions of engagement of any person, or any person belonging to a class of persons, who may be engaged under subsection (1)(*b*).

(3) The Commissioner may—
- (*a*) grant, or make provision for the grant of, pensions, gratuities and retirement benefits to employees;
- (*b*) provide other benefits for the welfare of employees and their dependants;
- (*c*) authorize payments, whether or not legally due, to the personal representatives of a deceased employee or to any person who was dependent on such employee at his death.

(4) The Commissioner may—
- (*a*) establish, manage and control; or
- (*b*) enter into an arrangement with any company or association for the establishment, management and control by that company or association either alone or jointly with the Commissioner of,

any fund or scheme for the purpose of providing for the pensions, gratuities, benefits and payments referred to in subsection (3).

(5) The Commissioner may make contributions to and may require employees to make contributions to any fund or scheme referred to in subsection (4).

(6) In this section "employees" (僱員) includes any class of employee which the Commissioner specifies and in subsection (3) includes former employees.

10. Delegations by Commissioner

(1) Subject to subsection (2), the Commissioner may delegate in writing any of his functions or powers under this Ordinance to any prescribed officer subject to such terms and conditions, if any, as he thinks fit and specified in the delegation.

(2) The Commissioner shall not delegate any of his functions or powers under—
- (*a*) subsection (1);
- (*b*) any provisions of any regulations made under this Ordinance which are specified in the regulations as provisions which shall not be subject to subsection (1);
- (*c*) any provisions of Schedule 2 which are specified in that Schedule as provisions which shall not be subject to subsection (1).

(3) A delegate of the Commissioner—
- (*a*) shall perform the delegated functions and may exercise the delegated powers as if the delegate were the Commissioner; and
- (*b*) shall be presumed to be acting in accordance with the relevant delegation in the absence of evidence to the contrary.

11. Establishment of Personal Data (Privacy) Advisory Committee

(1) There is hereby established a committee by the name of the Personal Data (Privacy) Advisory Committee for the purpose of advising the Commissioner upon any matter relevant to the privacy of individuals in relation to personal data or otherwise relevant to the operation of this Ordinance.

(2) The Committee shall consist of—

(*a*) the Commissioner, who shall be the chairman; and

(*b*) not less than 4 or more than 8 other persons, appointed by the Secretary for Home Affairs, of whom—

(i) not less than 1 shall have not less than 5 years' experience in the processing of data; and

(ii) not more than 1 shall be a public officer.

(3) The members of the Committee appointed under subsection (2)(*b*) shall hold office for such period and upon such terms as the Secretary for Home Affairs specifies in their respective appointments or from time to time.

(4) A member of the Committee appointed under subsection (2)(*b*) may resign at any time by notice in writing delivered to the Secretary for Home Affairs.

(5) The Committee may regulate its procedure.

PART III

CODES OF PRACTICE

12. Approval of codes of practice by Commissioner

(1) Subject to subsections (8) and (9), for the purpose of providing practical guidance in respect of any requirements under this Ordinance imposed on data users, the Commissioner may—

(*a*) approve and issue such codes of practice (whether prepared by him or not) as in his opinion are suitable for that purpose; and

(*b*) approve such codes of practice issued or proposed to be issued otherwise than by him as in his opinion are suitable for that purpose.

(2) Where a code of practice is approved under subsection (1), the Commissioner shall, by notice in the Gazette—

(*a*) identify the code concerned and specify the date on which its approval is to take effect; and

(*b*) specify for which of the requirements under this Ordinance the code is so approved.

(3) The Commissioner may—

(*a*) from time to time revise the whole or any part of any code of practice prepared by him under this section; and

(*b*) approve any revision or proposed revision of the whole or any part of any code of practice for the time being approved under this section,

and the provisions of subsection (2) shall, with the necessary modifications, apply in relation to the approval of any revision under this subsection as they apply in relation to the approval of a code of practice under subsection (1).

(4) The Commissioner may at any time withdraw his approval from any code of practice approved under this section.

(5) Where under subsection (4) the Commissioner withdraws his approval from a code of practice approved under this section, he shall, by notice in the Gazette, identify the code concerned and specify the date on which his approval of it is to cease to have effect.

(6) References in this Ordinance to an approved code of practice are references to that code as it has effect for the time being by virtue of any revision of the whole or any part of it approved under this section.

(7) The power of the Commissioner under subsection (1)(*b*) to approve a code of practice issued or proposed to be issued otherwise than by him shall include power to approve a part of such a code and, accordingly, in this Ordinance "code of practice" (實務守則) may be read as including a part of such a code.

(8) The Commissioner shall, not later than 6 months after the day on which this section comes into operation (or within such further period, not exceeding 6 months, as the Secretary for Home Affairs may allow), approve a code of practice under subsection (1) in respect of all or any requirements referred to in that subsection in so far as such requirements relate to personal data which are personal identifiers.

(9) The Commissioner shall, before approving a code of practice under subsection (1) or any revision or proposed revision of the code under subsection (3), consult with—

(*a*) such bodies representative of data users to which the code or the code as so revised, as the case may be, will apply (whether in whole or in part); and

(*b*) such other interested persons,

as he thinks fit.

(10) For the avoidance of doubt, it is hereby declared that different codes of practice may be approved under subsection (1) (including any code of practice referred to in subsection (8)) for different classes of data users, and may be so approved for the same or different requirements referred to in subsection (1).

13. Use of approved codes of practice in proceedings under this Ordinance

(1) A failure on the part of any data user to observe any provision of an approved code of practice shall not of itself render the data user liable to any civil or criminal proceedings but where in any proceedings under this Ordinance a data user is alleged to have contravened a requirement under this Ordinance, being a requirement for which there was an approved code of practice at the time of the alleged contravention, subsection (2) shall have effect with respect to such code in relation to those proceedings.

(2) Any provision of a code of practice which appears to a specified body to be relevant to a requirement under this Ordinance alleged to have been contravened shall be admissible in evidence in the proceedings under this Ordinance concerned and if it is proved that there was at any material time a failure to observe any provision of the code which appears to that body to be relevant to any matter which it is necessary to prove in order to establish a contravention of such requirement, that matter shall be taken as proved in the absence of evidence that such requirement was in respect of that matter complied with otherwise than by way of observance of that provision.

(3) In any proceedings under this Ordinance, a code of practice which appears to a specified body to be the subject of a notice under section 12 shall be taken to be the subject of such notice in the absence of evidence to the contrary.

(4) In this section—

"proceedings under this Ordinance" (根據本條例進行的法律程序) includes any criminal proceedings where a data user is alleged to have committed an offence by reason of a contravention of a requirement under this Ordinance;

"specified body" (指明當局) means—

(*a*) a magistrate;
(*b*) a court; or
(*c*) the Administrative Appeals Board.

PART IV

DATA USER RETURNS AND REGISTER OF DATA USERS

14. Data user returns

(1) Subject to subsection (2), the Commissioner may, by notice in the Gazette, specify a class of data users to which this section shall apply.

(2) The Commissioner shall, before specifying a class of data users in a notice under subsection (1), consult with—

(*a*) such bodies representative of data users belonging to that class; and

(*b*) such other interested persons,

as he thinks fit.

(3) This section shall not apply to a data user except a data user belonging to a class of data users specified in a notice under subsection (1) which is in force.

(4) A data user shall submit to the Commissioner a data user return—

(*a*) in the specified form;

(*b*) containing the prescribed information required by the return in relation to the data user;

(*c*) in the case of—

(i) a data user which belongs to the class of data users concerned on the day on which the notice under subsection (1) specifying that class commences, not earlier than 3 months before, and not later than, each anniversary of that day;

(ii) a data user which first belongs to the class of data users concerned on a day after the day on which the notice under subsection (1) specifying that class commences, not earlier than 3 months before, and not later than, each anniversary of that first-mentioned day; and

(*d*) accompanied by the prescribed fee.

(5) The Commissioner shall cause a notice to be published not less than once during every period of 6 months—

(*a*) in—

(i) the Gazette; and

(ii) not less than 1 Chinese language newspaper (and in the Chinese language) and not less than 1 English language newspaper (and in the English language), each of which shall be a newspaper circulating generally in Hong Kong; and

(*b*) subject to subsection (6), specifying the places at which and the hours during which data user returns are available to be obtained by data users for the purposes of this section.

(6) The Commissioner shall not exercise his power under subsection (5)(*b*) to specify places which are Government offices unless and until he has the approval in writing of the Secretary for Home Affairs to do so.

(7) The Commissioner shall cause data user returns to be available to be obtained by data users—

(*a*) free of charge; and

(*b*) at the places and during the hours specified in the last notice published under subsection (5).

(8) Where any prescribed information contained in a data user return submitted under subsection (4) to the Commissioner by a data user changes subsequent to the submission, then the data user shall serve a notice in writing on the Commissioner specifying such change—

(*a*) if, but only if—

(i) such information is specified in the return as information to which this subsection applies; and

(ii) the return contains, or has annexed to it—

(A) a copy of this subsection; or

(B) a statement summarizing the requirement imposed by this subsection on the data user; and

(*b*) not later than 30 days after such change.

(9) It is hereby declared that—

(*a*) a notice under subsection (1) is subsidiary legislation;

(*b*) where a data user belongs to 2 or more classes of data users specified in 2 or more notices under subsection (1) which are in force, then, for the purposes of this section, that data user shall be deemed to belong only to that class of data users specified in the first of those notices to be published in the Gazette; and

(*c*) subsection (3) shall not operate to prejudice the generality of section 67(4)(*c*).

(10) In this section and section 15, "prescribed information" (訂明資訊) means any information specified in Schedule 3.

15. Register of data users

(1) The Commissioner shall use—

(*a*) data user returns submitted to him under section 14(4); and

(*b*) any notices served on him under section 14(8),

to keep and maintain a register of data users which have submitted such returns.

(2) The register shall—

(*a*) be in the form of a database; and

(*b*) contain, in respect of each data user who has submitted a data user return under section 14(4), such particulars of the information supplied in that return as the Commissioner thinks fit.

(3) The Commissioner may, by notice in writing served on a data user, require the data user to submit a notice in the prescribed form containing such prescribed information in relation to the data user as the Commissioner may reasonably require in order to keep and maintain the register in so far as it relates to that data user, and the data user shall so submit the second-mentioned notice within such period (being a period of not less than

30 days after service of the first-mentioned notice) and in such manner as the Commissioner requires in the first-mentioned notice.

(4) Where any prescribed information submitted to the Commissioner under subsection (3) by a data user changes subsequent to the submission, then the data user shall serve a notice in writing on the Commissioner specifying such change—

(*a*) if, but only if—

(i) such information is specified in the notice concerned under that subsection as information to which this subsection applies; and

(ii) the notice referred to in subparagraph (i) contains, or has annexed to it—

(A) a copy of this subsection; or

(B) a statement summarizing the requirement imposed by this subsection on the data user; and

(*b*) not later than 30 days after such change.

(5) If the Commissioner is satisfied that a person has ceased to be a data user, he may delete from the register any particulars contained therein relating to that person in that person's capacity as a data user.

(6) A person who has ceased to be a data user may, by notice in the specified form served on the Commissioner, request the Commissioner to delete from the register the particulars contained therein relating to that person in that person's capacity as a data user, and the Commissioner shall, not later than 3 months after the date on which he receives that notice, comply with that request unless it has been withdrawn by that person.

16. Inspection of register

(1) The Commissioner shall provide facilities for making the particulars contained in the register available for inspection—

(*a*) by any person;

(*b*) in visible and legible form;

(*c*) during ordinary office hours; and

(*d*) free of charge.

(2) The Commissioner shall—

(*a*) on receipt of an application in the specified form from a person; and

(*b*) on payment of the prescribed fee,

provide a copy in writing of the particulars contained in the register in respect of the data user, or the class of data users, specified in the application.

17. Register shall not limit, etc. operation of this Ordinance

(1) For the avoidance of doubt, it is hereby declared that—

(*a*) whether or not the register contains any particulars;

(*b*) any particulars contained in the register,

in respect of a data user shall not of itself—

(i) limit, restrict or qualify the operation of any of the provisions of this Ordinance (including section 2(5) and the data protection principles) in relation to the data user;

(ii) exempt the data user from the operation of any of the provisions of this Ordinance.

(2) Subsection (1) shall not prejudice the operation of any limitation, restriction, qualification or exemption provided for in the other provisions of this Ordinance.

PART V

Access to and Correction of Personal Data

18. Data access request

(1) An individual, or a relevant person on behalf of an individual, may make a request—

(*a*) to be informed by a data user whether the data user holds personal data of which the individual is the data subject;

(*b*) if the data user holds such data, to be supplied by the data user with a copy of such data.

(2) A data access request under both paragraphs of subsection (1) shall be treated as being a single request, and the provisions of this Ordinance shall be construed accordingly.

(3) A data access request under paragraph (*a*) of subsection (1) may, in the absence of evidence to the contrary, be treated as being a data access request under both paragraphs of that subsection, and the provisions of this Ordinance (including subsection (2)) shall be construed accordingly.

(4) A data user who, in relation to personal data—

(*a*) does not hold the data; but

(*b*) controls the use of the data in such a way as to prohibit the data user who does hold the data from complying (whether in whole or in part) with a data access request which relates to the data,

shall be deemed to hold those data, and the provisions of this Ordinance (including this section) shall be construed accordingly.

19. Compliance with data access request

(1) Subject to subsection (2) and sections 20 and 28(5), a data user shall comply with a data access request not later than 40 days after receiving the request.

(2) A data user who is unable to comply with a data access request within the period specified in subsection (1) shall—

(*a*) before the expiration of that period—

(i) by notice in writing inform the requestor that the data user is so unable and of the reasons why the data user is so unable; and

(ii) comply with the request to the extent, if any, that the data user is able to comply with the request; and

(*b*) as soon as practicable after the expiration of that period, comply or fully comply, as the case may be, with the request.

(3) A copy of the personal data to be supplied by a data user in compliance with a data access request shall—

(*a*) be supplied by reference to the data at the time when the request is received except that the copy may take account of—

(i) any processing of the data—

(A) made between that time and the time when the copy is supplied; and

(B) that would have been made irrespective of the receipt of the request; and

(ii) subject to subsection (5), any correction to the data made between that time and the time when the copy is supplied;

(*b*) where any correction referred to paragraph (*a*)(ii) has been made to the data, be accompanied by a notice stating that the data have been corrected pursuant to that paragraph (or words to the like effect); and

(*c*) as far as practicable, be—

(i) intelligible unless the copy is a true copy of a document which—

(A) contains the data; and

(B) is unintelligible on its face;

(ii) readily comprehensible with any codes used by the data user adequately explained; and

(iii) in—

(A) subject to sub-subparagraph (B), the language specified in the request or, if no language is so specified, the language in which the request is made (which may be the Chinese or English language in either case);

(B) a language other than the language specified in the request or, if no language is so specified, the language in which the request is made, if, but only if—

(I) the language in which the data are held is not the language specified in the request or, if no language is so specified, the language in which the request is made, as the case may be; and

(II) subject to section 20(2)(*b*), the copy is a true copy of a document which contains the data;

(iv) without prejudice to the generality of subparagraph (iii) but subject to subsection (4), be in the form, or one of the forms, if any, specified in the request;

(v) where subparagraph (iv) is not applicable, in such form as the data user thinks fit.

(4) Where—

(*a*) a data access request specifies the form or forms in which a copy of the personal data to be supplied in compliance with the request is or are sought; and

(*b*) the data user concerned is unable to supply the copy in that form or any of those forms, as the case may be, because it is not practicable for the data user to do so,

then the data user shall—

(i) where there is only one form in which it is practicable for the data user to supply the copy, supply the copy in that form accompanied by a notice in writing informing the requestor that that form is the only form in which it is practicable for the data user to supply the copy;

(ii) in any other case—

(A) as soon as practicable, by notice in writing inform the requestor—

(I) that it is not practicable for the data user to supply the copy in the form or any of the forms, as the case may be, specified in the request;

(II) of the forms in which it is practicable for the data user to supply the copy; and

(III) that the requestor may, not later than 14 days after the requestor has received the notice, specify in writing one of the forms referred to in sub-subparagraph (II) in which the copy is to be supplied; and

(B) as soon as practicable, supply the copy—

(I) in the form specified in the response, if any, to the notice referred to in subparagraph (A);

(II) if there is no such response within the period specified in subparagraph (A)(III), supply the copy in any one of the forms referred to in subparagraph (A)(II) as the data user thinks fit.

(5) Subparagraph (ii) of paragraph (*a*) and paragraph (*b*) of subsection (3) shall expire on the 1st anniversary of the appointed day.

20. Circumstances in which data user shall or may refuse to comply with data access request

(1) A data user shall refuse to comply with a data access request—

(*a*) if the data user is not supplied with such information as the data user may reasonably require—

(i) in order to satisfy the data user as to the identity of the requestor;

(ii) where the requestor purports to be a relevant person, in order to satisfy the data user—

(A) as to the identity of the individual in relation to whom the requestor purports to be such a person; and

(B) that the requestor is such a person in relation to that individual;

(*b*) subject to subsection (2), if the data user cannot comply with the request without disclosing personal data of which any other individual is the data subject unless the data user is satisfied that the other individual has consented to the disclosure of the data to the requestor; or

(*c*) in any other case, if compliance with the request is for the time being prohibited under this Ordinance.

(2) Subsection (1)(*b*) shall not operate—

(*a*) so that the reference in that subsection to personal data of which any other individual is the data subject includes a reference to information identifying that individual as the source of the personal data to which the data access request concerned relates unless that information names or otherwise explicitly identifies that individual;

(*b*) so as to excuse a data user from complying with the data access request concerned to the extent that the request may be complied with without disclosing the identity of the other individual, whether by the omission of names, or other identifying particulars, or otherwise.

(3) A data user may refuse to comply with a data access request if—

(*a*) the request is not in writing in the Chinese or English language;

(*b*) the data user is not supplied with such information as the data user may reasonably require to locate the personal data to which the request relates;

(*c*) the request follows 2 or more similar requests made by—
   (i) the individual who is the data subject in respect of the personal data to which the request relates;
   (ii) one or more relevant persons on behalf of that individual; or
   (iii) any combination of that individual and those relevant persons,

and it is unreasonable in all the circumstances for the data user to comply with the request;

(*d*) subject to subsection (4), any other data user controls the use of the data in such a way as to prohibit the first-mentioned data user from complying (whether in whole or in part) with the request;

(*e*) the form in which the request shall be made has been specified under section 67 and the request is not made in that form; or

(*f*) in any other case, compliance with the request may for the time being be refused under this Ordinance, whether by virtue of an exemption under Part VIII or otherwise.

(4) Subsection (3)(*d*) shall not operate so as to excuse a data user from complying with the data access request concerned—

(*a*) in so far as the request relates to section 18(1)(*a*), to any extent;

(*b*) in so far as the request relates to section 18(1)(*b*), to any extent that the data user can comply with the request without contravening the prohibition concerned.

21. Notification of refusal to comply with data access request

(1) Subject to subsection (2), a data user who pursuant to section 20 refuses to comply with a data access request shall, as soon as practicable but, in any case, not later than 40 days after receiving the request, by notice in writing inform the requestor—

(*a*) of the refusal;

(*b*) subject to subsection (2), of the reasons for the refusal; and

(*c*) where section 20(3)(*d*) is applicable, of the name and address of the other data user concerned.

(2) Where—

(*a*) a data user has pursuant to section 20 refused to comply with a data access request; and

(*b*) the refusal also relates to section 18(1)(*a*) by virtue of section 63,

then the data user may, in the notice under subsection (1) concerned, in place of the matters of which the data user is required to inform the requestor under that subsection, inform the requestor that the data user has no personal data the existence of which he is required to disclose to the requestor (or words to the like effect).

22. Data correction request

(1) Subject to subsection (2), where—

(*a*) a copy of personal data has been supplied by a data user in compliance with a data access request; and

(*b*) the individual, or a relevant person on behalf of the individual, who is the data subject considers that the data are inaccurate,

then that individual or relevant person, as the case may be, may make a request that the data user make the necessary correction to the data.

(2) A data user who, in relation to personal data—

(*a*) does not hold the data; but

(*b*) controls the processing of the data in such a way as to prohibit the data user who does hold the data from complying (whether in whole or in part) with section 23(1) in relation to a data correction request which relates to the data,

shall be deemed to be a data user to whom such a request may be made, and the provisions of this Ordinance (including subsection (1)) shall be construed accordingly.

(3) Without prejudice to the generality of sections 23(1)(*c*) and 25(2), if a data user, subsequent to the receipt of a data correction request but before complying with the request pursuant to section 24 or refusing to comply with the request pursuant to section 25, discloses to a third party the personal data to which the request relates, then the user shall take all practicable steps to advise the third party that the data are the subject of a data correction request still under consideration by the user (or words to the like effect).

23. Compliance with data correction request

(1) Subject to subsection (2) and section 24, a data user who is satisfied that personal data to which a data correction request relates are inaccurate shall, not later than 40 days after receiving the request—

(*a*) make the necessary correction to those data;

(*b*) supply the requestor with a copy of those data as so corrected; and

(*c*) subject to subsection (3), if—

(i) those data have been disclosed to a third party during the 12 months immediately preceding the day on which the correction is made; and

(ii) the data user has no reason to believe that the third party has ceased using those data for the purpose (including any directly related purpose) for which the data were disclosed to the third party, take all practicable steps to supply the third party with a copy of those data as so corrected accompanied by a notice in writing stating the reasons for the correction.

(2) A data user who is unable to comply with subsection (1) in relation to a data correction request within the period specified in that subsection shall—

(*a*) before the expiration of that period—

(i) by notice in writing inform the requestor that the data user is so unable and of the reasons why the data user is so unable; and

(ii) comply with that subsection to the extent, if any, that the data user is able to comply with that subsection; and

(*b*) as soon as practicable after the expiration of that period, comply or fully comply, as the case may be, with that subsection.

(3) A data user is not required to comply with subsection (1)(*c*) in any case where the disclosure concerned of the personal data to the third party consists of the third party's inspection of a register or other like document—

(*a*) in which the data are entered or otherwise recorded; and

(*b*) which is available for inspection by the public,

but this subsection shall not apply if the third party has been supplied with a copy, certified by or under the authority of the data user to be correct, of the data.

24. Circumstances in which data user shall or may refuse to comply with data correction request

(1) Subject to subsection (2), a data user shall refuse to comply with section 23(1) in relation to a data correction request if the data user is not supplied with such information as the data user may reasonably require—

(*a*) in order to satisfy the data user as to the identity of the requestor;

(*b*) where the requestor purports to be a relevant person, in order to satisfy the data user—

(i) as to the identity of the individual in relation to whom the requestor purports to be such a person; and

(ii) that the requestor is such a person in relation to that individual.

(2) Subsection (1) shall not apply to a data correction request where the requestor is the same person as the requestor in respect of the data access request which gave rise to the data correction request.

(3) A data user may refuse to comply with section 23(1) in relation to a data correction request if—

(*a*) the request is not in writing in the Chinese or English language;

(*b*) the data user is not satisfied that the personal data to which the request relates are inaccurate;

(*c*) the data user is not supplied with such information as the data user may reasonably require to ascertain in what way the personal data to which the request relates are inaccurate;

(*d*) the data user is not satisfied that the correction which is the subject of the request is accurate; or

(*e*) subject to subsection (4), any other data user controls the processing of the personal data to which the request relates in such a way as to prohibit the first-mentioned data user from complying (whether in whole or in part) with that section.

(4) Subsection (3)(*e*) shall not operate so as to excuse a data user from complying with section 23(1) in relation to the data correction request concerned to the extent that the data user can comply with that section without contravening the prohibition concerned.

25. Notification of refusal to comply with data correction request, etc.

(1) A data user who pursuant to section 24 refuses to comply with section 23(1) in relation to a data correction request shall, as soon as practicable but, in any case, not later than 40 days after receiving the request, by notice in writing inform the requestor—

(*a*) of the refusal and the reasons for the refusal; and

(*b*) where section 24(3)(*e*) is applicable, of the name and address of the other data user concerned.

(2) Without prejudice to the generality of subsection (1), where—

(*a*) the personal data to which a data correction request relates are an expression of opinion; and

(*b*) the data user concerned is not satisfied that the opinion is inaccurate,

then the data user shall—

(i) make a note, whether annexed to that data or elsewhere—

(A) of the matters in respect of which the opinion is considered by the requestor to be inaccurate; and

(B) in such a way that those data cannot be used by a person (including the data user and a third party) without the note being drawn to the attention of, and being available for inspection by, that person; and

(ii) attach a copy of the note to the notice referred to in subsection (1) which relates to that request.

(3) In this section, "expression of opinion" (意見表達) includes an assertion of fact which—

(*a*) is unverifiable; or

(*b*) in all the circumstances of the case, is not practicable to verify.

26. Erasure of personal data no longer required

(1) A data user shall erase personal data held by the data user where the data are no longer required for the purpose (including any directly related purpose) for which the data were used unless—

(*a*) any such erasure is prohibited under any law; or

(*b*) it is in the public interest (including historical interest) for the data not to be erased.

(2) For the avoidance of doubt, it is hereby declared that—

(*a*) a data user shall erase personal data in accordance with subsection (1) notwithstanding that any other data user controls (whether in whole or in part) the processing of the data;

(*b*) the first-mentioned data user shall not be liable in an action for damages at the suit of the second-mentioned data user in respect of any such erasure.

27. Log book to be kept by data user

(1) A data user shall keep and maintain a log book—

(*a*) for the purposes of this Part;

(*b*) in the Chinese or English language; and

(*c*) such that any particulars entered in the log book pursuant to this section are not erased therefrom before the expiration of—

(i) subject to subparagraph (ii), 4 years after the day on which they were so entered;

(ii) such longer or shorter period as may be prescribed, either generally or in any particular case, by regulations made under section 70.

(2) A data user shall in accordance with subsection (3) enter in the log book—

(*a*) where pursuant to section 20 the data user refuses to comply with a data access request, particulars of the reasons for the refusal;

(*b*) where pursuant to section 21(2) the data user does not comply with section 21(1), particulars of the prejudice that would be caused to the interest protected by the exemption concerned under Part VIII if the existence or non-existence of the personal data to which the data access request concerned relates were disclosed;

(*c*) where pursuant to section 24 the data user refuses to comply with section 23(1) in relation to a data correction request, particulars of the reasons for the refusal;

(*d*) any other particulars required by regulations made under section 70 to be entered in the log book.

(3) The particulars required by subsection (2) to be entered by a data user in the log book shall be so entered—

(*a*) in the case of particulars referred to in paragraph (*a*) of that subsection, on or before the notice under section 21(1) is served in respect of the refusal to which those particulars relate;

(*b*) in the case of particulars referred to in paragraph (*b*) of that subsection, on or before the notice under section 21(1) is served in respect of the refusal to which those particulars relate;

(*c*) in the case of particulars referred to in paragraph (*c*) of that subsection, on or before the notice under section 25(1) is served in respect of the refusal to which those particulars relate;

(*d*) in the case of particulars referred to in paragraph (*d*) of that subsection, within the period specified in regulations made under section 70 in respect of those particulars.

(4) A data user shall—

(*a*) permit the Commissioner to inspect and copy the log book (or any part thereof) at any reasonable time; and

(*b*) without charge, afford the Commissioner such facilities and assistance as the Commissioner may reasonably require for the purposes of such inspection and copying.

28. Imposition of fees by data user

(1) A data user shall not impose a fee for complying or refusing to comply with a data access request or data correction request unless the imposition of the fee is expressly permitted by this section.

(2) Subject to subsections (3) and (4), a data user may impose a fee for complying with a data access request.

(3) No fee imposed for complying with a data access request shall be excessive.

(4) Where pursuant to section 19(3)(*c*)(iv) or (v) or (4)(ii)(B)(II) a data user may comply with a data access request by supplying a copy of the personal data to which the request relates in one of 2 or more forms, the data user shall not, and irrespective of the form in which the data user complies with the request, impose a fee for complying with the request which is higher than the lowest fee the data user imposes for complying with the request in any of those forms.

(5) A data user may refuse to comply with a data access request unless and until any fee imposed by the data user for complying with the request has been paid.

(6) Where—

(*a*) a data user has complied with a data access request by supplying a copy of the personal data to which the request relates; and

(*b*) the data subject, or a relevant person on behalf of the data subject, requests the data user to supply a further copy of those data,

then the data user may, and notwithstanding the fee, if any, that the data user imposed for complying with that data access request, impose a fee for supplying that further copy which is not more than the administrative and other costs incurred by the data user in supplying that further copy.

29. Service and language of certain notices

Without prejudice to the generality of section 68, where pursuant to a data access request or data correction request a data user is required to, or may, inform a requestor of any matter by notice in writing, then the requestor shall be deemed not to be so informed unless and until the requestor is served with the notice—

(*a*) in the language in which the request is made if that language is Chinese or English;

(*b*) in any other case, in the Chinese or English language as the data user thinks fit.

PART VI

MATCHING PROCEDURES AND TRANSFERS OF PERSONAL DATA, ETC.

30. Matching procedure not to be carried out except with consent of data subject, etc.

(1) A data user shall not carry out, whether in whole or in part, a matching procedure—

(*a*) unless and until each individual who is a data subject of the personal data the subject of that procedure has given his prescribed consent to the procedure being carried out;

(*b*) unless and until the Commissioner has consented under section 32 to the procedure being carried out;

(*c*) unless the procedure—

(i) belongs to a class of matching procedures specified in a notice under subsection (2); and

(ii) is carried out in accordance with the conditions, if any, specified in the notice; or

(*d*) unless it is required or permitted under any provision of any Ordinance specified in Schedule 4.

(2) For the purposes of this section, the Commissioner may, by notice in the Gazette, specify—

(*a*) a class of matching procedures;

(*b*) subject to subsection (3), the conditions, if any, subject to which a matching procedure belonging to that class shall be carried out.

(3) The Commissioner shall, before specifying any conditions in a notice under subsection (2), consult with—

(*a*) such bodies representative of data users to which the conditions will apply (whether in whole or in part); and

(*b*) such other interested persons,

as he thinks fit.

(4) It is hereby declared that a notice under subsection (2) is subsidiary legislation.

(5) Subject to subsection (6), a data user shall not take adverse action against an individual in consequence (whether in whole or in part) of the carrying out of a matching procedure—

(*a*) unless the data user has served a notice in writing on the individual—

(i) specifying the adverse action it proposes to take and the reasons therefor; and

(ii) stating that the individual has 7 days after the receipt of the notice within which to show cause why that action should not be taken; and

(*b*) until the expiration of those 7 days.

(6) Subsection (5) shall not operate to prevent a data user from taking adverse action against an individual if compliance with the requirements of that subsection would prejudice any investigation into the commission of an offence or the possible commission of an offence.

31. Matching procedure request

(1) A data user proposing to carry out, whether in whole or in part, a matching procedure may make a request—

(*a*) in the specified form;

(*b*) to the Commissioner; and

(*c*) seeking the Commissioner's consent under section 32 to the carrying out of that procedure.

(2) Where 2 or more data users may each make a matching procedure request in respect of the same matching procedure, then any of those data users may make such a request on behalf of all those data users, and the provisions of this Ordinance (including subsection (1)) shall be construed accordingly.

(3) Without prejudice to the generality of subsection (2), it is hereby declared that a matching procedure request may be made in relation to 2 or more matching procedures, or a series of matching procedures, and the other provisions of this Ordinance (including section 32) shall be construed accordingly.

32. Determination of matching procedure request

(1) The Commissioner shall determine a matching procedure request—
- (*a*) not later than 45 days after receiving the request; and
- (*b*) by taking into account the prescribed matters applicable to the request and—
  - (i) where he is satisfied as to those matters, serving a notice in writing on the requestor stating that he consents to the carrying out of the matching procedure to which the request relates subject to the conditions, if any, specified in the notice;
  - (ii) where he is not so satisfied, serving a notice in writing on the requestor stating—
    - (A) that he refuses to consent to the carrying out of the matching procedure to which the request relates; and
    - (B) such of those matters in respect of which he is not so satisfied and the reasons why he is not so satisfied.

(2) For the avoidance of doubt, it is hereby declared that a consent in a notice under subsection (1)(*b*)(i) to the carrying out of a matching procedure to which a matching procedure request relates shall not operate to prevent a data user who is neither the requestor nor, where section 31(2) applies to the request, any data user on whose behalf such request was made, from carrying out, whether in whole or in part, the procedure.

(3) An appeal may be made to the Administrative Appeals Board—
- (*a*) against—
  - (i) any conditions specified in a notice under subsection (1)(*b*)(i); or
  - (ii) any refusal specified in a notice under subsection (1)(*b*)(ii); and

(*b*) by the requestor on whom the notice was served or any data user on whose behalf the matching procedure request concerned was made.

(4) In this section, "prescribed matter" (訂明事宜) means a matter specified in Schedule 5.

33. Prohibition against transfer of personal data to place outside Hong Kong except in specified circumstances

(1) This section shall not apply to personal data other than personal data the collection, holding, processing or use of which—

(*a*) takes place in Hong Kong; or

(*b*) is controlled by a data user whose principal place of business is in Hong Kong.

(2) A data user shall not transfer personal data to a place outside Hong Kong unless—

(*a*) the place is specified for the purposes of this section in a notice under subsection (3);

(*b*) the user has reasonable grounds for believing that there is in force in that place any law which is substantially similar to, or serves the same purposes as, this Ordinance;

(*c*) the data subject has consented in writing to the transfer;

(*d*) the user has reasonable grounds for believing that, in all the circumstances of the case—

(i) the transfer is for the avoidance or mitigation of adverse action against the data subject;

(ii) it is not practicable to obtain the consent in writing of the data subject to that transfer; and

(iii) if it was practicable to obtain such consent, the data subject would give it;

(*e*) the data are exempt from data protection principle 3 by virtue of an exemption under Part VIII; or

(*f*) the user has taken all reasonable precautions and exercised all due diligence to ensure that the data will not, in that place, be collected, held, processed or used in any manner which, if that place were Hong Kong, would be a contravention of a requirement under this Ordinance.

(3) Where the Commissioner has reasonable grounds for believing that there is in force in a place outside Hong Kong any law which is substantially similar to, or serves the same purposes as, this Ordinance, he may, by notice in the Gazette, specify that place for the purposes of this section.

(4) Where the Commissioner has reasonable grounds for believing that in a place specified in a notice under subsection (3) there is no longer in force any law which is substantially similar to, or serves the same purposes as, this Ordinance, he shall, either by repealing or amending that notice, cause that place to cease to be specified for the purposes of this section.

(5) For the avoidance of doubt, it is hereby declared that—

(*a*) for the purposes of subsection (1)(*b*), a data user which is a company incorporated in Hong Kong is a data user whose principal place of business is in Hong Kong;

(*b*) a notice under subsection (3) is subsidiary legislation; and

(*c*) this section shall not operate to prejudice the generality of section 50.

34. Use of personal data in direct marketing

(1) A data user who—

(*a*) has obtained personal data from any source (including the data subject); and

(*b*) uses the data for direct marketing purposes,

shall—

(i) the first time he so uses those data after this section comes into operation, inform the data subject that the data user is required, without charge to the data subject, to cease to so use those data if the data subject so requests;

(ii) if the data subject so requests, cease to so use those data without charge to the data subject.

(2) In this section—

"direct marketing" (直接促銷) means—

(*a*) the offering of goods, facilities or services;

(*b*) the advertising of the availability of goods, facilities or services; or

(*c*) the solicitation of donations or contributions for charitable, cultural, philanthropic, recreational, political or other purposes,

by means of—

(i) information or goods sent to any person by mail, facsimile transmission, electronic mail, or other similar means of communication, where the information or goods are addressed to a specific person or specific persons by name; or

(ii) telephone calls made to specific persons.

35. Repeated collections of personal data in same circumstances

(1) A data user who—

(*a*) has complied with the provisions of data protection principle 1(3) in respect of the collection of any personal data from the data subject ("first collection"); and

(*b*) on any subsequent occasion again collects personal data from the data subject ("subsequent collection"),

is not required to comply with those provisions in respect of the subsequent collection if, but only if—

(i) to comply with those provisions in respect of that subsequent collection would be to repeat, without any material difference, what was done to comply with that principle in respect of the first collection; and

(ii) not more than 12 months have elapsed between the first collection and the subsequent collection.

(2) For the avoidance of doubt, it is hereby declared that subsection (1) shall not operate to prevent a subsequent collection from becoming a first collection if, but only if, the data user concerned has complied with the provisions of data protection principle 1(3) in respect of the subsequent collection.

PART VII

INSPECTIONS, COMPLAINTS AND INVESTIGATIONS

36. Inspections of personal data systems

Without prejudice to the generality of section 38, the Commissioner may carry out an inspection of—

(*a*) any personal data system used by a data user; or

(*b*) any personal data system used by a data user belonging to a class of data users,

for the purposes of ascertaining information to assist the Commissioner in making recommendations—

(i) to—

(A) where paragraph (*a*) is applicable, the relevant data user;

(B) where paragraph (*b*) is applicable, the class of data users to which the relevant data user belongs; and

(ii) relating to the promotion of compliance with the provisions of this Ordinance, in particular the data protection principles, by the relevant data user, or the class of data users to which the relevant data user belongs, as the case may be.

37. Complaints

(1) An individual, or a relevant person on behalf of an individual, may make a complaint to the Commissioner about an act or practice—

(*a*) specified in the complaint; and

(*b*) that—

(i) has been done or engaged in, or is being done or engaged in, as the case may be, by a data user specified in the complaint;

(ii) relates to personal data of which the individual is or, in any case in which the data user is relying upon an exemption under Part VIII, may be, the data subject; and

(iii) may be a contravention of a requirement under this Ordinance (including section 28(4)).

(2) Where 2 or more individuals may each make a complaint about the same act or practice, then any of those individuals, or any relevant person on behalf of any of those individuals, may make such a complaint on behalf of all those individuals, and the provisions of this Ordinance (including subsection (1)) shall be construed accordingly.

(3) A complaint shall be—

(*a*) in writing in the Chinese or English language; or

(*b*) in such other form as the Commissioner may accept.

(4) It shall be the duty of the Commissioner and each prescribed officer who has been employed under section 9(1)(*a*) to provide appropriate assistance to an individual, or a relevant person on behalf of an individual, who wishes to make a complaint and requires assistance to formulate the complaint.

38. Investigations by Commissioner

Where the Commissioner—

(*a*) receives a complaint; or

(*b*) has reasonable grounds to believe that an act or practice—

(i) has been done or engaged in, or is being done or engaged in, as the case may be, by a data user;

(ii) relates to personal data; and

(iii) may be a contravention of a requirement under this Ordinance,

then—

(i) where paragraph (*a*) is applicable, the Commissioner shall, subject to section 39, carry out an investigation in relation to the relevant data user to ascertain whether the act or practice specified in the complaint is a contravention of a requirement under this Ordinance;

(ii) where paragraph (*b*) is applicable, the Commissioner may carry out an investigation in relation to the relevant data user to ascertain whether the act or practice referred to in that paragraph is a contravention of a requirement under this Ordinance.

39. Restrictions on investigations initiated by complaints

(1) Notwithstanding the generality of the powers conferred on the Commissioner by this Ordinance, the Commissioner may refuse to carry out or continue an investigation initiated by a complaint if—

(*a*) the complainant (or, if the complainant is a relevant person, the individual in respect of whom the complainant is such a person) has had actual knowledge of the act or practice specified in the complaint for more than 2 years immediately preceding the date on which the Commissioner received the complaint, unless the Commissioner is satisfied that in all the circumstances of the case it is proper to carry out or continue, as the case may be, the investigation;

(*b*) the complaint is made anonymously;

(*c*) the complainant cannot be identified or traced;

(*d*) none of the following conditions is fulfilled in respect of the act or practice specified in the complaint—

(i) either—

(A) the complainant (or, if the complainant is a relevant person, the individual in respect of whom the complainant is such a person) was resident in Hong Kong; or

(B) the relevant data user was able to control, in or from Hong Kong, the collection, holding, processing or use of the personal data concerned,

at any time the act or practice was done or engaged in, as the case may be;

(ii) the complainant (or, if the complainant is a relevant person, the individual in respect of whom the complainant is such a person) was in Hong Kong at any time the act or practice was done or engaged in, as the case may be;

(iii) in the opinion of the Commissioner, the act or practice done or engaged in, as the case may be, may prejudice the enforcement of any right, or the exercise of any privilege, acquired or accrued in Hong Kong by the complainant (or, if the complainant is a relevant person, the individual in respect of whom the complainant is such a person); or (*e*) the Commissioner is satisfied that the relevant data user has not been a data user for a period of not less than 2 years immediately preceding the date on which the Commissioner received the complaint.

(2) The Commissioner may refuse to carry out or continue an investigation initiated by a complaint if he is of the opinion that, having regard to all the circumstances of the case—

(*a*) the complaint, or a complaint of a substantially similar nature, has previously initiated an investigation as a result of which the Commissioner was of the opinion that there had been no contravention of a requirement under this Ordinance;

(*b*) the act or practice specified in the complaint is trivial;

(*c*) the complaint is frivolous or vexatious or is not made in good faith; or

(*d*) any investigation or further investigation is for any other reason unnecessary.

(3) Where the Commissioner refuses under this section to carry out or continue an investigation initiated by a complaint, he shall, as soon as practicable but, in any case, not later than 45 days after receiving the complaint, by notice in writing served on the complainant accompanied by a copy of subsection (4), inform the complainant—

(*a*) of the refusal; and

(*b*) of the reasons for the refusal.

(4) An appeal may be made to the Administrative Appeals Board—

(*a*) against any refusal specified in a notice under subsection (3); and

(*b*) by the complainant on whom the notice was served (or, if the complainant is a relevant person, the individual in respect of whom the complainant is such a person, or either).

40. Commissioner may carry out or continue investigation initiated by complaint notwithstanding withdrawal of complaint

Where the Commissioner is of the opinion that it is in the public interest so to do, he may carry out or continue an investigation initiated by a complaint notwithstanding that the complainant has withdrawn the complaint and, in any such case, the provisions of this Ordinance shall apply to the complaint and the complainant as if the complaint had not been withdrawn.

41. Commissioner to inform relevant data user of inspection or investigation

(1) The Commissioner shall, before carrying out an inspection or, subject to subsection (2), an investigation, by notice in writing served on the relevant

data user, inform the data user of his intention to carry out the inspection or investigation, as the case may be.

(2) The Commissioner is not required to comply with subsection (1) in the case of any investigation in respect of which he has reasonable grounds to believe that to so comply may prejudice the purposes of the investigation.

42. Power of entry on premises for the purposes of an inspection or investigation

(1) Subject to subsections (3) and (8), the Commissioner may, for the purposes of an inspection—

(*a*) where the personal data system, or any part thereof, the subject of the inspection is situated in—

(i) non-domestic premises, enter the premises at any reasonable time;

(ii) domestic premises, enter the premises with the consent of any person (other than a minor) resident therein;

(*b*) carry out in the premises the inspection.

(2) Subject to subsections (3) and (8), the Commissioner may, for the purposes of an investigation—

(*a*) enter any premises—

(i) occupied by the relevant data user; or

(ii) in which is situated the personal data system, or any part thereof, used by the relevant data user;

(*b*) carry out in the premises the investigation.

(3) Subject to subsections (4) and (5), the Commissioner shall, not less than 14 days before exercising his power under subsection (1) or (2) in respect of any premises, by notice in writing served on the relevant data user, inform the data user—

(*a*) of the premises in respect of which he proposes to exercise that power; and

(*b*) that the power will not be so exercised before the expiration of 14 days after service of the notice.

(4) Without prejudice to the generality of subsection (5), where any domestic premises are specified in a notice under subsection (3) in respect of which the Commissioner proposes to exercise his power under subsection (2), then the Commissioner shall not exercise that power in respect of those premises unless and until a person (other than a minor) resident therein consents thereto before the expiration of 14 days after service of the notice.

(5) The Commissioner may, pursuant to a warrant issued under subsection (6), exercise his power under subsection (2) in respect of the premises specified in the warrant without complying with subsection (3).

(6) A magistrate may, if satisfied by information upon oath by the Commissioner or any prescribed officer that there are reasonable grounds for believing that the purposes of any investigation may be substantially prejudiced if the Commissioner were required to comply with subsection (3) before exercising his power under subsection (2) in respect of any premises, issue a warrant—

(*a*) in the form specified in Part 1 of Schedule 6; and
(*b*) in respect of those premises.

(7) A magistrate may, if satisfied by information upon oath by the Commissioner or any prescribed officer that there are reasonable grounds for believing that the purposes of an investigation may be substantially prejudiced if the Commissioner is prevented by the operation of subsection (4) from exercising his power under subsection (2) in respect of any domestic premises, issue a warrant—

(*a*) in the form specified in Part 2 of Schedule 6; and
(*b*) authorizing the Commissioner to exercise that power in respect of those premises.

(8) The Commissioner shall not exercise his power under subsection (1) or (2) in respect of any premises in such a way as to unduly disrupt any operations being carried out in the premises, whether by the relevant data user or any other person.

(9) Where the Commissioner exercises his power under subsection (1) or (2), the relevant data user shall, without charge, afford the Commissioner such facilities and assistance as the Commissioner may reasonably require for the purposes of the inspection or investigation concerned.

(10) Where the Commissioner, pursuant to a warrant issued under subsection (6), exercises his power under subsection (2) in respect of the premises specified in the warrant, he shall produce the warrant for inspection by any person found in those premises who questions his authority to exercise that power in respect of those premises.

(11) In this section and Schedule 6—

"domestic premises" (住宅處所) means any premises which are constructed or intended to be used for habitation;

"non-domestic premises" (非住宅處所) means any premises other than domestic premises;

"premises" (處所) means—

(*a*) any building where no part of the building is separately occupied, and includes any land appertaining to the building;
(*b*) in any other case, any part of a building which is separately occupied, and includes any land appertaining to such part.

43. Proceedings of Commissioner

(1) Subject to the provisions of this Ordinance, the Commissioner may, for the purposes of any investigation—

(*a*) be furnished with any information, document or thing, from such persons, and make such inquiries, as he thinks fit; and

(*b*) regulate his procedure in such manner as he thinks fit.

(2) Any hearing for the purposes of an investigation shall be carried out in public unless—

(*a*) the Commissioner is of the opinion that, in all the circumstances of the case, the investigation should be carried out in private; or

(*b*) if the investigation was initiated by a complaint, the complainant requests in writing that the investigation be carried out in private.

(3) Counsel and solicitors shall not have any right of audience before the Commissioner at any hearing for the purposes of an investigation, but may appear before him if he thinks fit.

(4) It shall not be necessary for the Commissioner to hold any hearing for the purposes of an investigation and no person shall be entitled to be heard by the Commissioner.

(5) If at any time during the course of an investigation it appears to the Commissioner that there may be sufficient grounds for him to make any report or recommendation that may criticize or adversely affect any person he shall give to the person an opportunity to be heard.

44. Evidence

(1) Subject to subsection (2) and section 45, the Commissioner may, for the purposes of any investigation, summon before him any person who—

(*a*) in the opinion of the Commissioner, is able to give any information relevant to those purposes;

(*b*) where the investigation was initiated by a complaint, is the complainant (or, if the complainant is a relevant person, the individual in respect of whom the complainant is such a person, or both),

and may examine any such person and require him to furnish to the Commissioner any information and to produce any document or thing which, in the opinion of the Commissioner, is relevant to those purposes and which may be in the possession or under the control of any such person.

(2) Where—

(*a*) an investigation has been initiated by a complaint;

(*b*) the complaint relates, whether in whole or in part, to personal data referred to in section 61(1);

(*c*) the Commissioner has, for the purposes of that investigation, under subsection (1)(*a*) summoned before him a person; and

(*d*) that person asserts, in response to any requirement under subsection (1) by the Commissioner to furnish him with information or to produce a document or thing, that—

(i) to comply with that requirement would directly or indirectly disclose the identity of the individual from whom those data were collected (whether in whole or in part); or

(ii) he is not required to comply with that requirement by virtue of any common law privilege,

then—

(i) notwithstanding any other provision of this Ordinance, the Commissioner shall not serve an enforcement notice on that person in relation to that requirement;

(ii) the Commissioner may, not later than 28 days after that assertion is made known to him, make an application to the High Court for an order directing that person to comply with that requirement;

(iii) the High Court may make the order if, but only if, it is satisfied, having regard to all the circumstances (including the circumstances of the complainant), that—

(A) if the act or practice specified in the complaint were proven to be a contravention of a requirement under this Ordinance, the contravention would be of sufficient gravity to warrant that person complying with the requirement referred to in paragraph (*d*);

(B) that investigation would be substantially prejudiced if the requirement referred to in paragraph (*d*) were not complied with;

(C) it is in the public interest, having regard to the benefit likely to accrue to that investigation, that the requirement referred to in paragraph (*d*) be complied with; and

(D) in any case to which paragraph (*d*)(ii) is applicable, the common law privilege asserted does not apply; and

(iv) on the hearing of the application, the Commissioner, that person and the complainant shall each be entitled to be heard on the application and to call, examine and cross-examine any witness.

(3) Where—

(*a*) a person has complied with a requirement referred to in subsection (2)(*d*) the subject of an assertion referred to in that subsection; and

(*b*) the result (whether in whole or in part) of the investigation to which that requirement relates is that the Commissioner is of the opinion that the individual concerned referred to in subsection

(2)(*d*)(i) has not contravened a requirement under this Ordinance in relation to the matter the subject of the complaint which initiated the investigation,

then, notwithstanding any other provision of this Ordinance, neither the Commissioner nor any prescribed officer shall disclose the identity of that individual to the complainant.

(4) The High Court may, of its own volition or on an application made to it for the purpose, by order reverse, vary or discharge an order made under subsection (2)(iii) or suspend the operation of such an order.

(5) Provision may be made by rules of court—

(*a*) with respect to applications to the High Court under subsection (2)(iii) or (4);

(*b*) generally with respect to procedure before the High Court in relation to any such application.

(6) Subsection (5) is without prejudice to the generality of any existing power to make rules.

(7) The Commissioner may administer an oath for the purposes of an examination under subsection (1) if he thinks fit.

(8) It is hereby declared that—

(*a*) no obligation to maintain secrecy or other restriction, imposed by law, upon the disclosure of any information, document or other thing, that is or has been in the possession or under the control of any person referred to in subsection (1), shall apply to its disclosure for the purposes of an investigation; and

(*b*) any requirement by the Commissioner that any such information, document or thing as is referred to in paragraph (*a*) be disclosed or produced for the purposes of an investigation shall be sufficient authority for its disclosure or production to the Commissioner.

(9) The Commissioner may pay the reasonable expenses of complainants (including, if the complainant is a relevant person, the individual in respect of whom the complainant is such a person) and witnesses incurred during the course of an investigation.

45. Protection of witnesses, etc.

(1) Every person shall have the same privileges in relation to the giving of information, the answering of questions, and the production of documents and things, for the purposes of an investigation, as witnesses have in civil proceedings in the Supreme Court but any rule of law which authorizes or requires the withholding of any document or thing, or the refusal to answer any question, on the ground that the disclosure of the document or thing or the answering of the question, as the case may be, would be injurious to the public interest, shall not apply in respect of any investigation.

(2) Except on the trial of any person for perjury in respect of his sworn testimony, or for an offence under this Ordinance, no statement made or answer given by that or any other person in the course of any investigation shall be admissible in evidence against any person, before any magistrate or in any court or at any inquiry or in any other proceedings, and no evidence in respect of an investigation shall be given against any person.

(3) Where the giving of any information or the answering of any question or the production of any document or thing would involve the disclosure, without the consent of the Governor, of the deliberations of the Executive Council, the Commissioner shall not require the information or answer to be given or, as the case may be, the document or thing to be produced.

46. Commissioner, etc. to maintain secrecy

(1) Subject to subsections (2) and (3), the Commissioner and every prescribed officer shall maintain secrecy in respect of all matters that come to their actual knowledge in the performance of their functions and the exercise of their powers under this Part.

(2) Subsection (1) shall not operate so as to prevent the Commissioner or any prescribed officer from—

(*a*) disclosing in the course of proceedings—

(i) for an offence under this Ordinance; and

(ii) before any court or magistrate,

any matter relevant to those proceedings;

(*b*) reporting evidence of any crime to such authority as he considers appropriate;

(*c*) disclosing to a person any matter referred to in subsection (1) which, in the opinion of the Commissioner or prescribed officer, may be ground for a complaint by that person.

(3) Subject to subsection (4), the Commissioner may disclose in any report made by him under this Ordinance any matter that in his opinion ought to be disclosed in order to establish grounds for his findings and recommendations other than a matter the disclosure of which in his opinion would involve the disclosure of personal data that are exempt from data protection principle 6 by virtue of an exemption under Part VIII.

(4) The Commissioner shall not publish a report under this Ordinance after completing an inspection or investigation unless—

(*a*) a copy of the report in the form in which it is to be published has been supplied to the relevant data user;

(*b*) that copy is accompanied by a notice in writing inviting the data user to advise the Commissioner, in writing and not later than 28 days after being served with the copy, whether—

(i) in the opinion of the data user there is any matter in the copy the disclosure of which would involve the disclosure of personal data that are exempt from the provisions of data protection principle 6 by virtue of an exemption under Part VIII; and

(ii) the data user objects to the disclosure of the matter; and

(*c*) either—

(i) the period referred to in paragraph (*b*) has expired without the Commissioner receiving any such advice; or

(ii) such advice is received by the Commissioner and—

(A) the Commissioner deletes from the report the matter the subject of the advice; or

(B) the Commissioner decides not to delete that matter from the report and—

(I) the period referred to in subsection (6) expires without the data user making an appeal under that subsection against that decision; or

(II) such an appeal is unsuccessful or withdrawn.

(5) Where the Commissioner makes a decision referred to in subsection (4)(*c*)(ii)(B), he shall serve on the relevant data user who gave the advice concerned a notice in writing—

(*a*) stating his decision;

(*b*) informing the data user that he may appeal under subsection (6) against that decision; and

(*c*) accompanied by a copy of this section.

(6) An appeal may be made to the Administrative Appeals Board against a decision of the Commissioner referred to in subsection (4)(*c*)(ii)(B) by the relevant data user not later than 14 days after the notice under subsection (5) stating that decision has been served on the data user.

47. Persons to be informed of result of inspection or investigation

(1) Where the Commissioner has completed an inspection, he shall, in such manner and at such time as he thinks fit, inform the relevant data user of—

(*a*) the result of the inspection;

(*b*) any recommendations arising from the inspection that the Commissioner thinks fit to make relating to the promotion of compliance with the provisions of this Ordinance, in particular the data protection principles, by the data user;

(*c*) any report arising from the inspection that he proposes to publish under section 48; and (*d*) such other comments arising from the inspection as he thinks fit to make.

(2) Where the Commissioner has completed an investigation, he shall, in such manner and at such time as he thinks fit, inform the relevant data user of—

(*a*) the result of the investigation;

(*b*) any recommendations arising from the investigation that the Commissioner thinks fit to make relating to the promotion of compliance with the provisions of this Ordinance, in particular the data protection principles, by the data user;

(*c*) any report arising from the investigation that he proposes to publish under section 48;

(*d*) whether or not he proposes to serve an enforcement notice on the data user in consequence of the investigation; and

(*e*) such other comments arising from the investigation as he thinks fit to make.

(3) Where the Commissioner has completed an investigation initiated by a complaint, he shall, in such manner and at such time as he thinks fit, inform the complainant of—

(*a*) the result of the investigation;

(*b*) any recommendations made to the relevant data user under subsection (2)(*b*);

(*c*) any report arising from the investigation that he proposes to publish under section 48;

(*d*) any comments made by or on behalf of the relevant data user on any such recommendations or report;

(*e*) whether or not he has served, or proposes to serve, an enforcement notice on the relevant data user in consequence of the investigation;

(*f*) if the Commissioner has not so served, and does not propose to so serve, such enforcement notice, his right to object thereto under subsection (4); and

(*g*) such other comments arising from the investigation as he thinks fit to make.

(4) The complainant (or, if the complainant is a relevant person, the individual in respect of whom the complainant is such a person, or either) may appeal to the Administrative Appeals Board against a decision of the Commissioner—

(*a*) to the effect that he has not served, and does not propose to serve, an enforcement notice on the relevant data user in consequence of the investigation concerned; and

(*b*) of which the complainant was informed in the notice concerned under subsection (3) served on him.

48. Reports by Commissioner

(1) Subject to subsection (3), the Commissioner may, after completing an inspection where section 36(*b*) is applicable, publish a report—

(*a*) setting out any recommendations arising from the inspection that the Commissioner thinks fit to make relating to the promotion of compliance with the provisions of this Ordinance, in particular the data protection principles, by the class of data users to which the relevant data user belongs; and

(*b*) in such manner as he thinks fit.

(2) Subject to subsection (3), the Commissioner may, after completing an investigation and if he is of the opinion that it is in the public interest to do so, publish a report—

(*a*) setting out—

(i) the result of the investigation;

(ii) any recommendations arising from the investigation that the Commissioner thinks fit to make relating to the promotion of compliance with the provisions of this Ordinance, in particular the data protection principles, by the class of data users to which the relevant data user belongs; and

(iii) such other comments arising from the investigation as he thinks fit to make; and

(*b*) in such manner as he thinks fit.

(3) Subject to subsection (4), a report published under subsection (1) or (2) shall be so framed as to the prevent the identity of any individual being ascertained from it.

(4) Subsection (3) shall not apply to any individual who is—

(*a*) the Commissioner or a prescribed officer;

(*b*) the relevant data user.

49. Cases in which sections 47 and 48 shall not apply

Where—

(*a*) the Commissioner has completed an investigation (and whether or not the investigation was initiated by a complaint);

(*b*) the result of the investigation is that the act or practice the subject of the investigation is not a contravention of a requirement under this Ordinance because of an exemption under Part VIII; and

(*c*) the interest protected by that exemption would be likely to be prejudiced if sections 47 and 48 applied in relation to the investigation,

then—

(i) those sections shall not apply in relation to the investigation; and

(ii) the Commissioner shall, in such manner and at such time as he thinks fit—
(A) inform the relevant data user of the result of the investigation and such other comments arising from the investigation as he thinks fit;
(B) if the investigation was initiated by a complaint, inform the complainant that the result of the investigation is that he is satisfied that the act or practice the subject of the investigation is not a contravention of a requirement under this Ordinance (or words to the like effect).

50. Enforcement notices

(1) Where, following the completion of an investigation, the Commissioner is of the opinion that the relevant data user—
(*a*) is contravening a requirement under this Ordinance; or
(*b*) has contravened such a requirement in circumstances that make it likely that the contravention will continue or be repeated,

then the Commissioner may serve on the relevant data user a notice in writing—
(i) stating that he is of that opinion;
(ii) specifying the requirement as to which he is of that opinion and the reasons why he is of that opinion;
(iii) directing the data user to take such steps as are specified in the notice to remedy the contravention or, as the case may be, the matters occasioning it within such period (ending not earlier than the period specified in subsection (7) within which an appeal against the notice may be made) as is specified in the notice; and
(iv) accompanied by a copy of this section.

(2) In deciding whether to serve an enforcement notice the Commissioner shall consider whether the contravention or matter to which the notice relates has caused or is likely to cause damage or distress to any individual who is the data subject of any personal data to which the contravention or matter, as the case may be, relates.

(3) The steps specified in an enforcement notice to remedy any contravention or matter to which the notice relates may be framed—
(*a*) to any extent by reference to any approved code of practice;
(*b*) so as to afford the relevant data user a choice between different ways of remedying the contravention or matter, as the case may be.

(4) Subject to subsection (5), the period specified in an enforcement notice for taking the steps specified in it shall not expire before the end of the period specified in subsection (7) within which an appeal against the notice may be

made and, if such an appeal is made, those steps need not be taken pending the determination or withdrawal of the appeal.

(5) If the Commissioner is of the opinion that by reason of special circumstances the steps specified in an enforcement notice should be taken as a matter of urgency—

(*a*) he may include a statement to that effect in the notice together with the reasons why he is of that opinion;

(*b*) where such a statement is so included, subsection (4) shall not apply but the notice shall not require those steps to be taken before the end of the period of 7 days beginning with the date on which the notice was served.

(6) The Commissioner may cancel an enforcement notice by notice in writing served on the relevant data user.

(7) An appeal may be made to the Administrative Appeals Board against an enforcement notice by the relevant data user not later than 14 days after the notice was served.

(8) Where the Commissioner—

(*a*) forms an opinion referred to in subsection (1) in respect of the relevant data user at any time before the completion of an investigation; and

(*b*) is also of the opinion that, by reason of special circumstances, an enforcement notice should be served on the relevant data user as a matter of urgency,

he may so serve such notice notwithstanding that the investigation has not been completed and, in any such case—

(i) the Commissioner shall, without prejudice to any other matters to be included in such notice, specify in the notice the reasons as to why he is of the opinion referred to in paragraph (*b*); and

(ii) the other provisions of this Ordinance (including this section) shall be construed accordingly.

PART VIII

EXEMPTIONS

51. Interpretation

Where any personal data are exempt from any provision of this Ordinance by virtue of this Part, then, in respect of those data and to the extent of that exemption, that provision neither confers any right nor imposes any requirement on any person, and the other provisions of this Ordinance which relate (whether directly or indirectly) to that provision shall be construed accordingly.

52. Domestic purposes

Personal data held by an individual and—

(*a*) concerned only with the management of his personal, family or household affairs; or

(*b*) so held only for recreational purposes,

are exempt from the provisions of the data protection principles, Parts IV and V and sections 36 and 38(*b*).

53. Employment—staff planning

Personal data which consist of information relevant to any staff planning proposal to—

(*a*) fill any series of positions of employment which are presently, or may become, unfilled; or

(*b*) cease any group of individuals' employment,

are exempt from the provisions of data protection principle 6 and section 18(1)(*b*).

54. Employment—transitional provisions

(1) Personal data—

(*a*) held by a data user—

(i) immediately before the appointed day;

(ii) who is the employer of the data subject; and

(iii) relating to the employment of the subject; and

(*b*) provided by an individual on the implicit or explicit condition that the subject would not have access to the data,

are exempt from the provisions of data protection principle 6 and section 18(1)(*b*) until the expiration of 7 years immediately following the enactment of this Ordinance.

(2) Personal data—

(*a*) to which subsection (1)(*a*) applies; or

(*b*) held by a data user—

(i) but not so held at any time before the appointed day;

(ii) who is the employer of the data subject; and

(iii) relating to the employment of the subject,

are exempt from the provisions of data protection principle 6 and section 18(1)(*b*) until 1 July 1996.

55. Relevant process

(1) Personal data the subject of a relevant process are exempt from the provisions of data protection principle 6 and section 18(1)(*b*) until the completion of that process.

(2) In this section—

"completion" (完成), in relation to a relevant process, means the making of the determination concerned referred to in paragraph (*a*) of the definition of "relevant process";

"relevant process" (有關程序)—

(*a*) subject to paragraph (*b*), means any process whereby personal data are considered by one or more persons for the purpose of determining, or enabling there to be determined—

(i) the suitability, eligibility or qualifications of the data subject for—

(A) employment or appointment to office;

(B) promotion in employment or office or continuance in employment or office;

(C) removal from employment or office; or

(D) the awarding of contracts, awards (including academic and professional qualifications), scholarships, honours or other benefits;

(ii) whether any contract, award (including academic and professional qualifications), scholarship, honour or benefit relating to the data subject should be continued, modified or cancelled; or

(iii) whether any disciplinary action should be taken against the data subject for a breach of the terms of his employment or appointment to office;

(*b*) does not include any such process where no appeal, whether under an Ordinance or otherwise, may be made against any such determination.

56. Personal references

Personal data held by a data user which consist of a personal reference—

(*a*) given by an individual other than in the ordinary course of his occupation; and

(*b*) relevant to another individual's suitability or otherwise to fill any position of employment or office which is presently, or may become, unfilled,

are exempt from the provisions of data protection principle 6 and section 18(1)(*b*)—

(i) in any case, unless the individual referred to in paragraph (*a*) has informed the data user in writing that he has no objection to the reference being seen by the individual referred to in paragraph (*b*) (or words to the like effect); or

(ii) in the case of a reference given on or after the day on which this section comes into operation, until the individual referred to in paragraph (*b*) has been informed in writing that he has been accepted or rejected to fill that position or office (or words to the like effect),

whichever first occurs.

57. Security, etc. in respect of Hong Kong

(1) Personal data held by or on behalf of the Government for the purposes of safeguarding security, defence or international relations in respect of Hong Kong are exempt from the provisions of data protection principle 6 and section 18(1)(*b*) where the application of those provisions to the data would be likely to prejudice any of the matters referred to in this subsection.

(2) Personal data are exempt from the provisions of data protection principle 3 in any case in which—

(*a*) the use of the data is for any of the purposes referred to in subsection (1) (and whether or not the data are held for any of those purposes); and

(*b*) the application of those provisions in relation to such use would be likely to prejudice any of the matters referred to in that subsection,

and in any proceedings against any person for a contravention of any of those provisions it shall be a defence to show that he had reasonable grounds for believing that failure to so use the data would have been likely to prejudice any of those matters.

(3) Any question whether an exemption under subsection (1) is or at any time was required in respect of any personal data may be determined by the Governor or Chief Secretary; and a certificate signed by the Governor or Chief Secretary certifying that the exemption is or at any time was so required shall be evidence of that fact.

(4) For the purposes of subsection (2), a certificate signed by the Governor or Chief Secretary certifying that personal data are or have been used for any purpose referred to in subsection (1) shall be evidence of that fact.

(5) The Governor or Chief Secretary may, in a certificate referred to in subsection (3) or (4), in respect of the personal data to which the certificate relates and for the reasons specified in that certificate, direct the Commissioner not to carry out an inspection or investigation and, in any such case, the Commissioner shall comply with the direction.

(6) A document purporting to be a certificate referred to in subsection (3) or (4) shall be received in evidence and, in the absence of evidence to the contrary, shall be deemed to be such a certificate.

(7) In this section—

"international relations" (國際關係) includes relations with any international organization;

"security" (保安) includes the prevention or preclusion of persons (including persons detained in accordance with the provisions of the Immigration Ordinance (Cap. 115)) entering and remaining in Hong Kong who do not have the right to enter and remain in Hong Kong.

58. Crime, etc.

(1) Personal data held for the purposes of—

(*a*) the prevention or detection of crime;

(*b*) the apprehension, prosecution or detention of offenders;

(*c*) the assessment or collection of any tax or duty;

(*d*) the prevention, preclusion or remedying (including punishment) of unlawful or seriously improper conduct, or dishonesty or malpractice, by persons;

(*e*) the prevention or preclusion of significant financial loss arising from—

(i) any imprudent business practices or activities of persons; or

(ii) unlawful or seriously improper conduct, or dishonesty or malpractice, by persons;

(*f*) ascertaining whether the character or activities of the data subject are likely to have a significantly adverse impact on any thing—

(i) to which the discharge of statutory functions by the data user relates; or

(ii) which relates to the discharge of functions to which this paragraph applies by virtue of subsection (3); or

(*g*) discharging functions to which this paragraph applies by virtue of subsection (3),

are exempt from the provisions of data protection principle 6 and section 18(1)(*b*) where the application of those provisions to the data would be likely to—

(i) prejudice any of the matters referred to in this subsection; or

(ii) directly or indirectly identify the person who is the source of the data.

(2) Personal data are exempt from the provisions of data protection principle 3 in any case in which—

(*a*) the use of the data is for any of the purposes referred to in subsection (1) (and whether or not the data are held for any of those purposes); and (*b*) the application of those provisions in relation to such use would be likely to prejudice any of the matters referred to in that subsection,

and in any proceedings against any person for a contravention of any of those provisions it shall be a defence to show that he had reasonable grounds for believing that failure to so use the data would have been likely to prejudice any of those matters.

(3) Paragraphs (*f*)(ii) and (*g*) of subsection (1) apply to any functions of a financial regulator—

(*a*) for protecting members of the public against financial loss arising from—

(i) dishonesty, incompetence, malpractice or seriously improper conduct by persons—

(A) concerned in the provision of banking, insurance, investment or other financial services;

(B) concerned in the management of companies;

(C) concerned in the management of occupational retirement schemes within the meaning of the Occupational Retirement Schemes Ordinance (Cap. 426); or

(D) who are shareholders in companies; or

(ii) the conduct of discharged or undischarged bankrupts;

(*b*) for maintaining or promoting the general stability or effective working of any of the systems which provide any of the services referred to in paragraph (*a*)(i)(A); or

(*c*) specified for the purposes of this subsection in a notice under subsection (4).

(4) For the purposes of subsection (3), the Governor may, by notice in the Gazette, specify a function of a financial regulator.

(5) It is hereby declared that—

(*a*) subsection (3) shall not operate to prejudice the generality of the operation of paragraphs (*a*), (*b*), (*c*), (*d*) and (*f*)(i) of subsection (1) in relation to a financial regulator;

(*b*) a notice under subsection (4) is subsidiary legislation.

59. Health

Personal data relating to the physical or mental health of the data subject are exempt from the provisions of either or both of—

(*a*) data protection principle 6 and section 18(1)(*b*);

(*b*) data protection principle 3,

in any case in which the application of those provisions to the data would be likely to cause serious harm to the physical or mental health of—

(i) the data subject; or
(ii) any other individual.

60. Legal professional privilege

Personal data are exempt from the provisions of data protection principle 6 and section 18(1)(*b*) if the data consist of information in respect of which a claim to legal professional privilege could be maintained in law.

61. News

(1) Personal data held by a data user—
(*a*) whose business, or part of whose business, consists of a news activity; and
(*b*) solely for the purpose of that activity (or any directly related activity),

are exempt from the provisions of—
(i) data protection principle 6 and sections 18(1)(*b*) and 38(i) unless and until the data are published or broadcast (wherever and by whatever means);
(ii) sections 36 and 38(*b*).

(2) Personal data are exempt from the provisions of data protection principle 3 in any case in which—
(*a*) the use of the data consists of disclosing the data to a data user referred to in subsection (1); and
(*b*) such disclosure is made by a person who has reasonable grounds to believe (and reasonably believes) that the publishing or broadcasting (wherever and by whatever means) of the data (and whether or not they are published or broadcast) is in the public interest.

(3) In this section—

"news activity" (新聞活動) means any journalistic activity and includes—
(*a*) the—
(i) gathering of news;
(ii) preparation or compiling of articles or programmes concerning news; or
(iii) observations on news or current affairs,
for the purpose of dissemination to the public; or
(*b*) the dissemination to the public of—
(i) any article or programme of or concerning news; or
(ii) observations on news or current affairs.

62. Statistics and research

Personal data are exempt from the provisions of data protection principle 3 where—

(*a*) the data are to be used for preparing statistics or carrying out research;

(*b*) the data are not to be used for any other purpose; and

(*c*) the resulting statistics or results of the research are not made available in a form which identifies the data subjects or any of them.

63. Exemption from section 18(1)(*a*)

Where a data access request relates to personal data which are or, if the data existed, would be exempt from section 18(1)(*b*) by virtue of section 57 or 58, then the data are also exempt from section 18(1)(*a*) if the interest protected by that exemption would be likely to be prejudiced by the disclosure of the existence or non-existence of those data.

PART IX

Offences and Compensation

64. Offences

(1) A data user who, in any—

(*a*) data user return submitted under section 14(4) to the Commissioner;

(*b*) notice under section 14(8) served on the Commissioner; or

(*c*) notice under section 15(3) or (4) submitted to or served on the Commissioner,

knowingly or recklessly supplies any information—

(i) which is false or misleading in a material particular; and

(ii) in purported compliance with that section,

commits an offence and is liable on conviction to a fine at level 3 and to imprisonment for 6 months.

(2) A person who, in any data access request or data correction request, supplies any information—

(*a*) which is false or misleading in a material particular; and

(*b*) which is so supplied for the purpose of having the data user concerned comply with the request,

commits an offence and is liable on conviction to a fine at level 3 and to imprisonment for 6 months.

(3) A person who, in any notice under section 15(6) served on the Commissioner, supplies any information—

(*a*) which is false or misleading in a material particular; and

(*b*) which is so supplied for the purpose of having the Commissioner comply with the request to which the notice relates,

commits an offence and is liable on conviction to a fine at level 3 and to imprisonment for 6 months.

(4) A data user who, in any matching procedure request submitted to the Commissioner, supplies any information—

(*a*) which is false or misleading in a material particular; and

(*b*) which is so supplied for the purpose of having the Commissioner consent to the matching procedure to which the request relates,

commits an offence and is liable on conviction to a fine at level 3 and to imprisonment for 6 months.

(5) A data user (including a data user first-mentioned in section 32(2)) who contravenes any condition specified in a notice under section 30(2) or 32(1)(*b*)(i) commits an offence and is liable on conviction to a fine at level 3.

(6) Any person who contravenes section 44(3) or 46(1) commits an offence and is liable on conviction to a fine at level 3 and to imprisonment for 6 months.

(7) Subject to subsection (8), any relevant data user who contravenes an enforcement notice served on the data user commits an offence and is liable on conviction to a fine at level 5 and to imprisonment for 2 years and, in the case of a continuing offence, to a daily penalty of $1,000.

(8) It shall be a defence for a relevant data user charged with an offence under subsection (7) to show that the data user exercised all due diligence to comply with the enforcement notice concerned.

(9) Any person who—

(*a*) without lawful excuse, obstructs, hinders or resists the Commissioner or any other person in the performance of his functions or the exercise of his powers under Part VII;

(*b*) without lawful excuse, fails to comply with any lawful requirement of the Commissioner or any other person under that Part; or

(*c*) makes a statement which he knows to be false or does not believe to be true, or otherwise knowingly misleads the Commissioner or any other person in the performance of his functions or the exercise of his powers under that Part,

commits an offence and is liable on conviction to a fine at level 3 and to imprisonment for 6 months.

(10) A data user who, without reasonable excuse, contravenes any requirement under this Ordinance (other than a contravention of a data protection principle) for which no other penalty is specified in this section commits an offence and is liable on conviction to a fine at level 3.

65. Liability of employers and principals

(1) Any act done or practice engaged in by a person in the course of his employment shall be treated for the purposes of this Ordinance as done or engaged in by his employer as well as by him, whether or not it was done or engaged in with the employer's knowledge or approval.

(2) Any act done or practice engaged in by a person as agent for another person with the authority (whether express or implied, and whether precedent or subsequent) of that other person shall be treated for the purposes of this Ordinance as done or engaged in by that other person as well as by him.

(3) In proceedings brought under this Ordinance against any person in respect of an act or practice alleged to have been done or engaged in, as the case may be, by an employee of his it shall be a defence for that person to prove that he took such steps as were practicable to prevent the employee from doing that act or engaging in that practice, or from doing or engaging in, in the course of his employment, acts or practices, as the case may be, of that description.

(4) For the avoidance of doubt, it is hereby declared that this section shall not apply for the purposes of any criminal proceedings.

66. Compensation

(1) Subject to subsection (4), an individual who suffers damage by reason of a contravention—

(*a*) of a requirement under this Ordinance;
(*b*) by a data user; and
(*c*) which relates, whether in whole or in part, to personal data of which that individual is the data subject,

shall be entitled to compensation from that data user for that damage.

(2) For the avoidance of doubt, it is hereby declared that damage referred to in subsection (1) may be or include injury to feelings.

(3) In any proceedings brought against any person by virtue of this section it shall be a defence to show that—

(*a*) he had taken such care as in all the circumstances was reasonably required to avoid the contravention concerned; or
(*b*) in any case where the contravention concerned occurred because the personal data concerned were inaccurate, the data accurately record data received or obtained by the data user concerned from the data subject or a third party.

(4) Where an individual suffers damage referred to in subsection (1) by reason of a contravention referred to in that subsection which occurred because the personal data concerned were inaccurate, then no compensation shall be payable under that subsection in respect of so much of that damage that has occurred at any time before the expiration of 1 year immediately following the day on which this section commences.

PART X

MISCELLANEOUS

67. Power of Commissioner to specify forms

(1) Subject to subsection (2), the Commissioner may specify the form of any document required under this Ordinance to be in the specified form and the form of such other documents required for the purposes of this Ordinance as he thinks fit.

(2) The Commissioner's power under subsection (1) shall be subject to any express requirement under this Ordinance for a form, whether specified or otherwise, to comply with that requirement, but that requirement shall not restrict the exercise of that power in respect of that form to the extent that, in the opinion of the Commissioner, his exercise of that power in respect of that form does not contravene that requirement.

(3) The Commissioner's power under subsection (1) may be exercised in such a way as to—

(*a*) include in the specified form of any document referred to in that subsection a statutory declaration—

(i) to be made by the person completing the form; and

(ii) as to whether the particulars contained in the form are true and correct to the best of that person's knowledge and belief;

(*b*) specify 2 or more forms of any document referred to in that subsection, whether as alternatives, or to provide for particular circumstances or particular cases, as the Commissioner thinks fit.

(4) A form specified under this section shall be—

(*a*) completed in accordance with such directions and instructions as are specified in the form;

(*b*) accompanied by such documents as are specified in the form; and

(*c*) if the completed form is required to be provided to—

(i) the Commissioner;

(ii) another person on behalf of the Commissioner; or

(iii) any other person,

so provided in the manner, if any, specified in the form.

68. Service of notices

A notice (howsoever described) which is required to be served under this Ordinance, or which may be served under this Ordinance, on a person (howsoever described) shall, in the absence of evidence to the contrary, be deemed to be so served if—

(*a*) in the case of an individual, it is—

(i) delivered to him;
(ii) left at his last known address for service, or at his last known place of residence or business, in Hong Kong;
(iii) sent by post to him at his last known address for service, or at his last known postal address, in Hong Kong; or
(iv) sent by telex, facsimile transmission or other similar method to him at his last known address for service, or at his last known postal address, or at his last known place of residence or business, in Hong Kong;

(*b*) in the case of a company, it is—
(i) given to or served on an officer of the company;
(ii) left at the company's last known address for service, or at its last known place of business, in Hong Kong;
(iii) sent by post to the company at its last known address for service, or at its last known postal address, in Hong Kong; or
(iv) sent by telex, facsimile transmission or other similar method to the company at its last known address for service, or at its last known postal address, or at its last known place of business, in Hong Kong;

(*c*) in the case of a partnership, it is—
(i) delivered, left or sent in accordance with paragraph (*a*) in respect of any partner who is an individual; or
(ii) given, served, left or sent in accordance with paragraph (*b*) in respect of any partner which is a company;

(*d*) in the case of a person ("attorney") holding a power of attorney under which the attorney is authorized to accept service in respect of another person, it is—
(i) delivered, left or sent in accordance with paragraph (*a*) where the attorney is an individual;
(ii) given, served, left or sent in accordance with paragraph (*b*) where the attorney is a company;
(iii) delivered, left or sent in accordance with paragraph (*a*) in respect of any partner who is an individual where the attorney is a partnership; or
(iv) given, served, left or sent in accordance with paragraph (*b*) in respect of any partner which is a company where the attorney is a partnership.

69. Regulations—fees

(1) The Commissioner may make regulations to prescribe the fees to be paid in respect of any matter, service or facility in respect of which a prescribed fee is payable to the Commissioner under this Ordinance.

(2) The amount of any fee prescribed in regulations made under subsection (1) shall not be limited by reference to the amount of administrative or other costs incurred or likely to be incurred in relation to providing the matter, service or facility to which such fee relates, and different fees may be so prescribed for the same matter, service or facility in order to provide for particular circumstances or particular cases specified in the regulations.

70. Regulations—general

(1) The Secretary for Home Affairs may make regulations for all or any of the following matters—

(*a*) the particulars to be entered in the log book of a data user, including particulars referred to in section 27(2)(*a*), (*b*) and (*c*);

(*b*) prescribing anything that is required or permitted to be prescribed under this Ordinance.

(2) Any regulations made under this section may—

(*a*) empower the Commissioner to grant exemptions from the regulations, either generally or in a particular case;

(*b*) make different provisions for different circumstances and provide for a particular case or class of case;

(*c*) be made so as to apply only in such circumstances as are prescribed by the regulations.

(3) Any regulations made under this section may prescribe offences in respect of contraventions of the regulations, and may provide for the imposition in respect of any such offence of a fine not exceeding level 3 and of imprisonment for a period not exceeding 2 years and, in the case of a continuing offence, to a daily penalty not exceeding $1,000.

71. Amendment of Schedules 2, 4 and 6

The Governor in Council may, by notice in the Gazette, amend Schedule 2, 4 or 6.

Consequential Amendments

Prevention of Bribery Ordinance

72. Public bodies

The Schedule to the Prevention of Bribery Ordinance (Cap. 201) is amended by adding—

"79. Privacy Commissioner for Personal Data.".

Administrative Appeals Board Ordinance

73. Schedule amended

The Schedule to the Administrative Appeals Board Ordinance (Cap. 442) is amended by adding—

"29. Personal Data (Privacy) Ordinance (Cap. 486)	A decision of the Privacy Commissioner for Personal Data— (*a*) to impose conditions on his consent to the carrying out of a matching procedure under section 32(1)(*b*)(i); (*b*) to refuse to consent to the carrying out of a matching procedure under section 32(1)(*b*)(ii); (*c*) to refuse under section 39(3) to carry out or continue an investigation initiated by a complaint; (*d*) not to delete under section 46(5) a matter from a report under the Ordinance; (*e*) not to serve an enforcement notice under section 47; (*f*) to serve an enforcement notice under section 50.".

SCHEDULE 1 [s. 2(1) & (6)]

DATA PROTECTION PRINCIPLES

1. **Principle 1—purpose and manner of collection of personal data**

(1) Personal data shall not be collected unless—
  (*a*) the data are collected for a lawful purpose directly related to a function or activity of the data user who is to use the data;
  (*b*) subject to paragraph (*c*), the collection of the data is necessary for or directly related to that purpose; and
  (*c*) the data are adequate but not excessive in relation to that purpose.

(2) Personal data shall be collected by means which are—
  (*a*) lawful; and
  (*b*) fair in the circumstances of the case.

(3) Where the person from whom personal data are or are to be collected is the data subject, all practicable steps shall be taken to ensure that—

(*a*) he is explicitly or implicitly informed, on or before collecting the data, of—

(i) whether it is obligatory or voluntary for him to supply the data; and

(ii) where it is obligatory for him to supply the data, the consequences for him if he fails to supply the data; and

(*b*) he is explicitly informed—

(i) on or before collecting the data, of—

(A) the purpose (in general or specific terms) for which the data are to be used; and

(B) the classes of persons to whom the data may be transferred; and

(ii) on or before first use of the data for the purpose for which they were collected, of—

(A) his rights to request access to and to request the correction of the data; and

(B) the name and address of the individual to whom any such request may be made,

unless to comply with the provisions of this subsection would be likely to prejudice the purpose for which the data were collected and that purpose is specified in Part VIII of this Ordinance as a purpose in relation to which personal data are exempt from the provisions of data protection principle 6.

2. **Principle 2—accuracy and duration of retention of personal data**

(1) All practicable steps shall be taken to ensure that—

(*a*) personal data are accurate having regard to the purpose (including any directly related purpose) for which the personal data are or are to be used;

(*b*) where there are reasonable grounds for believing that personal data are inaccurate having regard to the purpose (including any directly related purpose) for which the data are or are to be used—

(i) the data are not used for that purpose unless and until those grounds cease to be applicable to the data, whether by the rectification of the data or otherwise; or

(ii) the data are erased;

(*c*) where it is practicable in all the circumstances of the case to know that—

(i) personal data disclosed on or after the appointed day to a third party are materially inaccurate having regard to the purpose (including any directly related purpose) for which the data are or are to be used by the third party; and

(ii) that data were inaccurate at the time of such disclosure,

that the third party—

(A) is informed that the data are inaccurate; and

(B) is provided with such particulars as will enable the third party to rectify the data having regard to that purpose.

(2) Personal data shall not be kept longer than is necessary for the fulfillment of the purpose (including any directly related purpose) for which the data are or are to be used.

3. **Principle 3—use of personal data**

Personal data shall not, without the prescribed consent of the data subject, be used for any purpose other than—

(*a*) the purpose for which the data were to be used at the time of the collection of the data; or

(*b*) a purpose directly related to the purpose referred to in paragraph (*a*).

4. **Principle 4—security of personal data**

All practicable steps shall be taken to ensure that personal data (including data in a form in which access to or processing of the data is not practicable) held by a data user are protected against unauthorized or accidental access, processing, erasure or other use having particular regard to—

(*a*) the kind of data and the harm that could result if any of those things should occur;
(*b*) the physical location where the data are stored;
(*c*) any security measures incorporated (whether by automated means or otherwise) into any equipment in which the data are stored;
(*d*) any measures taken for ensuring the integrity, prudence and competence of persons having access to the data; and
(*e*) any measures taken for ensuring the secure transmission of the data.

5. **Principle 5—information to be generally available**

All practicable steps shall be taken to ensure that a person can—

(*a*) ascertain a data user's policies and practices in relation to personal data;
(*b*) be informed of the kind of personal data held by a data user;
(*c*) be informed of the main purposes for which personal data held by a data user are or are to be used.

6. **Principle 6—access to personal data**

A data subject shall be entitled to—

(*a*) ascertain whether a data user holds personal data of which he is the data subject;
(*b*) request access to personal data—
  (i) within a reasonable time;
  (ii) at a fee, if any, that is not excessive;
  (iii) in a reasonable manner; and
  (iv) in a form that is intelligible;
(*c*) be given reasons if a request referred to in paragraph (*b*) is refused;
(*d*) object to a refusal referred to in paragraph (*c*);
(*e*) request the correction of personal data;
(*f*) be given reasons if a request referred to in paragraph (*e*) is refused; and
(*g*) object to a refusal referred to in paragraph (*f*).

SCHEDULE 2

[ss. 5(7), 10(2)(*c*) & 71]

Finances, etc. of Commissioner

1. **Resources of Commissioner**

(1) The resources of the Commissioner shall consist of—

(*a*) all money—
  (i) paid by the Government to the Commissioner and appropriated for that purpose by the Legislative Council; and
  (ii) otherwise provided to the Commissioner by the Government; and

(*b*) all other money and property, including gifts, donations, fees, rent, interest and accumulations of income received by the Commissioner.

(2) The Secretary for the Treasury may give directions in writing of a general or specific character to the Commissioner in relation to the amount of money which may be expended by the Commissioner in any financial year and the Commissioner shall comply with those directions.

(3) For the avoidance of doubt, it is hereby declared that any remuneration or other benefit payable to, and any expenses of—

(*a*) the Commissioner; or

(*b*) any person employed or engaged under section 9(1) of this Ordinance,

shall be paid out of the resources of the Commissioner.

2. **Borrowing powers**

(1) Subject to subsection (2), the Commissioner may borrow by way of overdraft such money as he may require for meeting his obligations or performing his functions under this Ordinance.

(2) The Secretary for Home Affairs may, after consulting with the Secretary for the Treasury, give directions in writing of a general or specific character to the Commissioner in relation to the amount of money which may be borrowed under subsection (1) and the Commissioner shall comply with those directions.

(3) The Commissioner may with the approval of the Secretary for Home Affairs given after the Secretary has consulted with the Secretary for the Treasury borrow, otherwise than by way of overdraft, such money as he may require for meeting his obligations or performing his functions under this Ordinance.

(4) A person lending money to the Commissioner shall not be concerned to inquire whether the borrowing of the money is legal or regular or whether the money raised has been properly applied and shall not be prejudiced by any illegality or irregularity or by misapplication or non-application of the money.

3. **Investment of surplus funds**

(1) Subject to subsection (2), the Commissioner may invest money that is not immediately required to be expended.

(2) The Commissioner shall not invest money pursuant to subsection (1) except in such forms of investment as the Secretary for Home Affairs, after consulting with the Secretary for the Treasury, approves.

(3) Subsection (1) shall not be subject to section 10(1) of this Ordinance.

4. **Accounts, audit and annual report of Commissioner**

(1) The Commissioner shall cause proper accounts to be kept of all his financial transactions.

(2) The Commissioner shall, as soon as practicable after the expiry of a financial year, prepare a statement of the accounts of the Commissioner, which statement shall include an income and expenditure account and a balance sheet.

(3) The Commissioner shall appoint an auditor who shall, as soon as practicable, audit the accounts required under subsection (1) and the statement of accounts required under subsection (2) and shall submit a report on the statement to the Commissioner.

(4) The Commissioner shall, as soon as practicable and in any case not later than 9 months after the expiry of a financial year (or such further period as the Chief Secretary allows), furnish—

(*a*) a report on the activities of the Commissioner during that year including a general survey of developments, during that year, in respect of matters falling within the scope of the Commissioner's functions;

(*b*) a copy of the statement of accounts required under subsection (2); and

(*c*) the auditor's report on the statement,

to the Chief Secretary who shall cause the same to be tabled in the Legislative Council.

(5) This section shall not be subject to section 10(1) of this Ordinance.

5. **Director of Audit's examination**

(1) The Director of Audit may, in respect of any financial year, conduct an examination into the economy, efficiency and effectiveness with which the Commissioner has expended his resources in performing his functions and exercising his powers.

(2) Subject to subsection (3), the Director of Audit shall have a right of access at all reasonable times to all such documents as he may reasonably require for conducting an examination under this section and shall be entitled to require from any person holding or being accountable for any such document such information and explanation as he considers reasonably necessary for that purpose.

(3) Subsection (2) applies only to documents in the custody and control of the Commissioner.

(4) The Director of Audit may report to the President of the Legislative Council the results of an examination conducted by him under this section.

(5) Subsection (1) shall not operate to entitle the Director of Audit to question the merits of the policy objectives of the Commissioner.

6. **Exemption from taxation**

(1) The Commissioner shall be exempt from taxation under the Inland Revenue Ordinance (Cap. 112).

(2) For the avoidance of doubt, it is hereby declared that subsection (1) does not apply to or in relation to any remuneration, benefits or expenses referred to in section 1(3) paid out of the resources of the Commissioner to the Commissioner.

SCHEDULE 3 [s. 14(10)]

PRESCRIBED INFORMATION

1. The name and address of the data user.
2. A description of the kind of personal data in respect of which the data user is a data user.
3. A description of the purpose or purposes for which the personal data referred to in item 2 are or are to be collected, held, processed or used by the data user.
4. A description of any classes of persons to whom the data user discloses, intends to disclose or may wish to disclose the personal data referred to in item 2.
5. The names or a description of any places outside Hong Kong to which the data user transfers, intends to transfer or may wish to transfer, the personal data referred to in item 2.
6. The name and address of the individual to whom data access requests may be made to the data user.

SCHEDULE 4 [ss. 30(1)(*d*) & 71]

PROVISIONS OF ORDINANCES UNDER WHICH MATCHING PROCEDURES ARE REQUIRED OR PERMITTED

SCHEDULE 5 [s. 32(4)]

PRESCRIBED MATTERS

1. Whether the carrying out of the matching procedure is in the public interest.
2. The kind of personal data to be the subject of the matching procedure.
3. The likely consequences to a data subject if the matching procedure were to result in any adverse action taken against the data subject.
4. The practices and procedures, if any, that will be followed to enable a data subject to make a data correction request—
   (*a*) in respect any of the personal data produced or verified by the matching procedure;
   (*b*) before any adverse action is taken against the data subject.
5. The practices and procedures, if any, that will be followed to ensure, so far as is practicable, the accuracy of any personal data produced or verified by the matching procedure.
6. Whether any such data subject is to be informed of the procedure before it is first carried out.
7. Whether there is any practicable alternative to the matching procedure.
8. The benefits to be derived from carrying out the matching procedure.

SCHEDULE 6 [ss. 42(6), (7) & (11) & 71]

PART 1

WARRANT AUTHORIZING PRIVACY COMMISSIONER FOR PERSONAL DATA TO ENTER SPECIFIED PREMISES WITHOUT INFORMING RELEVANT DATA USER

To the Privacy Commissioner for Personal Data.

Having been satisfied by information upon oath/declaration* that there are reasonable grounds for believing that the purposes of an investigation under the Personal Data (Privacy) Ordinance (Cap. 486) in relation to .... [name of relevant data user] may be substantially prejudiced if you were required to comply with section 42(3) of that Ordinance before exercising your power under section 42(2) of that Ordinance in respect of the premises at ....

....

[address of premises occupied by the relevant data user/in which is situated the personal data system, or any part thereof, used by the relevant data user*]:

YOU ARE HEREBY AUTHORIZED, with such assistants as may be necessary, to exercise your power under section 42(2) of that Ordinance in respect of those premises without complying with section 42(3) of that Ordinance provided that such power is exercised before the expiration of 14 days after the date on which this warrant is issued.

Dated this .... day of .... 19........

....

(Signature) Magistrate

* Delete whichever is inapplicable.

PART 2

WARRANT AUTHORIZING PRIVACY COMMISSIONER FOR PERSONAL DATA TO ENTER SPECIFIED DOMESTIC PREMISES

To the Privacy Commissioner for Personal Data.

Having been satisfied by information upon oath/declaration* that there are reasonable grounds for believing that the purposes of the investigation into .... [name of relevant data user] may be substantially prejudiced if you are prevented by the operation of section 42(4) of the Personal Data (Privacy) Ordinance (Cap. 486) from exercising your power under section 42(2) of that Ordinance in respect of the domestic premises at ....

....

[address of domestic premises occupied by the relevant data user/in which is situated the personal data system, or any part thereof, used by the relevant data user*]:

YOU ARE HEREBY AUTHORIZED, with such assistants as may be necessary, to exercise that power in respect of those premises provided that such power is exercised before the expiration of 14 days after the date on which this warrant is issued.

Dated this .... day of .... 19........

....

(Signature) Magistrate

* Delete whichever is inapplicable.

Index